MY LIFE WITH THE SAMURAI

HOW I SURVIVED JAPANESE DEATH CAMPS

JOURNEYS 1941 - 1945

MY LIFE
WITH THE SAMURAI

HOW I SURVIVED
JAPANESE DEATH CAMPS

TONY COWLING

With best wishes
Tony Cowling
May your rice bowl always be full.

Cover design by Darian Causby and Tony Cowling
Art work by Murray Griffin
Escape 1944
Brush and brown ink and wash 30.1 * 25 cm
Australian War Museum (26464)

First published in1996 by Kangaroo Press Pty Ltd

3 Whitehall Road Kenthurst NSW Australia

2nd printing 2001 by Premium Printing

Vancouver British Columbia, Canada

Third printing 2003 by Premium Printing

Vancouver British Columbia Canada

ISBN 0 86417 813 3

Tony Cowling

3751 Lockhart Road, Richmond, BC, V7C 1M4.

www.anthonycowling.com

acowling@cowlingplus.com

Disclaimer

In reference to the word "Nips". A slang term denoting a person of Japanese descent, commonly used during the time of the events described. The use of this term is not intended to discriminate against the Japanese people in whole.

CONTENTS

INTRODUCTION   6

FOREWORD 8

ACKNOWLEDGEMENTS   10

CHAPTERS

1   SINGAPORE *Raffles and all that stuff*   11
2   JAVA *Incompetence, disaster, capture*   34
3   SEMARANG *Intro to slavery, a girl no less*   59
4   JARR MARKT CAMP *Three squares and a little looting*   79
5   THE BOAT TRIP *Bombs, gas, dysentery*   87
6   HARUKU 1 *The Camel's Humps*   93
7   HARUKU 2 *Beating and bombings*   106
8   HARUKU 3 *Whores and ham*   126
9   HARUKU AND AMBON *Dead Natives*   139
10 MUNA *The death camp*   160
11 CLOTHES AND SOAP *From near death to near life*   180
12 HOME *"Liberty is always dangerous"*   194

APPENDICES

1   CHRISTMAS LETTER, JAPANESE STYLE   202
2   DAD'S ESCAPE FROM SINGAPORE   203
3   EXTRACT FROM Dr. FORBES REPORT TO SINGAPORE
     WAR CRIMES TRIBUNAL   208
4   THE CODE OF BUSHIDO   209
5   INTERESTING FACTS OF THE PACIFIC WAR   220
6   TELEGRAM FROM CHURCHILL TO AIR VICE MARSHAL
     MALTBY   232

BIBLIOGRAPHY   233
INDEX   234

Introduction

I have written this book with two reasons in mind. First, when I visited the Imperial War Museum in London, England, in 1986 I was amazed to find an exceedingly sparse reference to the suffering of Prisoners in the Far East. The historical and humane aspect of how a nation treats its prisoners and the general population it is trying to influence is of some concern to all of us. Today, the fact that Japan is a powerful economic nation is all the more reason for people everywhere to be aware of the type of treatment they are only too happy to mete out to those that they wish to subjugate. It is most important that we are aware of the nature of the Japanese as they are unlikely to change, for the better, with the acquisition of power. In fact the contrary is true. The second reason for writing this book is to let my family know the consequences of war. The whole notion of settling difference by force must die with the knowledge that only the arms manufacturers and those that do not see any hostile action benefit from such a degrading activity. The young and idealistic are taken advantage of and forced to suffer the degeneracy that their elected leaders are morally bound to guide them away from.

In August/September, 1945 when the war was over for us I was able to find a checklist that measured about six inches long by one and a half inches wide. On this I made a lot of notes that I felt would be useful to me at some distant date. Little did I realise that close to forty five busy years would pass before I had the opportunity to sit down and organise the notes and try to answer the nagging question, WHY?

I have done an extraordinary amount of reading to try to solve the questions of why did they treat us in such an ugly fashion and why did the Western powers, particularly the British, act in such an unintelligent manner when they must have known the results of sacrificing thousands of human lives for political vanity. They claimed at the time that every day of delay was priceless. Prime Minister Churchill and General Wavell both ordered that officers and men should sacrifice their lives for the defence of the paper tiger fortress - - Singapore - - to preserve a Naval Base that was not capable of maintaining a non-existent Battle Fleet. It must never be forgotten that both Churchill and Wavell were many hundreds, or thousands, of miles distant from the action.

Initially the blame for the loss of Singapore was put upon the other ranks for their inability to face up to an overwhelming enemy. In actual fact the blame rests at the other end of the spectrum. Not only was the military leadership abysmal but the political will to unite a diverse population absolutely non existent. [See appendix "Interesting facts of the Pacific War]

I made notes of our camp life immediately after the "Bombs" were dropped. Some of the dates may be wrong but all the happenings occurred the way they are written. The death statistics on boats and in the later camps may be out by a fraction. The Dutch authorities have the best record of this entire period. Where possible these figures have been used to confirm my own and other British references.

For my wife Norma and our four sons, Christopher, Geoffrey, David and Michael together with their families, who have been spared the horrors of war, this is the story of how I spent my late teenage life and how the atom bombs gave me an opportunity to create an environment that has seen all my boys develop into such fine young men. Men that not only their mother and I are proud of but our whole community and country are blessed with.

With the publication of the second printing the world situation has changed considerably. The USA is once again the dominant economic and military power. Japan has been suffering an economic slow down for the past few years and China is gaining momentum as an industrial power. I have included two appendices which Kangaroo publishers were reluctant to include in the first printing. New information has come to light about the beheading of men on our neighbouring camp Amahai. Other small and insignificant changes have been made as a result of this information.

Foreword

When the Japanese overran most of the Far East in 1942, no fewer than 50,016 British service men were taken prisoner, most of them in Singapore. From Singapore, very many of them were taken up country to work as slaves on the notorious Siam railway, and it is with the calvary of these men that most people who take the trouble to study the history of those times today associate the terrible story of suffering under the Japanese of the Allied prisoners of war.

But that is by no means the whole story. When Singapore was on the verge of collapse, the remaining British, Australian and Dutch aircraft left on the untenable airfields were flown out to Sumatra and Java in the forlorn hope of carrying on the war from there. The eventual result was that a large number of Allied airmen fell captive to the Japanese in Java. From there, many were later dispatched like cargo in the holds of merchant ships to the Spice Islands of what is now Indonesia. 2071 of them were landed on the little island of Haruku, and put to work building an airstrip.

One of these airmen was Tony Cowling. His very readable book tells the story of how, as a young civilian in Singapore, he volunteered for the Royal Air Force and found himself a POW after only a few days in uniform. After only a matter of weeks he was chipping coral on the airfield site at Haruku, using the primitive hand tools with which the POWs were expected to level the hills.

Today, Haruku is a little paradise of a place, and to the recent visitor like myself it is difficult to imagine the conditions under which the POWs laboured for over a year. After only one month, a hundred men had died, after two months, two hundred men had died. By the time the airstrip was levelled and the survivors moved to the island of Ambon, approximately 126 men from Tony's work group of over 400 were still alive.

More slave labour on Ambon followed, then another wretched journey in the hold of a cargo ship to Muna near the south-eastern tip of Sulawesi. Here all the remaining Haruku slaves were reunited, there were only about 425 of them - a causality rate of almost 80%. As the Allied advance in the Far East gathered pace, the Japanese continued to move the prisoners further away from possible rescue, and the POWs on Muna found themselves yet again in the hold of a ship, bound this time for Maccassar and eventually a return to Java. The wonder is that the ship survived the marauding American submarines in the Java Sea, and escaped the fate of the Suez Maru, which was sent to the bottom in November 1943 with over 600 POWs on board.

Finally, in August 1945, the almost unbelievable happened, when the

Japanese thinned out and left the prison camp gates open. The war was over. For the prisoners this ended over forty four months of incarceration. It had been forty four months of great tribulation, but as Tony's account so well brings out, it had also been a time during which human spirit and comradeship among the prisoners had made it possible for many to survive conditions that might well otherwise have seen the end of all of them. It is an inspiring story, a story not without humour, and a story told with attractive modesty by a man who not only survives but did what he could to see that others survived.

Air Chief Marshal Sir Michael Armitage. KCB, CBE, RAF [RTD].
Former Commandant of the Royal College of Defence Studies, London.

Acknowledgements

I experienced most of the happenings in this book some fifty years ago and was very happy to put them aside whilst the business of earning a living and raising my family was the most important aspect of my life. Now with the help and enthusiasm of my wife Norma and our four boys, Christopher, Geoffrey, David and Michael and their lovely ladies the memoirs have become a matter of public record. For this I am grateful, as the record of how the Japanese treated their prisoners of war in this area of the world has seldom if ever been mentioned. Dr. A Forbes, MD. Dr. R. Phelps, MD and Lt. Dan Duff have all contributed to the details by allowing me to use their written records of these many camps. My friend Sgt. Pilot Ron Blackmore, now living in Zimbabwe contributed a couple of reminisces on the lighter side of life and the rules promulgated in Semarang Camp. After many rejections by publishers in North America and Europe my very good friend, Tom Coles, of Swansea, Wales, put me in touch with The Kangaroo press and David Rosenberg who have been good enough to take on the publishing project.

My family have all lent their expertise and contributed to the published document. My wife Norma has read the manuscript many times and made the corrections she felt were necessary. Christopher, of Cowling and Associates, computer consultants, has kept an eye on me and helped enormously with my computer ineptitude. Karen his talented wife has advised me on sequencing etc. Geoffrey has contributed to the humourous side of events that I saw only as a dictatorial part of our existence and corrected the manuscript many times. David and Michael have lent their untiring support to assist in the completed manuscript.

Fred and Elaine Vyse of Premium Printing have helped enormously in the final phase of organizing the second printing and been most patient in our business transactions.

1

SINGAPORE, RAFFLES

AND ALL THAT STUFF

I find a hundred thousand touching my heart,
and there is ringing in my ears like an
admonition eternal, an incessant call, "it must not be again."
WARREN HARDING

I arrived in Singapore, after a month of exotic cruising, on a beautiful day in May 1941. As the *President Taft* pulled alongside the wharf I strained my eyes to pick out my father in the crowd below. In that seething mass of happy, smiling, shouting faces I thought that I would recognise Dad. My heart was pounding at the very the idea of this reunion and the fact that he had given me the choice to leave school and join him in this distant part of the Empire. I had no inkling of what his plans were for me. I had not seen Dad for many years but felt sure that I would recognise him and had a feeling that he might recognise me. Soon after the docking was completed and the visitors were crowding on board I heard my name being called over the loudspeaker system for a meeting at the purser's office. Hurriedly, I raced there but could not recognise anyone. Soon an "uncle" I had no idea existed was introducing himself and apologising for the fact that my Dad could not be there to meet me. An important business meeting had kept him away. Much later in my life I realised that business was far more important to Dad than family. To waste time on a dock greeting a displaced son was not a profitable enterprise.

Singapore is the city of my birth. My parents and grandparents had been Empire Builders since before the turn of the century. Dad was a successful civil engineer and contractor and had lived in this part of the world since 1920. He was adviser and confidant to many of the Malay Sultans and a good friend of the "Great White Rajah-Vyner Brooke[1]." He knew the Far East and its languages, five of them fluently, with the assurance of a native potentate. His interests were far ranging. During the 1930s he had explored, on foot, the jungles of the Cameron Highlands in central Malaysia. Coming across a valley that was bathed in a magnificent blue light as the sun took wings to top the mountains, he was so impressed that he bought the valley and started Blue Valley Tea Estate which is still a thriving concern today. The estate is situated at the end of a twelve-mile road that he built from the village of Tanah Rata through virgin jungle with the sole purpose of supplying the estate-to-be. The road is an umbilical cord attaching five hundred acres of cultivation to the nearest civilisation. At the bulls eye of the jungle clearing is the manager's house, with the factory in the next ring and the estate houses branching off from this area. The shop that supplies all the people on the estate is situated between the factory and the residential area. The whole layout is convenient for the manager, whose house is situated on a two hundred foot knoll at the centre of the valley floor. The estate workers like it for the convenience it affords and the fact that they have a vegetable garden with each house.

Typical of English empire building families, Dad had sent me to school in England where he could conveniently forget about me, knowing that the prep' and public schools would instil into me all the right attitudes. As luck would have it I spent my summer holidays travelling- France, Denmark, Suez, and in 1939, to Canada. Hitler started his antics while I was enjoying some salmon fishing off the beautiful coast of British Columbia. My mother had brought me to Canada for two reasons; firstly her sister and her husband were living in Vancouver and she wanted to visit them, and secondly she felt that I should be taken out of school early in the year as the situation was not beneficial for me. This meant that we would have the required time to travel to Vancouver and return for the commencement of the school year that fall. I had a most enjoyable summer at my uncle's cottage on Qualicum Beach - fishing, hiking in the mountains and riding the railroad boxcars to Nanaimo and back. When September came and Hitler started ravaging Europe the whole kaleidoscope of events tumbled to a new position. For us it meant a drastic separation for an unknown period. My mother returned to England to look after my brothers. I was not allowed to accompany her on the basis that wartime England did not want to house and feed underage kids. I stayed with my uncle and aunt in Vancouver. Robbie and Babs had a most profound effect on my life. It was a totally new experience for them as they had three delightful daughters who behaved in a most civilised fashion, whereas I was a rotten little SOB.

Knowing my abhorrence for school and being well aware that my academic progress was average at best, Mother decided to indenture me to a farmer on Vancouver Island just North of Victoria. At Swallowfield Farm I had a real taste of the hard physical work involved in everyday farming. I was given an exceptionally small room that had as its only access a door that opened directly to the outside area between the barn and the pigsty. In spite of the fact that my parents were paying for me to be on the farm I was forced to work like a Trojan, with my only privilege being to saddle up the horses and ride on Sundays. After several months of this my uncle and aunt realised what was happening and advised my parents that the money spent on indentured labour would be far more worthwhile in giving me an education.

I attended St. George's School and found that it was just as bad for an over active boy as it had been in England. After a few fairly harmless antics that broke the school rules I was asked to leave at the end of the first year. Andy, a dayboy, had a nice little car with a "dicky" seat at the back. After lights out he would arrive at the bottom of the fire escape and give Glenny and me a whistle, at which time we would leave little dummies in our beds, leap onto the fire escape and head for the big time. If we were really flush we would have a hot chocolate at the Palomar on Burrard Street and then back to bed. For us it was a daring escapade but quite harmless. All the rules were similar to those that I had experienced in English schools - in fact Canadian private schools were patterned after the English public schools. The following year I was enrolled at University School in Victoria, which was reputed to exercise stronger discipline than St. George's. It was hoped that I would succumb to more acceptable forms of behaviour. Luckily the British Government intervened and denied my father the privilege of sending money from a sterling area to a gold area. Like a clarion call, in April 1942, my formal education came to a resounding stop. I must leave the gold area immediately and join my father in far off exotic Singapore. This torture of attending school was to be replaced with a life of adventure- much more exciting and totally enjoyable.

The *President Taft* had brought me from San Francisco via Hawaii and Shanghai. While we were in Hawaii we feasted our eyes on the incredible strength of the US navy in Pearl Harbour. So many war ships tied together in such a small area. A very impressive sight. In Shanghai my fellow Canadian passengers took me to an exclusive nightclub, The Mandarin, to celebrate my 17th birthday. A little too much champagne was an excellent introduction for an innocent youth into the ways of life in the Far East. In the taxi on the way back to the boat one of the fellows bought himself a most attractive young Chinese lady who joined us in the cab. During the ensuing bargaining procedure she demanded a down payment as a token of good faith. This was handed over enthusiastically resulting in her rapid exit at the next traffic light. It seems I was not the only one learning lessons that night.

With the hustle and excitement of Singapore just ahead of me, my "uncle" soon cleared me of all the entry formalities and I was being chauffeured to The Raffles Hotel, that bastion of prestige in the Far East. Dad had made arrangements for me to have a room next to his on the ground floor. All very convenient. That evening I met Dad. Although he had put on a little weight in the years since I had last seen him, he was his usual self, full of business schemes and ideas. He brought me up to date on his business plans over a most enjoyable meal at the hotel. Here I was introduced to his favourite drink - a "stengah" - scotch and soda.

Now as I sat on the veranda of the Raffles Hotel, sipping a "stengah," and feeling very much a man of the world, Dad outlined his plan of action for me. The very first thing to do was buy some suitable clothes and get rid of this heavy-duty cold weather stuff. He told me the name of his tailor and that I should get well fitted out - everything from a sharks skin tuxedo to work clothes. I would need at least a dozen white shorts and shirts, a topee [the hat, actually a pith helmet, that symbolised The White Raj], a couple of dress suits and a tux' for evening wear. This is what life is all about - to be enjoyed. Such a dramatic change from the humdrum of school to life in the fast lane in one more tumble of this wonderful kaleidoscope.

Dad's plan was for me to take a work crew up to Kerilla Estate in Kelantan with a couple of D8 tractors, clear the old existing rubber and burn it prior to re-planting. This sounded wonderful to me as I would actually be in charge of the whole job, with full responsibility. Dad, in his wisdom, had arranged for me to have the best foreman in the company. He was Managing Director of the Gammon Malaya Ltd. the biggest construction company in the Far East. This company was Dad's pride and joy - his life's work. He had decided to bid on this rubber-clearing job with me in mind for three reasons. Firstly, he did not want me under foot, secondly he figured that I would gain a lot of experience working independently with a good crew and thirdly the job was an easy one for a beginner to handle. I was not due to go north for at least four months so I had plenty of time to enjoy the delights of Singapore in the evenings and catch up on my Malay during the day. As a child in Singapore I had mostly Malay and Chinese playmates. Consequently I spoke Malay and Cantonese like my little friends.

I wasted no time in initiating my new tuxedo. Jacqueline, the daughter of one of my father's friends, and I soon became very friendly and spent many evenings dancing at the roof top, open air restaurant at Kallang Airport or at the Tanglin Club. Our weekends were spent watching Dad's horses racing, usually in Singapore. Sometimes a nice flight to Kuala Lumpur or Penang would top off a week getting used to this tropical climate. At the racetracks in Singapore and Up-country we were treated very favourably, as we spent our time in the owners' compounds where there were plenty of servants to fill our every wish. Jacqueline, with her long blond hair and flashing eyes turned heads wherever we went. When the horses were not racing we could be found on the courts of the Tanglin Club, or playing polo at the Singapore Swimming Club, where I became quite proficient at playing water polo and signing for a variety of exotic drinks. The plebeian method of paying cash for drinks was out of the question. The call of "Boy" would bring a waiter running and eager to set up a new round of drinks. This was so much more enjoyable than being at school in Vancouver. I was revelling in freedom and the luxurious life.

It was soon time for me to meet my work crew and make arrangements for the equipment to be sent north. My job at Kerilla Estate involved a new concept in land clearing. A large two hundred yard one inch wire hawser would be hitched to the two D8 tractors, which in turn would be placed with a row of rubber trees between them. The centre of the hawser would then be raised twenty feet off the ground and lodged in the middle branches of the trees. With equal strain on the tractors the line would tighten and the trees would fall like dominoes. We soon discovered that the tractors were powerful enough to span two rows of trees and adopted this modification to great advantage.

The Sakai Express was the only means of getting from Singapore to Kota Bharu by land. The nearest town, Kota Bharu, is situated on the north east coast of Malaya and is located just below the Siam [Thailand] border. It was Malaya's most isolated town. The railway passed the edge of Kerilla rubber estate where a loading platform had been conveniently built for supplying the estate — there was not a station for many miles in either direction. Loading the equipment in Singapore, with all the facilities readily at hand, was a snap. The off loading at a railway siding in the jungle with only a platform made for comparatively light merchandise was my first challenge. Needless to say I left this in the capable hands of Chota, the foreman. He managed in fine style and soon had the tractors rumbling on their way through the rubber estate. The Malay tractor drivers impressed me with their skill and daring. They seemed to have no fear of the tractors turning over. On several occasions I wanted Chota to stop the off loading as it appeared inevitable that the tractors would tumble down the embankment, resulting in severe injuries and real recovery problems. He would wave me aside with assurances that all was under control. I soon learned to respect his judgement and many times during the coming months called on him to get me out of some nasty predicament as I learned to drive the tractors myself.

I met the estate manager and his wife, Mr. & Mrs. Gregory, a conservative English couple who had spent many years as rubber planters in Malaya. They gave me a large airy room in their bungalow with my own private bathroom. The bathroom was a novelty for me. The room itself was about twelve feet square with a fifteen-foot ceiling, and two doors. One led to the bedroom and the other to the outside. In the centre of the stone floor was a four-inch diameter drain hole. The room was bare of all furnishings except for a large vase. This must have held at least ten gallons of water. It stood about two and a half feet tall, one foot diameter at the base swelling to two feet about two thirds of the way up and then narrowing off to about eighteen inches at the top. This was my bath water and surprisingly cold. Every day the water carrier would fill the vase with fresh well water. Abdul Aziz's sole job in life was to carry water from the well to the manager's house and make sure that there was always plenty of it. The method of bathing was to dip a large scoop into the vase and then sluice the water over one's body. A primitive form of shower.

A few days later I met the assistant manager, Tom, and his attractive wife, Joan. We soon became firm friends. Tom was about twenty-eight years old with a slight build and a good facility with both Malay and Tamil, for most of the workers (tappers) on the estate were from Southern India and spoke Tamil. Joan was younger than Tom and having a hard time settling into the life of ease that is the lot of the planter's wife — especially in such an isolated area. A lady with an active and sporting life in England now found herself with enough servants to look after the house and grounds and only sedentary pursuits available to her. The estate was sandwiched between the Kelantan River and the Siamese [Thailand] border, a truly isolated part of the Empire. It was not easy to get into town and usually meant an overnight stay, so most of our fun was locally initiated. It was so late when we had finished dinner that first night that I did not get around to seeing where my men were located. My transportation around the estate was a BSA motorbike that gave me many moments of great excitement, but I soon mastered it. My first trip the following day was slow and wobbly. I met Chota and the crew at the estate office and found that the men were quite happy with their quarters.

Mr. Gregory took us out to the area to be cleared, showed us the perimeter and then left us to do our damndest. From this day on he did not worry about our progress. Occasionally he would visit us in the field and watch fascinated as the old rubber came tumbling down like a house of cards. The trees would then be bulldozed into neat rows and set ablaze. Once the entire area was cleared it would be planted with new rubber. The trees we were clearing were well past their most productive stage.

My small work force of Malays who had been working in Singapore now found themselves housed in a remote rubber estate in the least developed of the Malay States. The Malayan people are pastoral by nature and I believe that they rather enjoyed this sudden change from the big city life. I do not know how the group was selected, apart from Chota the foreman, but they settled into the life of semi isolation very nicely. There is always a large, appealing selection of young ladies of many nationalities on most estates. This fact, together with the variety of entertaining skills that are part of the estate life, made the world just hum along as if there was not a care or worry in sight. I was getting in a lot of reading during the quiet evenings and loved walking to the edge of the estate where I could frequently hear and occasionally see wild elephants browsing in the jungle. Monkeys were a constant source of amusement but had to be treated with great respect. A group of them in the rubber trees yelling and swinging just overhead was frightening. I always had the feeling that they were just enjoying themselves and rather pitied me and my earth - bound limitations, but showed this distaste in a most agitated way. I carried a really stout stick at all times to counteract the lesser hazards, such as huge spider webs spun between the trees. If I was lucky enough to see the webs before walking into them, I walked around them. If by chance I walked into a web then there was violent flailing with the stick and I broke loose. I always had a great dislike for spiders and did not relish the thought of being caught in a web knowing that a huge spider was somewhere in the trees watching my every move. These big bird-eating spiders create webs that will span a distance of eighteen feet, the space between rubber trees, with an elasticity that is quite extraordinary

A sidelight of my job that I had not anticipated, but my father had warned me was bound to happen, was that the men came to me with their problems. Being their supervisor, regardless of age, I was the man they would turn to in case of trouble. I learned that Chota, my foreman, had three wives and was considering a fourth. He was keen to get one of them on to the estate and wanted my assistance in making the necessary arrangements. Abdul and Ronowegino had similar requests. The others were bachelors and had more of a yearning to get time off for longer visits to Kota Bharu.

The night of Sunday 7 December we retired after a quiet evening of reading, with the idea of an early start on Monday. I normally started the crew working just after 6:00 am so that we got a good start on the day before the tropical sun would beat down on us and slow our progress. Soon after midnight I was awakened by what I thought to be thunder, but it did not have that pause between thunderclaps that is usual. No need to worry as I would soon find what kind of thunder it was. Mr. Gregory was a terrific source of information and knowledgeable in the weather patterns in this area. The thunder was just an incessant series of loud bangs, some of them quite sharp and some muffled. After a most disturbing night I got up early as there was little point in just tossing and turning. After the usual sluice down in my magnificent bathroom I showed up for breakfast only to find the manager glued to the radio and warning me that the Japanese had landed on the coast a few miles to the east of us. He told me that the Malays and others local inhabitants were streaming through the estate getting out of the way of the fighting and the rapidly advancing invaders. The estate was surrounded by jungle on three sides and the river on the fourth so the natives reached the end of their journey when they arrived on Kerrila.

My God! It was this close to us! The thunder was explained - a heavy naval barrage to soften up the defence. I hopped onto my bike and found Chota, and a couple of mechanics, told them that we must immobilise the two D8 tractors immediately. I thought the easiest and fastest way to do this was to take off the fuel injection pumps. He agreed, so we raced out to the field and did just that. I left him there thinking that I would be back before they had finished and went back to the house for some breakfast and an update on the news. The manager and his wife had been advised, by runner, that we must leave the estate at the very first opportunity. I packed a small suitcase, for the only way out of the estate now was by the river. The manager, and his wife, with Tom, Joan, and I all piled into the company launch that was used only for emergencies. We moved slowly up stream, each of us with what we could carry of our possessions in a small bag, wondering quietly what the world had come to.

We were completely stunned. Living in this isolated area of Malaya we had no idea of what was developing around us. I am sure the manager knew much more than he had told us about the international situation, but now we found ourselves heading out of our peaceful world, being chased by a war hungry, blood thirsty bunch of fanatics. It was just too much to comprehend. Literally overnight our world had drastically changed. Somebody was turning my kaleidoscope in the wrong direction. All those bright colours were tumbling the wrong way. Going up river in the launch I felt very bad about leaving my crew behind without so much as a farewell. The one saving grace was that I had paid them on Saturday - as usual, in cash. What would be their fate? No launch for them.

What would we do now? There was no road to Singapore, the Japanese were between us and the sea and behind us was dense jungle. The manager told us that we were headed for the nearest little town on the river, Kuala Krai. After a slow and very quiet journey, bucking the river all the way, we docked at a shaky little landing and wondered what we would find here. This was the only place to stop as any further progress up the river would take us into dense jungle. Also at this point the railroad came inland from Kota Bharu and met the main North South line. True there was a village here full of happy Malays who no doubt had not yet heard of the disaster that was so close to them. We walked up the riverbank and soon found Army headquarters, an advanced HQ that was controlling the fighting front. We all volunteered and were soon found jobs. The major was most reluctant to give me any work at all, but I insisted and at last he decided that I would be useful as a cipher clerk working in the HQ. Tom, who spoke Malay and Tamil fluently, was asked to go on a reconnaissance trip to the front with one of the officers. I heard them discussing the fact that a front did not really exist. If they went straight down the road they could probably drive right into Kota Bharu without any resistance. The Japanese were everywhere, but where? During this early stage of the fighting they were keeping well off the roads. Tom was to be the first of a long list of friends who did not survive, for this was his first and last reconnaissance. We were far enough behind the lines not to hear the action, but so closely associated with the action that we lived it. An occasional Brewster Buffalo fighter flew over, but more often we saw Japanese Zeros so we had to take cover.

I found it easy to master the job of cipher clerk and soon felt very important running around the HQ with great enthusiasm and privy to mighty military secrets. Lt Col C.A. Hendricks, commanding officer of the 1st Hyderabads was killed by his troops when he tried to stop them leaving their defencive positions on the Kota Bharu airfield. Inspite of this bad news I thought, "It's just a matter of time before we get organised and throw the little people out of Malaya." I felt sure the Japanese had made the greatest mistake they possibly could in attacking the British Empire. Kota Bharu was attacked some hours before Pearl Harbour[2]. We were so involved in our own catastrophe that the treachery of Pearl Harbour was a distant disaster that we did not hear about until the following day. I am afraid that we did not share Churchill's enthusiasm that the war was now won. History has shown that one of Churchill's ambitions was to involve the Americans actively in the hostilities.

It did not take long for the Japanese to threaten our HQ position so the major insisted that I get out of there via a train that was presently on its way north. Under these conditions the train would stop well south of the fighting and all civilians would pile on in typical Oriental fashion. The major had a Japanese POW who was to be taken to Singapore for interrogation. He gave me a Smith & Weston .38 revolver and told me that the prisoner must be kept tied and in sight at all times. Prior to the train leaving he had a change of heart, took away my weapon, and put the prisoner in the care of some returning wounded soldiers. Under heavy guard he made the long trip to Singapore on the same train. Mr. and Mrs. Gregory and Joan had been evacuated earlier. In spite of my confidence that we would soon be winning, something seemed to be terribly wrong. We had left the estate in such haste and were now going even further south. Little did I know that the Japanese had crossed the peninsula and were advancing at a more rapid rate down the west coast.

After some twenty-four hungry hours on the train I phoned my Dad at the hotel and he sent the car to pick me up. Once again I took up residence at Raffles Hotel in the room next to my father. Now it was most important for me to be close to him as he had been made stone deaf in front line fighting during WW1. After retiring for the night and removing his hearing aid he had no idea when the air raid sirens sounded. He had two very big teak shelters constructed of 6inch by 6inch timber. They resembled coffins, with the opening on the side for easy access. These were installed in our rooms so that we need not go out into the big drainage ditches, so characteristic of Singapore, for shelter during a raid.

My next job, a few days before Christmas, was to go up the west coast and meet the heavy-duty construction equipment that was being brought down to Singapore. Dad's contracts on Sungei Patani and Butterworth involved the use of many Turnapulls, tractors, and other valuable equipment. This was now destined for work on the airfields of Singapore. I was to relieve any drivers who might be exhausted, as they had been on the road since the initial East coast attack. The company project engineers were in charge of the evacuation of the equipment. The idea was to get the equipment to Kuala Lumpur, well south of the fighting. Here they felt it would be safe to give the men a rest before moving on to Singapore. The average speed of our convoy moving south was approximately five miles per hour. Any faulty equipment was left with a mechanic on the roadside for immediate repairs. Our Malay and Chinese staff were excellent at jury rigging and usually had the machinery moving in short order. In Kuala Lumpur I had taken over the controls of a large Turnapull to relieve one of the exhausted drivers. When crossing a main intersection I had an unfortunate collision with a large army truck. Normally at these intersections there would be a Malay policeman directing traffic but now during these troubled times police were being used for other duties. There were no casualties involved in our little altercation and the police did not want to know about it. Just by the very nature and design of a Turnapull I was bound to come off on the winning side of anything the army had in Malaya, for there was not a single tank in the country.

At Kuala Lumpur there was the possibility of loading the equipment on to rail transport for a much faster move south. This option did not materialise. It was Christmas Day when I completed all the arrangements in Kuala Lumpur so I thought a quick drive back to Singapore, about two hundred miles, would make my Dad very happy and give me a chance to drive like mad with a reasonable excuse for doing so. I drove like fury in order to get to the hotel before dinner was over and give Dad a Christmas surprise. I did not make it until very late. He was furious. He implied that I was neglecting my job and the men I was responsible for and asked me to return right away. However, after a couple of drinks and chatting about the situation in general, I stayed the night and left for the north early Boxing Day. When I finally arrived in Singapore a week later he gave me a very nice, stainless steel, automatic watch for a Christmas present.

With the Japanese advancing at such a great speed I approached the HQ of the Royal Malayan Air Force in Kuala Lumpur and asked if I could join up for pilot training. The squadron leader in charge told me in all sincerity "as soon as we throw the little Bastards out of here we will be happy to take you on." The situation did not look too promising so I continued the journey south with the company equipment. Even as a seventeen year old I was beginning to doubt that we would "throw the little bastards out."

Several days later we got all the equipment safely to Singapore, where it could be put to good use on the different aerodromes that were still under construction, Tengah and Sambawang. It was not long before we were made aware of the New Zealand Air Force construction unit that was operating on the island. Now under wartime military regulations it appeared that the New Zealanders wanted our equipment — all the big earth moving equipment. It soon came under their control and I was left without any really significant work. I assisted my Dad and became a general messenger boy on many different jobs.

On one occasion when the now usual Japanese flight of twenty-seven bombers[3] flew over Tengah airfield I found myself in the middle of the field as they approached. I knew there were some slit trenches near the rubber trees on a slight rise to one side of the runway. This was my only hope. With a frantic dash I started a life and death sprint across the grassed area between the runway and the safety of a slit trench. A soon as I hit the bottom of the trench I was almost buried alive with the debris thrown up by a very near hit. The whistling crescendo of bombs so close is devastating. I had little time to worry about it as I now had to fight my way out of the earth covering me.

The following day I witnessed an extraordinary sight when the sirens sounded. As all the labourers started swarming off the airfield Robert Kinloch, one of the supervisors, stood in the gate way and started punching any one who tried to get past him. This gate was a truck entrance and must have been at least twelve feet wide. Since he was opposed by more than two hundred Chinese "coolies" he soon realised the foolishness of his patriotic efforts and was swept along with them to safer ground.

Early in January I was working on Sambawang aerodrome when much to my surprise and great delight, Chota, my Malay foreman from Kerilla estate, walked very proudly across the runway with his hand outstretched and a big smile on his face. He had moved fast after I had left him taking off the fuel injectors. He told me that he had two objectives - to keep the crew together, and get to Singapore. He figured that the easiest way to cross the river was over the bridge. However, this meant bucking the tide of oncoming refugees, joining the group that was heading south and gambling on the fact that the bridge was still standing. This he did successfully. With this big obstacle behind him he could take his time, or so he thought! He had not reckoned on the speed of the enemy advance and soon realised that he would have to put all his ingenuity to work to keep ahead of them. There were of course no train schedules at this time and with the trains running by guess and by God it was not easy to hitch a lift. He was well aware of the value of the fuel injectors and clung on to them like glue.

Eventually he arrived in Singapore with the crew intact and reported to the company offices. He had seen my Dad that morning, who told him how worried I was about leaving him behind. Dad had sent him out to the aerodrome to see me, so now I took him to the local coffee shop where we had a long chat. He was ecstatic to be back in Singapore with his three wives. He was forgiving and did not chastise me for leaving him behind. I thanked him for doing my job of getting the others out of that rotten situation. He was most grateful.

About a week after this I was back at Sambawang where Chota was now foreman of the mechanics maintaining the heavy earth moving equipment. We had a Bucyrus Erie tractor that was a standard reddish colour but had many rust marks on it. One of the men in the shop was at loose ends so Chota told him to get a can of red paint and touch up the rust marks. It was impossible to match the paint so the end result was a chicken pox Bucyrus Erie tractor - a unique piece of equipment that was recognisable amongst a hundred of its twin brothers. It was soon back on the job and working at peak efficiency in spite of its appearance.

I was still enjoying the wonderful life of Singapore. To bring in the New Year Jacquie and I had dinner under the stars at Kallang airport and then moved on to the Tanglin Club to take part in the dancing, and ring in the wonderful prospects of 1942 in the traditional style. As I learned soon after joining the RAF, the troops were enjoying life at the Worlds: The Great World, The New World and The Happy World. Taxi dancing was the rage and of course some of the girls were amiable to a little further enjoyment for the night. There was no cover charge; one just bought a number of tickets and after selecting the girl of one's choice, enjoyed the evening. Many soldiers and airmen found that after spending a fortune on tickets and dancing the night away, that they had chosen a nice girl who did not want go out for the night. *C'est la vie*. Tiger Beer in nice big quart bottles and a good variety of almost anything that tickled your fancy was always available. The social status of the individual did not matter in the merry-making of Singapore in these last desperate days. The majority of servicemen were enjoying themselves if they were in the city. Those poor devils in the front line were being hounded to death, if not by the Japanese, then by our own stupidity. The disorganisation and chaos, being administered by World War One senior officers has come to light, as we, the men who suffered for this, are speaking out, not only to record the facts for history but to preserve the memory of lives that were thrown away by pompous politicians and incompetent officers. Deaths of fine young men who had misplaced faith in their officers.

The Japanese were continuing their advance at an incredible rate and I was so close to military age that I volunteered. I was mad keen on flying so off to the RAF I went. Their organisation seemed to be pretty loose as they rejected me as being too young. They had only asked my age and no paper work had been initiated. I let two weeks go by hoping that they might forget me, as the number of white people joining the RAF as privates in Singapore was few and far between. Two weeks later, on the 23rd of January, I told them I was 18 and was accepted into the RAF - a proud moment.

I went to the Seletar Transit Camp, was processed into the Royal Air Force, given a uniform and told that I would soon be posted to South Africa for flying training. Seletar transit camp is situated close to the north shore of Singapore Island and about fifteen miles from the city. Dad had allowed me to keep a company car, which made my visits to the hotel easy. It also assured me of many friends who wanted to get a quick ride into the city and an easy ride back again at night. Most of the white people in Singapore who were of military age were in the volunteer forces, the army and the navy being the popular choices. I know of only six people who joined the RAF as other ranks. There must have been many more in the officer category. I had been in the COTC {Canadian Officers Training Corps} in Canada and so my basic training was advanced enough for me to take my place amongst the other Air Force "erks" [Lowest ranks in the RAF], and participate in Gregson's "X" Party training. Squadron Leader Gregson was an ex-sergeant major from World War 1, a military man who ran a tight unit based on strict discipline. He would review the troops on parade most mornings, inspect rifles and make sure that all ranks were dressed and shined in the appropriate manner. He created "X" Party, later known as 'Gregson's Grenadiers', from the men in this transit camp to become a mobile demolition squad. As the Japanese were advancing so fast it appeared that no previous provisions had been made by the RAF for demolition of petrol and ammunition that was stored in isolated areas. Gregson's plan was for us to be ready at a moment's notice to carry out a scorched earth policy. This seemed to be an ideal job for me while I was waiting for pilot training. I would see a fair amount of action and at the same time not be immersed in it.

Seletar runway was in direct line, as the Swordfish flies, with the transit camp sleeping quarters. The Swordfish[4] would fly out to sea on take off in the evening and invariably come right over our sleeping huts on their return around midnight. It seems that the Japanese had captured one of these planes on a northern airfield, or had something very similar to it, which they used on these return flights with great effect. As we lay on our bunks at night we would count the number of aircraft coming back, to check up on how many had made it successfully, and listen to their characteristic landing noises. On many occasions the last aeroplane, probably a *captured* Swordfish or Vildebeeste, did not land but dropped his bombs and flew off. The first time this happened everybody was caught unawares. The second time there was a good barrage to meet him. However, I believe he got away with it until the very last night raid on the camp.

The fight all the way down the Malayan peninsula was an uneven contest from the start of the campaign. We had no experience in jungle fighting, whereas the Japanese had been fighting in China for the last ten years. Most of the Japanese units fighting in Malaya had been trained in jungle warfare in Indochina or Formosa.

Their espionage was so easy it should not be called by this name. Japanese were allowed virtually free access to all military areas. Japanese Nationals owned rubber estates and tin mines throughout Malaya, many of them being active or retired military officers. The average military policeman did not know the difference between a Japanese, a Malay or a Chinese person. Of course the authorities believed that security was tight and on paper it probably looked good. However the man guarding the gate is the ultimate authority. All military bases had a very convenient photography shop just outside the gate with an exceptionally helpful staff to pry out details of "how many men, How many aeroplanes," etc. Close by would be situated a barber's shop for the same purpose. Invariably these were run by Japanese. They could tour the country at leisure. They owned businesses throughout the country and, significantly, on the desolate East Coast. The detailed maps used by the advancing Japanese were far superior to those held by the British forces. The ability of the Japanese to mingle with the Malay and Chinese population meant they could infiltrate or flank the fighting front with comparative ease. Their unscrupulous use of women and children as shields brought into effect a new aspect of fighting our men were not accustomed to [Chippington—Singapore the Inexcusable Betrayal]. The mines and estates owned and operated by the Japanese must have played a part in the overall espionage picture. They had all the advantages and freedoms of travelling in a peacetime country. Every day we heard stories through the military grape vine of butchery and slaughter of innocent people. There were so many eyewitness accounts of the most atrocious tortures that it made the German treatment of the Jews pale by comparison.

Unknown to me, my father was interested in keeping an eye on all his equipment, a very large investment. He had spoken to various senior officers, as he was well connected with the military, and I soon found myself attached to the New Zealand construction unit. Because of the vagaries of the services I never did get to see any of my father's heavy earth moving equipment while I was attached to the New Zealanders. And far more important to me at the time, I was not being paid. If one makes a major move in the services it takes a long time for the paperwork to catch up with the individual being moved. With the *laissez faire* attitude of the personnel staff and the fact that I transferred to another National Air Force created unusual problems and delays.

As an AC2 in the RAF in Singapore I found myself in some strange situations.

I lived in the Raffles Hotel, but The Raffles Hotel was out of bounds to all "other ranks." It was for officers only. The most distinguished part of an "erk's" dress is his forage cap. With this on, a man is immediately known to be in the services. Khaki shirt and shorts were not uncommon civilian wear so, by the simple expedient of removing my cap, I could make my way into the Raffles undetected by the ever watchful military police stationed outside. Even after getting into the hotel I was, on occasion, challenged by some junior naval officer who was too pompous for his own good. Upon declaring that I lived in the hotel, he invariably raised his voice and demanded proof of this ridiculous pronouncement. It was too easy to walk him over to the desk and get the staff to confirm my situation, much to his embarrassment. Dad was so well known that any time he approached the foyer of the hotel the watchman would call out the licence number of his car and the chauffeur would immediately drive to the entrance to pick him up. This so impressed me that after the war I was able to identify this car by its licence plate number. When Dad asked me why I should remember the number after so many incredible adventures had transpired I was able to rattle it [7696] off in Malay without hesitation.

Jack Dobbie and I became very good friends. Jack had joined up just a few weeks before I had. He was a rubber planter in Borneo when the Japanese attacked Malaya. Without a moment's hesitation he quit his job, flew to Singapore, and joined up. He spoke Malay with such fluency that he could easily mimic different accents. This always raised eyebrows with the surprised Malays he spoke to. He could have made a unique contribution to the war effort if he had not been so hasty in joining the RAF as an erk. His knowledge of South East Asia, its culture and people could have contributed to the overall effort in a far more purposeful way than running around blowing up ammunition and petrol dumps. He was a big fellow over 6ft 2in and two hundred pounds. He looked on me as a younger brother, as he was in his thirties, and considered that a young fellow of seventeen should at least be taught the ways of the world by some one with a little sophistication. It was great fun to spend an evening with Jack at the Great World or the Happy World where he would charm the Malay dance girls with his impeccable command of the language. Invariably the next morning on the CO's inspection parade I would have to cover for him and pray that he would turn up before the allocation of duties for the day. He only let me down once when I had answered his name on roll call and he did not show up for daily duty assignment. Gregson was far too experienced to have the simple answer of 'here' or 'present' as a response to the roll call. We had to give the last three digits of our service numbers. Since Jack and I had joined up within a few weeks of each other it was easy for me to remember his number - 785101.

As the Japanese advanced down the Malayan peninsula the New Zealand unit proved to be the smartest ancillary unit of all those in this war zone. In late January or early February we were ordered to evacuate immediately. On the morning the order to evacuate was announced we were milling about camp waiting for a new assignment when we were told in no uncertain terms that a ship was alongside the dock in Singapore harbour, a very dangerous situation as we were experiencing many air raids everyday. All personnel would carry only a backpack and side pack with our kit bags being transported by truck to the dock. The evacuation parade would be formed in exactly one hour. It turned out that a large passenger ship had disembarked some fresh desert trained troops for the final defence of Singapore. Singapore city was surrounded by rubber trees, swamp and jungle. Troops were still arriving in this stricken city a few days before the Japanese landed fifteen miles to the north.

Since the Japanese had complete command of the air, our ship had to load and leave in the shortest possible time. A short time after receiving our orders we were loaded into trucks and wheeled off to the docks. I had a full kit bag and backpack. Quite apart from my military kit I had re-equipped myself with civilian clothing, as it was far easier to enter the Raffles as a civilian. I moved with the unit on to a ship that was waiting to take us away. I boarded the ship with my fellow airmen, was assigned a bunk, stowed my kit, and went on deck to watch the cast-off proceedings. I had been leaning over the rail for about five minutes when one of the fellows rushed up to me and said my name was being called over the Tanoy [loud speaker] system. Why, of all the troops on board, would they want me? I was totally mystified and trying to puzzle this one out as I ran to the purser's, now adjutant's, office. I must get off the ship immediately. No time to get my kit - just "get off." The gangway already had the crane hooked to it and the ship was on the very verge of departure. Repeat "no time to get your kit - get off the ship." This was the second time in as many months that I had lost all. Once again newfound friends were lost without so much as a farewell. I never did hear what happened to my kit. Soon after arriving back at camp I wrote to the RNZAF HQ in Auckland, New Zealand, but didn't receive a reply. I discovered after the war that my Dad had written to the RNZAF in an effort to regain all my belongings, but without any luck. It appeared that as a member of the RAF my attachment to the RNZAF was for a temporary period only and subject to this hasty recall.

Back at the Transit camp things were heating up. I was reissued with Air Force uniforms but no consideration was given to the loss of my personal belongings. I became an enthusiastic member of "X" party again. The Japanese were very close to Singapore now and Gregson could see an expanded role for his small mobile unit - The Grenadiers.

Now, at the end of January, that the war was well in progress and the enemy at the gates of the city, the men in camp had a chance to look back at the situation before the Japanese attacked, it was painfully obvious what an efficient system of passive espionage they had. Many men recalled having such a friendly chat with the man in the photographer's shop and boasting about the capabilities of the Brewster Buffalo. And telling that really good barber, who always had a nice hot, sweet, cup of coffee ready for you, the "little insignificant" details of life on the base. With a little encouragement these details could be expanded to include who knows what? Many of the civilian employees on the bases were Japanese. The recruiting agents and security guards did not know how to identify Japanese who worked as "Malays" inside the military installations.

After the outbreak of hostilities some of our fighter aircraft went aloft with screwdrivers neatly slipped into the barrels of their machine guns. At night, tiles of some buildings were removed so that a gigantic arrow would be formed to point to that night's target. I personally witnessed the explosion of a Blenheim bomber over Singapore Island a few months before the hostilities began. The inquiry into this "accident" was held while I was tucked away on Kerilla Estate in Kelantan so I knew nothing of it. Apparently I was the only witness.[5]

Gregory Board an Australian Buffalo pilot is quoted in *"The World's Worst Aircraft"* by James Gilbert, saying 'Intelligence briefings almost daily by the most learned of men, who came in from the other side of the Japanese bamboo curtain, and told us that the best of the Japanese fighters were old fabric-covered biplanes which wouldn't stand a chance against the Buffalos. With this ringing promise of slaughtering the Japanese in the air should they get too big for their britches, we concentrated on flying and learning different methods of drinking gin-and-tonic. The entire squadron was wiped out to a man'.

After the Argyll & Sutherland Highlanders piped their way across the causeway on the 31st January, and a small hole was blown in the middle of it to impede the advance of the Japanese, we became quite busy doing a hundred and one jobs to assist both military and civilian authorities in the death clutches of a dying city. Our nights were anything but quiet. Seletar Transit camp was situated on the north slope of Singapore Island facing the northeast and the State of Johore. The Japanese set up their heavy artillery in front of us, and the defenders their heavy artillery behind us. It seemed that the most effective time for them to shell each other was after dark, usually just after we had jumped into our bunks for the night. I spent the first two nights of this incredible artillery battle in the slit trench just outside the hut. But it seemed that there was a pattern to this unbelievable barrage of shells. The shells that fell short or went astray had a different whine to them. When they fell close to camp there was a definite and distinctive tone involved. But this was a life and death situation. A stray shell could put many of us six feet under. I wanted to be secure in my own mind that

I knew what I was doing. On the third night, after much encouragement by Jack and my other friends in the unit, I had enough trust in my judgement to stay in my bunk when the shelling started. Even with this newfound skill our nights were pretty sleepless. The intensity of both barrages was awesome. We did not actually sleep at this time although we thought we did. The shelling was so intense that we heard every shell passing both north and south. This was the trick of "sleeping." You could actually identify the shells that were falling short and scramble for the slit trench before impact. A sleepless period on the border of life and death. A magnificent way to heighten one's awareness and a tool that would contribute to survival during the next few years.

It was not many days now before we were moved out of camp. The Japanese landing at 10:30 p.m. on the night of the 8th February had been strongly resisted[6], but they had been advancing continuously for the past nine weeks so there was a certain feeling that the inevitable was soon to take place. I managed to drive into Singapore on the night of February 11th for a quick visit with my Dad. He gave me the good news that Jacqueline had been evacuated and was on her way out of the war zone but no one knew of her destination.[7] I implored him to leave the city by any means he could. With all his connections he should be able to arrange some method of evacuation. I felt that his Navy friends might be able to help him. The air was controlled by the Japanese, as it had been from Day One, and the army was fighting a desperate last-ditch battle to save the city. I left the car at the hotel and hitched my way back to camp. The driver who picked me up was drunk as a skunk and was watching the sky instead of the road. I asked him what he was watching so he explained that with the blackout regulations in effect and a bright moon overhead the best way to make progress was to drive by the gap between the trees. A great deal of the land between the city and Seletar was planted with rubber. This nice neat arrangement of trees meant that there was a regular gap to the sky that followed the road. It helped to have one too many under the belt to drive comfortably in this fashion. We got back to the barracks without incident, proving that necessity is the mother of invention.

The naval base [which my Dad had a large hand in building] and Seletar aerodrome were now evacuated. Jack got word that the NAFFI[8] had been abandoned without any of the stock being moved. He mentioned this to the C.O. and volunteered to rescue the stores before they fell into Japanese hands. He got permission to take a three ton truck with a volunteer crew into the base and liberate them. About ten o'clock that morning I found myself on the back of a three-ton truck happily going down the North Slope into Seletar air base. I thought the driver was over doing it a bit as we seemed to be going hell for leather down the slope. All was well as we pulled up alongside the canteen. The plan was to load all the bulk stores - cartons of cigarettes, chocolates, liquor by the case, and a wide variety of other "stuff," all easily handled with the maximum movement in the minimum of time. Soon the truck was loaded and we started our journey up the hill and back to camp. Of course we were discussing the spoils of the escapade. Each of us would have the choice of a carton of goodies for himself and several cartons of chocolates would be put into the barracks for the good of all. The rest of the loot would be surrendered and turned into the camp NAFFI. The commanding officer had given permission for the digression so we were bound to show a good return for the risks taken.

The Japanese must have been watching us from their artillery observation post in Johore[9] as we proceeded up the main road. This was an ideal situation for their artillery as the slope we drove down faced north with an uninterrupted view directly to their gun emplacements, facing south. After we had loaded the truck and were on our way out of the base, the shelling started. The Japanese straddled the road with a heavy barrage of shells, but we managed to get back to camp safely. The Japanese must have thought we were after some really top-secret equipment to have paid that much attention to us. They ruined the road for any further attempt to rescue stores. The value of shells expended far exceeded the value of one truck in spite of its highly desirable cargo.

The twenty-four hour air raids were knocking Singapore to smithereens. Many of the roads were so scarred with craters that they were impassable. Hundreds of buildings were in shambles. The city was host to all the evacuees from the Malaya peninsula. This presented a double problem - thousands upon thousands of people in a city with hundreds of houses, hotels, shops, apartments and other buildings destroyed.

The Japanese were dropping anti-personnel bombs which had the nasty effect of ripping out your guts as you lay on the ground for protection. They were designed in such a fashion that on explosion the fragments would rip along the surface of the ground and tear any one in the prone position to pieces. They also dropped "tins of cigarettes." These would invariably be picked up by children playing in the rubble after an air raid. In fact the cigarette tins were in themselves small bombs, powerful enough to maim a child, usually blowing off both hands, but not enough power to kill outright. Prior to and during the hostilities most cigarettes were sold in tins of fifty. These tins were sealed to prevent moisture absorption.

On one of our calls to demolish a petrol dump I remember driving down a road with gas and oil stored on either side of it. The road and dump had just been bombed with the result that the road was covered in oil. Our truck hit the oil patch travelling at approximately forty miles per hour and made two complete turns before the vehicle was through the oil and on the dry surface again. The driver did not have time to react to the situation so we carried on as if nothing had happened. Our demolition had been done for us by a couple of stray bombs. Whose, we wondered? The front line was just in the rubber trees to the north of us so the bombs could well have been from our own aircraft. We drove back over this same oil-marred road but with far greater caution.

On another occasion we rushed out to Tengah aerodrome to demolish their entire 'ammo' depot. This was early in the morning of the 9th or 10th February. When we were close to the depot the road was blocked with vehicles going in the opposite direction. The resulting traffic jam was soon spotted by Japanese dive bombers, turning us into a prime target before reaching our destination. We now got off the vehicle and added our fire power of ten .303 rifles to the Bofors that formed the ground defence of Tengah and the hundreds, probably thousands, of air force and army men in the area. We individually claimed to have shot down the dive-bomber that failed to pull out of his final dive. Who knows? When the immediate danger passed we found out that the Bofors protecting the airfield were being used in the horizontal position as the advancing Japanese were in the rubber plantation on the north side of the airfield. The ground defence boys had done as much damage as possible to the stocks of ammunition and petrol, so we returned to base satisfied that between us we had knocked down a Japanese dive-bomber. Air Force ground defence were doing a magnificent job against an advancing enemy, in spite of the fact that all their training had been concentrated on air defence, not ground attack.

The next day we formed a defensive line behind some army units, but this did not last long. I was terrified from the moment we crept into our positions with bayonets fixed and loaded down with ammunition. Fighting the enemy in the air was a test of skill, not the same as this ridiculous business with cold steel in your hands. Our only protection was to take cover behind very young rubber trees. There were no slit trenches, foxholes or other cover. It seemed to me that experienced infantry men would find it hard to fight under these conditions. We were soon pulled out and ordered into the city. There were huge palls of smoke covering the whole of Singapore. Thousands of people wandered the streets. The noise was incredible - shells, bombs, machine gun fire, Japanese Zeros everywhere. The place was stinking with dead bodies. Broken water mains were involuntarily cleaning the streets. Labour battalions were organised to keep the city running, but they seemed only to work where the danger was least. We were sent to the dock area to assist in any way that was needed. The bombing here was intense, as the ships in port represented excellent targets. Some of them had been badly damaged and were abandoned.

Our orders had been vague. Nobody needed any assistance. There were hoards of civilians who had been pressed into this area as the free territory of Singapore shrank into the very small city and dock district. We were wandering around the godowns (warehouses) looking for I know not what. There was any amount of arms and ammunition. I soon found myself with a Thompson automatic (Dillinger style) complete with three bandoleers of ammo; a sten gun with five pouches of clips and of course my .303 rifle. I could not get rid of this as I had signed for it. We may be losing thousands of lives, dozens of aeroplanes, battleships, etc. but I had signed for my rifle and was honour bound to keep it until death do us part.

Soon we were formed up in four ranks and told that the CO had managed to find a skipper who could navigate a small coastal steamer to Batavia (Jakarta), Java. The first hazard to overcome was our own minefield. It was not the type of job anyone would like to tackle without detailed charts. All we had to do was man the ship and defend it. The whole unit was ordered aboard the SS *Ipoh*. It soon was apparent why we had been lucky enough to secure a means of evacuation. The *Ipoh* had a marked list to the starboard and was close to, if not on her last trip. She had suffered a near hit in a recent bombing raid and had been abandoned. There was not a soul on board so we took over with great relish. *Ipoh* was in good condition as far as the upkeep was concerned. She was clean and tidy which indicated to us that she had only very recently been abandoned. It appeared that the bombs had been dropped to the seaward side of the ship as she was tied to the dock, a lucky break for us as the damage would have been much worse if the bombs had fallen close on the dock side. We were not the only unit to board this crippled ship. Soon it was crowded with every conceivable type of person getting out of this smouldering city. Navy, army and civilians crowded every inch of space to be found. I was soon to find out that not too many of the airmen on board were keen to work their way to freedom. The call went out for volunteers to man and stoke the furnaces. The coalbunker was just about full, but there were few volunteers to man and stoke the furnaces. While there were obvious dangers to being below the water line, surely this was preferable to being taken a prisoner by the Japanese. But only a handful volunteered. I was amazed that everybody was not scrambling to get a shovel in their hands so that we could get out of this burning city. I soon found myself wielding a large shovel and feeding the insatiable boilers. With the intense heat surrounding us we drank warm water directly from a rusty bucket that we found in the boiler room.

During the campaign to date we had all heard stories of Japanese brutality. How they had doused Chinese civilians [mostly country folk] with petrol, set them on fire and then put out the flames with boiling water - premeditated torture. How the Japanese had tied individuals' hands behind their backs and then tied them to high branches of trees and beaten them to death. How they had disembowelled pregnant village women. The stories were endless and had proved to us that we were fighting an inhumane enemy.

The best job was the defence of the ship. Here one was stationed on the top deck with the incredible amount of small arms that we had picked up on the docks, plus a few Bren guns and maybe even a few point five-inch machine guns. There was also a lot of booze to go along with this. I volunteered for the stoke hold and soon found myself nearly naked, sweating like a trooper, and shovelling coal like there was no tomorrow. Boy, was that ever hard work, but I knew we were putting the miles between us and the Japanese.

After enough stokers had been found to give us originals a break I would spend my spare time as close to the top deck as I could. We were strafed and bombed by all kinds of Japanese aircraft and put up a very good defence. The amount of ammo' shot off was quite beyond belief. We did not see any of the fighters go down but knew that they must have been hit. Nothing could have survived our barrages without some damage. The *Empire Star*, a regular passenger vessel, full of troops, passed us in broad daylight, only to be heavily bombed before she reached the horizon. We were fortunate, as the squadron of 27 bombers that flew directly overhead, but out of range of our small arms, could obviously see the much bigger target and attacked that. We saw the *Empire Star* survive the attack but had no idea if it had been damaged. Japanese bombers were now so completely in control of the air that they flew at only about five thousand feet or less. Prior to this they were usually at twenty thousand feet plus.

The following day more bombers came over but again they let us go. We concluded that our list was so bad the Japanese must have thought we were sinking. The normal time for this trip was thirty-six hours. We took three days and were happy to be in Batavia, where a really strong fight could be organised. If the rumours of squadrons of Hurricane and Kittyhawk fighters arriving in Java were true we would soon have the Japanese in a defensive position.

One thing I clearly remember about the retreat from Kota Bharu to Singapore was that we always had to take cover when we heard aircraft approaching. At first we checked to see if our Buffaloes were up there, but it did not take long to realise that the sound of aircraft meant the Japanese were on the way. The cry "its one of ours" was seldom heard.

1   Sir Charles Vyner de Windt Brooke 1874—1963. Son of the first "White Raja" who was given land [Sarawak] for helping the Sultan quell an uprising. In 1941 he initiated a constitution to create a self-governing state. This was delayed by the Japanese aggression and not finalised until 1962.

2   This was not the first attack of the Japanese against the allies. Michael Montgomery in his excellent book "*Who Sank the Sidney*" Australia: Cassell, 1983 mentions the first attack as being on the 19th November 1941.

3   The Japanese system of bombing became known as "Pattern Bombing". They invariably flew in squadrons of twenty-seven bombers and let their "Bombs Away" on one command. As the campaign progressed and they became aware that there was no aerial opposition these flights

numbered up to 100 aircraft.

4   The Swordfish [and the Vildebeeste] was probably the oldest aircraft in the RAF. Operational in 1934 it was scheduled for retirement in 1939. A biplane with a single open fore and aft cockpit for the pilot and air-gunner. It was powered by a Bristol Pegasus 30, 9-cylinder radial engine with a top speed of 138 mph. The armament consisted of a .303 firing through the propeller and a rear mounted .303 machine gun. The rear gunner stood in the open cockpit to operate the machine gun. The Japanese Navy Zero was powered by Nakajima Sakae 21, 14 cylinder radial engine top speed 340 mph. Armed with 2* 20mm cannon and 2 machine guns.

5   The acts of sabotage and the ease of infiltrating our units would make an extremely interesting book. Unfortunately a lot of the information is of a personal nature and shunned by the official records.

6   Lt - Gen. A.E.Percival the Army Commander in Malaya and Singapore had been advised to expect a landing on the Westside of the causeway. He insisted on concentrating his troops on the Eastside. The landing took place on the Westside at 10:30 pm on the 8th February against the 22nd Australian Brigade. Due to the preceding heavy artillery barrage the surface telephone lines had all been severed and the searchlights to cover this action could not be active without specific orders from HQ.

7   Jacqueline was not evacuated. She moved with her parents to Saigon, a former French colony occupied by the Japanese since July 1941. She spent the remainder of the war in relative freedom. We continued our friendship for a short period after the war.

8   Naffi is the acronym for the Navy, Army, Air Force Institute. Canteen facilities for soft drinks, a light snack, etc.

9   This Observation Post was in the Sultan's Palace in the town of Johore. This situation is a classic microcosm of the Far East campaign. The British would not consider shelling the Palace whereas the Japanese would not hesitate to destroy anything that may impede their conquest of the Far East.

2

JAVA

INCOMPETANCE, DISASTER, CAPTURE

You are lost that is why you are free.

FRANZ KAFKA

We arrived at Batavia in one piece, with the old ship still listing heavily to starboard but without food or water on board. The Dutch authorities asked us to move on to Australia but our officers refused on the grounds that we had no provisions. The end result was that we went ashore and were found billets in King William School. This school was already housing other contingents of RAF who had arrived prior to us, many being reinforcements directly from the UK. We heard the good news that forty-eight Hurricanes had been flown off the aircraft carrier *Indomitable* and were now operating out of P1 and P2 in Sumatra. These designations covered the two air strips located near Palembang, the large oil-producing centre in South Sumatra, one of the main targets of the entire Japanese aggression. P2 was reputed to be the only airstrip in the Far East the Japanese did *not* know about.

We were soon finding our way around this city although the language was a bit of a problem. I spoke Malay and found that I could converse reasonably with both the Dutch and the Indonesians. My first priority was to find out if my father had been able to get out of Singapore. The Hotel Des Indes was the best hotel in Batavia so I raced off to leave a note at the reception desk. Their attitude was not reassuring. Being the lowest rank in the air force did not create much of an impression in this prestige-loving part of the world. The reception desk clerks accepted my note with a great deal of scepticism.[1]

It was about the day after we arrived in Batavia, 15th February, we learned that Singapore had fallen. What a crushing defeat! Soldiers had been disembarking at the docks just a few days before the city capitulated.[2] How could this have happened to the British Empire? How could our senior officers be so misinformed? And even worse, why did the general public know so little of what was happening? My strong patriotic sense was beginning to question —

why were we in this pickle? As a seventeen year old in uniform there seemed to be many questions arising, the answers to which I had always taken for granted. Surely our leaders always told the truth? Is this not basic to leadership?[3]

A quick look at the calendar showed that the whole campaign had lasted ten weeks to the day. My strong patriotic belief in the British Empire was being slowly ground down by these horrible people. General Sir A. Wavell was in command and now in Java, so we still had hopes that someone could turn the tide. We heard that squadrons of Hurricanes were on the way to reinforce Java. In fact some had taken off from their aircraft carrier and had landed at Palembang (P1). The grape vine news told us that several squadrons of Hurricanes would be located there. The chances of their success were minimal as the personnel were directly from England where goods and services were immediately available. The setting of P1 and P2 was the opposite of anything one could find in England. Palembang 1 was essentially a jungle airstrip without the basic necessities to keep a fighter squadron in the air. Men who had just arrived from an English winter in the pleasant British countryside with a pub on every corner now found themselves in the tropical jungle of one of the remotest islands in the world. No pubs here. No maintenance facilities, no electricity, limited, unreliable transportation and only the crudest of accommodation. The men were up to the challenge but the leaders were incapable of organising an effective infrastructure. Maybe their hands were tied by the international aspect of organising resistance on foreign soil, or perhaps they were overwhelmed by the enormity of the situation or just totally out of their depth. The fastest and the only fighter in Singapore and Malaya had been the Brewster Buffalo, an aircraft the American Forces had rejected years previously. Now we were getting first class fighter aircraft without the basic requirements (including a good, reliable electrical supply and some transport system to cover the large areas of these two 'dromes) to operate the maintenance equipment. Who was running this war? Did they really think we could win here with outdated aircraft and unreliable or non-existent maintenance equipment?

As we had settled into the school in Batavia we heard the most terrible stories from Singapore. In the military hospital the Japanese had killed nurses, doctors and patients alike. They had captured the hospital and instead of keeping it as a place for wounded and sick people they treated it as a killing ground. Patients confined to bed and nurses trying to administer to them were bayoneted for the glory of the Samurai warriors. Many patients, orderlies, nurses, and doctors, unarmed and considering themselves safe, were slaughtered in cold blood, mostly bayoneted to death. This in the name of Bushido? Of the many nurses who escaped or were fortunately evacuated from the various military hospitals in Singapore sixty five sailed on the *Vyner Brooke* and were sunk off

Banka Island. After many hours in the water twenty-two nurses and one civilian lady ended up on Radji beach. Some hours later 20 British soldiers arrived on the same beach. One of the men decided to get some help for the wounded and managed to find a patrol of fifteen Japanese under the command of an officer. When the Japanese arrived on the scene the officer separated the men from the women and ordered them to move over a nearby hill. Most of the men were bayoneted to death. A few who tried to escape were shot. On return to the beach, the Japanese soldiers under the command of their officer ordered all of the nurses into the water. When they had waded out to about waist height machine gun fire mowed them down. Nurse Bullwinkel was the only survivor of this absolutely needless and senseless killing. The code of Bushido or cold-blooded murder? (I had the privilege of meeting Nurse Bullwinkel in Australia some forty-four years after this incident).

The Chinese population was gathered on the *padang* (park) in central Singapore, herded onto trucks, taken to the Changi area, then down to the beach, at low tide mark and machined gunned — not just a few truck loads, but approximately seventy thousand unarmed men and boys. The conquering Samurai were living up to their code as warrior captains.[4]

For the next nine days I called at the Hotel Des Indes as late in the day as possible as I naively thought this was the most advantageous time to find my Dad. No such luck! All the inquiries that I made of people who had subsequently arrived from Singapore proved to be fruitless. I feared for my Dad's life if he was interned by the Japanese. He would soon run out of batteries for his hearing aid and that would make an already difficult life almost impossible.

During the day we were employed on the docks doing a variety of jobs. I was working alongside *H.M.S. Exeter* when a squadron of twenty-seven Japanese bombers came over. To have a cruiser tied to the dockside must have seemed the ultimate in targets for them. For us, on the dock, it was an ear splitting episode never to be forgotten. The *Exeter* was fighting back with all she had and believe me that is a lot of firepower. Her chances seemed slim as it was Japanese air power that had recently sunk both the *Prince of Wales* and the *Repulse* in two hours of heavy action — action where the victims were free to manoeuvre at their own will. The squadron passed over and with them went our terrifying moments of sound and action. The cruiser was still in one piece and we were still alive. As soon as the raid finished the cruiser and our work party moved with remarkable speed to clear this hot area. The *Exeter* lived for only a few more days as she clashed with the full force of the Japanese navy in the Java Sea Battle and was sunk a few days later in Sunda Straits.

We had only been in Batavia for nine or ten days when the order came for us to move. Our only luxury in Batavia was a restaurant we had discovered that served steak, egg and chips for one guilder, a meal of great proportions that satisfied our meagre budgets. I only visited there once but it made a nice change from the rations of the day. On arrival in Batavia I had to relinquish my small armoury and was once again reduced to the issue .303 rifle, the slowest firing of my three weapons. Understandably we all had to use the same type of weapon or the requirements for ammunition could not have been fulfilled. By this time I had accumulated a full backpack and side pack of possessions. I had learned the hard way not to have more kit than I could carry.

Orders had a way of being compromised soon after they had been decided on at the highest level. This was common knowledge but the effort at secrecy had to be maintained, resulting in us being kept at arms' length from the true situation - especially involving our movements. It appears that the Japanese knew where we were going and the purpose of the journey. We were loaded into a train and moved south to Purwakarta, a village in south central Java. Here we were housed in tobacco drying sheds for the next ten days. We were obviously putting in time, as the only official activities we had were to keep fit. This was a rural area of Java so our only recreation was to visit the local village. This rather appealed to me as I could get to know the people better and practice my Malay. Actually it was now Indonesian, a similar language. I had a great respect for the Malay people and was keen to find the same qualities in the Indonesians. The Malays have an easy attitude to life, which is frequently interpreted by the Westerners as being unambitious and lazy. In fact it is a deep realisation that life is for living and not for continual stressful striving. The Javanese do not have the same attitude to life as the Malays. They are more emotional and inclined to an impulsive temperament.

A loudspeaker system had been installed at the end of the tall drying sheds that housed us. One morning we were assembled beside the speakers and told that Winston Churchill was going to address us. We huddled around in the bright sunlight and waited for him to start. Much to our surprise he told us that we were going to fight to the last man. That we would never surrender and that the eyes of the world were upon us.

I am afraid that the morale of the troops was not up to this sort of announcement, especially considering the fact that he was some nine thousand miles away from the action. Many of the men present had arrived in Singapore or Java just a few weeks and even days before this speech. This meant that thousands of men were being sacrificed for what? Why had they come to fight to the last man when the result was already known? How could he do this? We were staggered. Did this war mean that we were to be sacrificed on the cross of foolishness, for politics? If so, why? Who was deciding our fate and why were they so stupid in dealing with us? My faith in the British Empire was being shattered rapidly. There was not a grain of intelligence in the way we were being treated.

The next day, 5th March 1942, in keeping with this strange war, we were marched to the railway station and told that we were going to Tjilatjap, a port on the south coast, where a boat was to evacuate us to Australia. Most of the RAF fellows I was with were highly trained aircraft maintenance personnel. Many of them were pre-war regular airmen with more than one trade to their name. I gathered that, as a potential pilot, I was to be included with the highly trained. The only catch to this last piece of good news was that we would have to leave our arms and ammunition behind. This was a good thing, we thought, as it must mean that the senior officers were serious about our safe journey to, and evacuation from, Tjilatjap. We were told that the Dutch army was short of arms and ammunition and that our arms would be immediately transferred to them. They were preparing for the fight of their lives and they would fight to the last man. Lucky Devils?

We stacked our arms in true military fashion on the platform and then we were ordered to board the cattle cars. Being an outdoor type I got permission from our sergeant to sit on the brake platform at the end of the railway car that I had been assigned to. I was on the left hand (north) side as the train pulled slowly out of the station. We chugged along at a slow rate with the old steam engine belching out copious quantities of smoke. The iron and wood brake platform that I found myself sitting on was hard, but this was easy to take as I could stand up and stretch my legs whenever I felt like it. In spite of the continual stream of cinders that wafted by me there was an inexhaustible supply of fresh air. I thought of my last train journey down the length of Malaya when I had known for sure that I was running away from the rapidly advancing Japanese army. I was on the run again but did not know where I, or the enemy, was. It was impossible for me to find a map of the island and in spite of a good general knowledge of the Far East I had no idea of the geography of Java or Indonesia with its hundreds of islands.

Taffy had decided to join me and was sitting on the right hand (south) side of our little platform. We watched the sun go down, nothing spectacular this evening. Soon after dark we went through a clearing in the jungle and I was struck with the incredibly beautiful sight of millions of fireflies twinkling throughout the whole of the cleared area. The moon was high enough to show a clear delineation of the coconut palms swaying in the breeze against the skyline. The whole effect was so enjoyable it inscribed itself on my mind for a lifetime. I sat with my back against the railing of the platform and just soaked in this scene. Taffy was also an outdoor type. He was tall and lean and had been in the air force about a year. Coming from the south of Wales he enjoyed a good singsong and contributed heartily. Now he was thanking his lucky stars that he had chosen to stay on the outside with me. There is nothing appealing about traveling in an old, dirty, airless boxcar. I put my hands over my ears to block out the chugging of the engine to further enjoy this exquisite scene. Swaying palms, - moonlight, and a million individual fire flies each flashing its own signal around this little clearing. I was soaking up the tranquility of the scene when there was a shuddering explosion. I heard the whirring noise of a missile flying through the air, so reminiscent of Singapore, and then a fantastic explosion just ahead of our boxcar.

A mortar bomb had been fired, signaling the start of an attack. Machine guns and rifle fire raked the train. Without any arms we were sitting ducks for the enemy. Parachute troops must have been dropped and surrounded the railway. We were in the thick of it.[5] I grabbed my helmet and curled into a vertical fetal position trying to hide behind this ridiculously small protection. There were troops running beside me - - Japs or Brits? For a moment I thought the Japs were running beside the train in an effort to board it and massacre all on board. This type of suicidal practice was quite in keeping with their fanatical attitude. The train was still moving but slowing down as if all power were lost - coasting. We guessed that the mortar bomb that had triggered this massacre had exploded near the engine and holed the steam boiler. But why were people running beside us? Did they know we were without arms? It seemed that those who were in the cattle cars had panicked. Not wanting to be trapped or to be such an ideal target, they jumped out hoping to find some cover. By the time we realised what had happened we were through the worst of it. The engine was out of steam and we came to a complete halt. We were past the jungle clearing and out of the way of the Japanese for the time being. We looked for some one to organise us but the officers had taken off down the tracks at high speed. The senior NCOs told us to gather what belongings we could and follow the officers, who were going in the right direction. There was no real organisation. We just took off down the railroad tracks with as much as we could carry, knowing that the Japs would be following as soon as possible. I thought the finest officers in the world were in the RAF. Now they had abandoned us!

During the march along the railroad tracks many of the men who had left the train with full packs were soon lamenting the fact that they had so much kit. I had grabbed my back and side packs as Taffy had, but I lost him in the race down the tracks. Being a great deal taller than I am, and with an excellent incentive for fast movement, I should imagine he was ahead of me. Decisions had to be made rapidly as to which pack to discard first. With the Japanese on our tail nobody had time to think about the details of unpacking and selecting the treasures that should be kept. In this respect I was ahead of the game - all my remaining possessions were rather mundane and limited. I carried them all. The only object of real value that I possessed was the watch that my father had given me for Christmas just ten weeks ago. This was securely around my wrist.

After marching for what seemed hours, straining to hear if the invaders were catching us, we arrived at a station immediately adjacent to a bridge. We had caught up with our officers, some of whom were negotiating with the Dutch army guard in a little hut next to the railroad bridge. Like sheep we lined up to wait word that we were allowed to cross the bridge. We did not have a single gun amongst the whole group so there seemed little point in staying on the fighting side of the bridge. After milling about in the dark for some considerable time a decision was reached and we proceeded across in single file. All men had to stack their kit before being allowed on to the approaches of the bridge. This rather ominous procedure seemed a repeat performance of what had happened at the station before getting on to the train? All arms had been taken from us just before we were attacked by the Japanese. Now without kit we were to cross the river with the Japanese hot on our tail. How would the kit be taken over? Surely it would be easier for each man to carry his own kit? With the Japanese in relentless pursuit it seemed to be a senseless waste of our few possessions and a dangerous recovery mission later in the night or following day. Once over the river no one would return unarmed to face a ruthless and fanatic enemy.

There was a narrow maintenance track, near to, but separated from the railway lines, no doubt used by the local population, on to which we were herded and the crossing began. I had just passed the centre of the bridge when a Dutch soldier elbowed his way past me going in the opposite direction. He had fought his way past all the men on this narrow track to the centre point of the bridge, not easy to do as the feeling between the English and the Dutch was not the best. He was being called an unhealthy variety of names when there was a huge explosion right behind us. I, with the fellows immediately around me, was blown to the far side of the river and landed on the relatively soft bank, unhurt. The Dutch soldier had sacrificed his life in a desperate and heroic attempt to save all the RAF personnel on the bridge.

What in the hell had happened now? Our immediate reaction was to get under cover as it appeared that the Japanese had caught up with us and were opening up with their mortar, soon to have their machine guns in action again. However it turned out that the Dutch had timed the bridge to blow at midnight and it had been deliberately demolished without warning us. How many men we lost on this occasion I do not know.[6]

While getting ourselves together and looking for the wounded we were ordered to move away from the river as quickly as possible. A small rescue party was to stay behind to search for those blown into the water, to get a rope across the river, and to assist the wounded and those still on the other side of the bridge. It was a difficult task in the middle of the night, in unfamiliar surroundings, without equipment.

We had seen only a few Dutch soldiers on guard. It is doubtful that they had equipment for a rescue operation. The man who had been rushing towards the centre of the bridge must have sacrificed his life in a vain and brave attempt to stop the bridge being blown. Being a member of the bridge guard he must have been familiar with the wiring and the fuse system. My guess is that he was trying to race the fuse to the detonators in a gallant and fearless attempt to save many RAF lives.

I joined the group on the line heading south. We proceeded at a good clip without our fifty pound packs. With the secrecy that surrounds war time movement of troops all we knew was that we were headed for the south coast town of Tjilatjap and evacuation to Australia. At daybreak we stopped by a little stream to get some water. Many of the fellows had been warned not to drink anything unless it was bottled or boiled. I felt that I was sufficiently accustomed to the Far East and could get away with a good drink of fresh stream water, and did. I doubt if there is a river or stream that is this close to the sea that is not highly contaminated. Rivers are used for all purposes - bathing, washing and toilets. There is always some enterprising character taking advantage of those who are gullible. Not more than one hundred yards from the stream a couple of fellows were selling fresh drinking water out of RAF bottles for five guilders a bottle. The five guilders covered the water only. They managed to get quite a few customers.

At this stopping point we discussed our position and what action should be taken to get us to Tjilatjap. Nobody knew the direction of our destination, other than south. No maps were available. Somebody had the idea that if we moved across country we would cut miles off the railway route, and not be so exposed to enemy aircraft. This was a totally wrong decision, though it was presented in such away that it seemed the only way to go. We started across country and soon found that we had to race for cover whenever Japanese aircraft came over. During the whole day we saw only one Hurricane and must have dived into the bushes for fifty Japanese planes. Progress was slow. From the 7th December to the 8th March, the entire Far East campaign, this was the only time I saw a Hurricane in flight.

March 7th was a repeat of the previous day. At night we lay on the ground and spent most of the time killing mosquitoes. By this time the group of us who had left the blown bridge had thinned out to just a few stragglers wandering aimlessly around not knowing where we were or what to do next. Each little group thought they had the best idea of how to get to the South coast. Some marched late into the night; others started before the sun was up. Each little party headed in the direction they felt would get them to their destination in the fastest time. I had long since lost my few friends and was trying to make my way south with a bunch of fellows who appeared to have answers. I came across three fellows huddled in a group and soon realised that two of them were tending the fellow lying on the ground with his guts torn out by a bomb fragment. There was nothing to be done so I kept going. I don't think he lasted too long. With a little more experience we would have known that traveling at night was far more effective than daytime travel.

On the morning of March 8th I came across the railway tracks again and followed them until I came to a large platform with the name Tasik Malaja on it. It did not mean a thing to me. I had no idea how this related to Tjilatjap. There were a few fellows squatting and lying around on the station so I joined them for a rest. It was much easier to sleep on the warm concrete surface with the bright sun on me than to combat all the insects of the night. The only thing I possessed at this time was a tin of condensed milk. Somebody produced a knife and we soon had it opened. There were four or five of us on the station when one of the others offered me a drink from a cup half filled with water. At this stage of my life I was still very polite and thought that he was offering me the water at his own expense - sharing it with me. I felt that we must all be very thirsty and so I refused his kind offer only to see him pour the water on to the hot concrete and watch it soak quickly into the sun-dried surface. Lessons in life were coming thick and fast.

I had been resting for a couple of hours when a truck drove to the station and told us that everybody must report to the school in the town. This was my first inkling that there was anyone around who had any authority and that the RAF was back in business. We were given instructions on how to get to the school but were leery of obeying them. I was all for going on down the railway but common sense prevailed and I joined the others. We got to the school and found a regular RAF organisation there. Also there was a large pile of shoes and boots on the grass of the school grounds. Anybody in need of footwear could help himself. This was my chance to get rid of my air force boots. I picked out a beautiful pair of thin-soled patent leather shoes - a sight to behold. I was so proud of the change I had made. Discarding my heavy RAF boots I slipped the lightweight patent leather shoes on. Just what was the RAF coming to, allowing "erks" to choose their own foot wear? If this lax attitude continued we would soon be wearing anything we could find! How true. Within a few hours we would be advised that Java had capitulated, which in turn made my choice of shoes a foolish mistake. I would soon be in need of a strong pair of boots.

Unknown to us Tasik Malaja (TM) was one of the aerodromes that was still operating with a full complement of RAF personnel, offering the heaviest resistance against the Jap invasion of the north coast. RAF Hurricanes had played their part in this action.

We were moved from the school to the aerodrome by trucks and paraded on the runway. Here for the first time in weeks I saw my CO from X Party, Wing Commander Gregson. He had been promoted. He had all the troops lined up on the runway and was telling us that the Dutch commander in chief had surrendered to the Japanese forces. We were now officially Prisoners of War. Just as he finished saying this the ominous sound of a Japanese bomber squadron approached directly over the runway, flying down the length of it at a height of two thousand feet. Gregson gave the order for the parade to stand to attention. We just heard this before his voice was drowned out by the roar of aircraft overhead. Not a man moved. I raised my eyes to see what type of aircraft they were when to my horror I saw the bomb bays opening. Not a soul moved. It was an incredible feeling - rigid discipline or instant death. I am sure that Wing Commander Gregson was one of the few RAF officers in Java who had the ability to command men so effectively under such dire circumstances. The bombers flew over and we, four thousand airmen, breathed a sigh of relief. If there had been any attempt to run from the parade the Japanese would not have hesitated to let their bombs away.

We were paraded at approximately 11:30am. The official surrender time must have been very close to noon on the 8th March 1942. How good were the Japanese communications? Was their lust for blood to be controlled on this occasion? All these thoughts and many more went through our heads at this time.

It was evening before I arrived at the hangars where we were to be housed. These were huge buildings with the front side open so that aircraft could be wheeled in. The floors were concrete. I had been separated from the fellows that I had met on the railway station and so I walked into prison camp a forlorn and lonely soul, not knowing where to claim a space for my own. I was hailed by some army men who saw me wandering around in a most dejected way. They invited me to join them so I threw in my lot with this bunch. They were army men of an ack ack unit (anti aircraft) that had been defending various RAF bases. A different crowd to the average RAF "erks". These fellows were mostly from Glasgow and tough as nails. Their whole outlook on life was different to most of the men I associated with in the RAF. You got what you could when you could and to hell with the rest of mankind. Their favourite saying was "Fuck you Jack, I'm fire proof." Yet they were the only group to befriend a lost comrade. I was most appreciative of their help and stayed with them until some form of organisation was brought to our motley gathering.

I was really interested in this aerodrome. This was the first and last time during my five years in the Air Force that I was on an operational fighting air strip and already it was too late - no operations and no fighting. However I took off for the dispersal hangars first thing the next morning and saw to my delight a Hurricane and many Kittyhawks. Many more Kittyhawks were still in their crates. There were also Hudson Bombers, Lodestars and quite a variety of other aircraft. I spent hours with these machines just wishing that I knew how to handle them. I did not know any pilots. I just had to imagine what it was like to fly one of these beauties. I got back to the hangar just in time to get something to eat. I was able to get myself a billy can and set of eating irons and so started building up my possessions from scratch. A few days later there was an attempt to get the entire camp into some kind of organisation. Our CO sent out the word that we former X Party and Seletar Transit camp personnel would form up a unit. This was great news for me. Wing Commander Gregson was an excellent CO and I was glad to be in his unit again. I would now meet my former buddies. A parade was called and various units assembled. Some order was returning in contrast to the mass confusion of the past few days.

I hailed Jack Dobbie from a distance and sure enough here were the others I had lost on the way - Humphrey, Taffy, Peter, and Jim. After the parade we had to gather together in the hangar and claim our unit space so that there could be some sort of discipline maintained over the different areas. I was more than pleased to do this as it would get me in touch with some knowledgeable people to tell me all about the fighter planes. I soon got Humphrey and Taffy to join me in an inspection of the fighters.

I met two fellows, Sergeants Blackmore and Penteney (Blackie and Penny), who were to become friends, as they were both fighter pilots. They both flew hurricanes and had just arrived from England. Penny had been on quite a few strafing raids over northern France and gave me some idea of what it was like to "slip the surly bonds of earth."[7] Blackie had recently been posted to a fighter squadron (232) but had not yet seen action in the Far East campaign. He had his pilots' textbook with him, which he loaned me, and I read voraciously at night. I firmly believed that in three months we would be free and then I would have a chance to square the odds with these little people. Also in these hangars were members of 211 and 84 squadrons (Blenheims). Both squadrons recently arrived from the Middle East as part of the sacrifice to total incompetence.

Life during the first month as a Prisoner was easy. We seldom saw any Japanese. We were under the command of our own officers. A Group Captain, I believe, was commanding the camp. We followed our own military rank structure. We were living on RAF rations, and there was plenty of fruit on the aerodrome or near by. I learned how to make jam out of papayas, bananas, pineapples and pumpkin. But, of course, the most important thing on our minds was ESCAPING.

My first thoughts along these lines were to try to get back to Singapore as a

POW and then escape and make my way to the Cameron Highlands where Dad had Blue Valley Tea Estate. I knew if I got there I would be able to see out the war in relative freedom. Blue Valley is isolated and of no military importance. It was too insulated from the rest of Malaya. The only access to the estate was by a single-track road eleven to twelve miles long, with a few Chinese vegetable gardeners near the Cameron Highlands end of it. My Dad always treated the labor force fairly and I felt sure that they would be fiercely loyal to him and consequently to me.[8] It was not a place that any occupying power would be likely to waste troops.

The first Japanese we saw were the conquering heroes of their God Emperor - the men who had captured South East Asia to create "The Greater East Asia Co-prosperity Sphere."[9] *Life* magazine was the popular magazine of the day and a frequently advertised product was suspenders for holding up one's socks. The Japanese soldiers interpreted these pictures to be the ultimate in style in the USA. When they dressed up to impress the local population they wore army khaki shorts with brightly coloured suspenders holding up their socks. The power of advertising and a little ignorance produced some really funny sights.

A few disturbing things were happening. Seven men who had been ordered to get some furniture for the officers' quarters were caught by the Japanese and tied to separate trees with their hands behind them and around the trees. Fed twice a day, they were kept like this for several days. The ants, flies and myriad other insects crawled all over them. The Japanese would throw the swill from their meals on them to make life more uncomfortable and encourage the local population to make fun of them. Under our new circumstances such frivolous orders from our officers had to be reassessed by both the giver and taker. Who was going to suffer this treatment for some officers who had already shown that their primary concern was their own safety and comfort?

It was apparent that any escape attempt must be carried out independently of the local population — almost an impossibility. Java is the world's most populated island. It had been a colony for over two hundred years, not a happy situation for many Javanese. With this high density of population and the industrious, agricultural nature of the Javanese one had little chance of being at large without the natives knowing about it. Our plan was to get into the mountains in central Java and set up camp there. After a lot of serious discussion and checking out our assets we were forced to abandon the idea. The Javanese farmers rise early in the morning to tend their fields and chat late into the night around a single hurricane lamp. It would have been out of the question to roam the countryside without being detected. The resources at our disposal were sadly lacking.

Daily more Japanese were coming into the area. I mentioned to Jack that

Taffy and I were considering escaping to the mountains and seriously planning along these lines. The mountains of Java are not as densely populated as the fertile plains and would afford us a better chance of survival. There was at least a possibility of being undetected and a potential for finding a co-operative group of natives or other escapees. We made a lot of inquiries throughout the camp and found that an excursion had been made and the native population was not at all friendly. Reception varied at every village. Some Headmen were most co-operative while others warned that it was dangerous to be seen at large. The Japanese had put a price on our heads, with the result that many people were only too happy to take advantage of the situation. Rumours persisted that a submarine would be surfacing at night off the coast east of Tjilatjap. We knew that the escape was a one-chance effort. It would result in success or death. With the native situation so uncertain our plan was reluctantly shelved. We had no idea that there was an underground movement being organised by the Dutch.[10]

One day Jack approached me and without so much as a word grabbed my arm and wheeled me off to a secluded spot behind the hangars. As we started walking in the direction of the derelict bombers he told me of a scheme that was coming to fruition - *to take off in one of the Lodestars*. The plan was to get the plane loaded with escapees, start the engines, run them for two minutes and then onto the runway and off for Darwin, maintaining a low level of flight until over the coast. A do or die adventure, as this "run up" time to test the engines was totally inadequate under normal circumstances. There was enough petrol to get to Darwin. It was a good bet that the radio was working, in which case contact could be made with Darwin and a position given in case of ditching. With a dark night take off it would be only a matter of minutes before the aeroplane reached the south coast of Java, after which it would be over the Indian ocean and difficult for Japanese fighters to find. What a proposition! If we got into the air successfully our chances were pretty good. I was really excited about this, but now he gave me the bad news. Priority for the passenger list must go to the fellows who had worked on the plane. Then there were people who had greater claim to this scheme than we did; people who had procured spare parts from the town or arranged for some other necessities. We were strictly a last choice as we had done nothing to assist in any way. Our only hope was that some of the priority men might chicken out at the last moment. We waited for someone to make the decision as to which night would be the most suitable for the operation. By day we kept our ears open as we knew that the mechanics would test the engines when the opportunity arose. Sure enough it happened when some Japanese aircraft flew low over the camp. We heard the unmistakable roar of the Wright radial engines as they kicked in. It lasted only long enough to let the mechanics know that the engines were able to start with the system they were using. We knew the scheme was under way but did not know how long it would take to mature.

By the middle of April the place was swarming with Japanese. At this time they were at the height of their conquests, having suffered only minor and temporary setbacks to gain possession of the entire South East Asia Co-prosperity Sphere. They decided that all prisoners should be taught Japanese military commands. If only Gilbert & Sullivan had witnessed this they would have had a sure fire winner on their hands.

Four thousand men were paraded on the runway in three ranks. This meant that from end to end we must have covered close to three quarters of a mile. At the middle point of this parade the Japanese commander stood on a box so that we could all see him. He was about 5ft. 2in. and must have spent his life on a horse in true Samurai style. You could pass a loaf of bread between his knees without any trouble at all. At fifty yard intervals he stationed a trusty lieutenant and they in turn had sergeants, corporals, and privates placed amongst us. This being our first encounter with the glorious conquering army of Dai Nippon, we were not too sure what to expect. We knew they were a cruel sadistic bunch but how would this affect us? With a snarling, slapping attitude they marched through our ranks to make sure not a sound was muttered or a happy face was encountered.

Now the exercise began. The commander yelled a command -"*Kioski.*" Nobody, of course, knew what he was talking about. There was no reaction. The lieutenants repeated the command and the fun started. The Japanese other ranks would come smartly to attention, for that was the command - Attention. But the commander had not made it clear to them that the command was for prisoners only and that the soldiers were to run amongst us making us obey the command. The lieutenants had to impress on the other ranks that these orders must not be obeyed by them. This was like trying to tell milk it must not curdle. They had been so thoroughly indoctrinated, and militarised, that the lieutenants had to slap many soldiers before they got the message. After about half an hour of this little pantomime, the commander was told by one of the POW officers that if he formed us into four ranks the whole parade would be much easier to handle. The Japanese commander fought this suggestion as the victor must not be advised by the vanquished. But after another half an hour this idea looked as if it might be of his own initiation. We were formed into four ranks, with the result that we spread out over little more than half a mile. Now the same antics continued. Having us so completely at their mercy the Japanese soldiers suddenly realised that we were sitting ducks for their depredations. They started ripping off watches, rings and anything that appealed to them. If you had an appealing belt it was stolen. I spotted this quickly and slipped off my watch putting it out of sight in my pocket. All that afternoon, in the boiling sun, the parade commander shouted orders. These were relayed to us through the chain of command and if you were unlucky enough to be standing next to one of the Japanese soldiers you were clipped over the ear for not obeying immediately. The soldiers would then rush about looking for anyone who did not obey the current command. It took time for one command to filter down through the ranks. Hardly had the slapping finished for one order when another order was given. In the midst of this cacophony of sound - orders, slapping, boots coming to attention, others standing at ease, lieutenants yelling at Sergeants, Sergeants at Corporals etc., total confusion reigned and we suffered the first indignities that, given a little time, would turn into atrocities. In this way we learnt that *kioski* = attention, *yasumey* = stand at ease, *ichi, ne, san, si,*= 1,2,3,4, etc. We were soon to learn basic phrases such as " I am going to the bathroom."

The smart way to do this would have been to write the orders on a piece of paper and circulate this to the troops before we were paraded. We would have paraded with a basic knowledge of Japanese military commands. Doing it their way entailed a lot of physical punishment and emphasised to us the differences between our two systems of discipline. It soon became apparent that the Japanese soldiers were amazingly ignorant peasants who sought out all opportunities to hit and slap us. We were the only people who were lower in life than they were. Slapping and beating are a part of the soldier's life in Japan. Their only form of discipline is physical punishment. This saves an awful lot of paper work and promotes physical abuse. The idea of writing an order and circulating it was totally foreign to their way of thinking.

The Samurai or warrior class is a different type of person in Japan than the warrior class in the West. In the Japanese army for a Samurai to beat, rape, or molest an innocent individual or one who is at a great disadvantage is considered normal. This was proved to us so many times in prison camp. The perpetrator of these crimes may not be a Samurai, but of course they were commanded by officers who aspired to this title. I hate to use the term warrior in connection with Samurai as the meanings in the east and the west differ so totally. In Japan the Samurai is a wanton killer without the least consideration for humanity. This wartime experience proved beyond doubt that their theory and practice are at complete odds. This way of conduct does not match our meaning of the word warrior — somewhat more noble, even honourable. Surely the only time a warrior class can prove itself is under actual fighting conditions. The Samurai proved to be uncivilised barbarians by any standards. Their contempt for surrendering fighting soldiers was quickly forgotten when they were in this position in August 1945. The honourable end to a Japanese soldier's fighting career, if not killed in battle, is to commit *hari kari*. Far less than one percent was true to their beliefs. To the people they subjugated, the only proven legacy of the Japanese Empire in the Far East (1942-1945) is one of uncontrolled brutality, murder, torture, rape, and plunder.

These afternoon parades continued for about two weeks. There seemed to be two outward purposes; learning basic Japanese commands, and learning their method of discipline. The discipline was reinforced daily, as they now required that a certain number of people form a working party. We worked near the camp, usually just outside the immediate camp boundary doing clean up jobs, digging drainage ditches, filling in bomb holes etc. We used our own rank system, so that a normal working party consisted of an officer, sergeant, and workers. When we got to the work site our officer would naturally receive the orders for the work to be done from the Japanese soldier in charge, and pass this to the Sergeant who would detail us to do the work for the day. The RAF Sergeant was our boss. The only trouble was that the Japanese did not want it this way. The Japanese soldier would tell us what to do. Whenever he changed his mind—which was quite frequently— he would not relay this through the chain of command, but use the direct method, straight to us. The first day this happened Sergeant Gent told the soldier, amidst a great amount of sign language and frantic gesticulations, that he would have to ask permission before changing our workload. The Japanese had no intention of asking a POW for permission to do anything. He picked up a *chunkel* (large oriental hoe) and chased the Sergeant until he felled him with a single well-aimed blow, then pounded him, as he lay helpless on the ground. Japanese discipline was on us in no uncertain terms. The officer in charge tried to intervene, only to be slapped for his good intentions. From this day on we knew what to expect. Beatings, beatings and more beatings.

The East West dichotomy was revealing itself in the only way the conquering Japanese knew how — brute force. Looking back with many years of hindsight one can see that the Japanese throughout history had only voluntarily had communications with the west in defence of their Empire against the Russians and to aid in the delivery of cheap manufactured goods. Both of these acts needed an aggressive attitude. At this early stage of our captivity it looked as if "Asia for the Asiatics" was not a sincere policy. Prisoners were not the only people being beaten. From out of the blue a totally foreign system of behaviour was being forced onto a population that was unprepared for the drastic change.

Bowing is a part of the Japanese culture. This was easy to observe but the finer points were hard to pick up. The lower on the social scale, the lower one has to bow. We were under the impression that any kind of bow showed that we were in effect saluting the conquerors. This was a great mistake especially if the Japanese soldier in question had just shown his complete subservience to one of his officers. The POW bow had to be lower than the bow the soldier had just made to the officer. This little intricacy did not impress itself on us for a long time. The result was many beatings. To us a bow was a bow and that was the end of it. To the Japanese soldier the angle of the bow and the depth of the bow were aspects to be closely scrutinised. They may have told this to us in the diatribe that preceded each slapping or beating but is was unintelligible.

The Japanese soldiers were of peasant stock and trained only to obey their God Emperor and their officers and NCOs. When the order came for them to move a convoy of three-ton trucks to Bandung they did not have enough soldiers who knew how to drive. They could ride bicycles but had not the least idea how to drive a truck. A call went out for volunteers to drive a convoy of British and Dutch trucks to Bandung. We would drive all day, spend the night there, and come back the next day in one of the trucks. I volunteered in a flash. Jack and Humphrey criticised me for assisting the enemy. I told them that my plan was to drive in such a way that I would ruin the transmission. This is not difficult. To use the gears in the wrong way and neglecting to use the clutch will make a mess of any mechanical transmission in short order. Luckily this proved to be easier than I thought. The convoy had only one free runner, and a Japanese soldier in the first and last vehicle. I was free to abuse this vehicle to my heart's content. I had often wondered if it was possible to change gears without using the clutch. I felt sure that by listening to the engine revs carefully one could easily slip from one gear to the next without difficulty. Now was my chance to experiment and lay the foundations for a "clutchless mechanical transmission." What a hope! It can be done but I don't recommend it, especially on a private vehicle. I am sure that they did not get much service out of that three tonner after a fifty-mile journey to Bandung through narrow mountainous roads. Jack joined me on this trip as he thought this was a first class idea. This meant that we left our "hosts" with two trucks of doubtful reliability. I do not know if any of the other fellows had the same intentions as we had, but I have no doubt that other drivers had similar ideas to mine.

When we arrived back in camp we realised that our situation as newly taken prisoners was being considered as a long-term possibility by the senior officers. Our doctors decided that VD would not be a good start to a man's life in POW camp. All four thousand prisoners were ordered to parade naked in the hangar. The camp doctors then walked through the parade and inspected our genitals. How much useful information they derived from this exercise is known only to them. To us it was another embarrassment. Maybe they were able to treat some infected individuals before the supply of medicines became acute or in many cases non-existent.

The camp was guarded at the main entrance without too much thought given to the massive perimeter area. This meant that prisoners could easily get out. Three of the camp officers decided to celebrate a birthday in the traditional fashion - a good meal and a couple of drinks in a nice restaurant. Off they went and had their celebration. They were caught by the Japanese. Next day they were tied to trees in the local park and used for live bayonet practice. They died with their hands tied behind their backs watching helplessly as Japanese soldiers bayoneted them - rushing at them screaming and shouting and plunging the bayonet into them until it stuck into the tree behind. Not once but hundreds of times. The code of Bushido? The way of the Samurai? A short while later Wing Commander Steadman, a highly respected officer who stood up for his men, disappeared. We never heard of him again.

The camp commander was a group captain who apparently got to hear of the Lodestar escape plan. He was most emphatic that it must not happen. He felt that now that we were getting to know the type of enemy we were up against the repercussions would be terrible. (There had been rumours that for every individual escapee there would be at least ten prisoners beheaded).[11] I have no doubt that he was correct. Someone was sent to the dispersal area to slash the tires of all the Lodestars. And so ended that little dream.

One day rice appeared in our lunch and Taffy suggested that we would soon be eating nothing but rice. This was shouted down with a lot of merriment, the thought was so ridiculous. We were living mostly on RAF rations and this was two months after the fall of Java. Work parties were a daily routine. Slappings and beatings were recognised as part of the way of life, but rice as the main staple of our meals was an absurd thought. They would not dream of feeding prisoners like their own troops! They had signed the Geneva Convention but not ratified it. They had also assured the American government that all prisoners would be treated according to international standards of behaviour. To us this meant three meals a day with meat, and potatoes or bread, especially in this most fertile area of the world.

The artists and entertainers in the camp arranged for an evening of theatre. They decorated a stage and wrote their own little skits that caused great merriment for all of us. We sat on the ground and watched enthusiastically as the officers and other ranks competed for the most amusing part of the evening show. The officers put on an excellent show. The feature being a chorus "We are the officers' working party—not very hail and not very hearty" sung to the appealing strains of a Gilbert & Sullivan ditty. The other ranks had a boisterous show of large breasted women amusing us with enlightened conversation and extraordinary antics. This was the only evening of live entertainment we had during what would become nearly four years of captivity.

An order came from our conquerors that all prisoners must have their heads shaved in true Japanese military style, by midnight May 6th — my 18th birthday. About May 4th men started getting their heads shaved. The first few to do this looked most peculiar and a new interest developed in the camp. Nobody had realised that there was such a difference in the shapes of the human skull. Now with no hair on our heads we saw a magnificent array of skull shapes. This must have been most interesting to the doctors and no doubt lead to much speculation as to what this wonderful variety of shapes covered in the way of grey matter. To us other ranks, it was just a source of wonder.

Jack arranged for me to have a fried egg, half a papaya, and two bananas as a birthday treat. We had both tried the thousand year old duck eggs - not exactly a tasty treat. These green-shelled duck eggs are buried in the low tide sands and left to mature. How long this takes I have no idea but I do know that the taste is stronger than a normal duck egg that has gone rotten. Maybe two years down the road we would have enjoyed these but that would have shown our desperation, not a sophisticated leap in taste. How rapidly my situation had changed from the previous year — celebrating my seventeenth birthday in Shanghai and topping it off with a little too much champagne. I had come into camp with nothing in the way of kit and, even more drastic, my wallet was empty. Jack was an operator and always seemed to have money to spend. He always had a scheme of some sort going, and I was able to pick up a few guilders doing some surplus *dhoby* (washing) for him. Knowing that the money in camp was with the officers he managed to talk his way into doing their *dhoby* and, if he felt generous or had too much to do, he would let me do some for a small payment. This was my only source of income at the time. About 7:00 pm on May 6th, as the light was fading, I had my head shaved. I was the last man in camp to do so but I felt that on this special day for me this was the only special thing I could do. It also turned out that I was the youngest of the four thousand POWs in camp.

There were many strange stories of vast amounts of money that had been taken from the banks and hidden, buried, distributed, and in one case, kept for escape purposes. We on Tasik Malaja had been the lucky recipients of a free issue of seven guilders - this without even a signature! A totally new outlook on the part of those in charge. Since joining the RAF I had to sign for everything except my meals. Now they gave me seven guilders for nothing. Of course the reason was that the senior officers did not want the Japanese to get the money. I had now been in the RAF for over three months and this was the second time I had been paid since arriving in Java.[12] At King William School I had received fifteen guilders advance, as they euphemistically called it! In Singapore soon after joining the RAF I had been transferred to the RNZAF. This made for some complications in the paper work. Then I was rapidly transferred back to the RAF. All this movement resulted in my not being paid. The total amount of money being handled by the camp must have been considerable. The officers obviously received more than we did and it would be prudent for the commanding officer to keep a sizeable amount for future contingencies, so one can only guess what the original amount of money had been.

We heard of an army staff sergeant who had managed to acquire a substantial amount of money and had immediately taken off to the south coast with six members of his unit. They intended to buy a boat and sail to Australia. None of them could speak Indonesian so communication was difficult. They found a suitable boat but did not have the slightest idea how to sail it. They indicated to the Indonesians that they would like to buy the boat and have some one go with them. They would pay him well. The staff sergeant flashed his roll of bills by way of confirmation. The Indonesians indicated they would think about this. The staff sergeant went below decks to talk to the others and check over this rather rough purchase. Eight Indonesians came on board and cast the lines off. They were under way. With the sail raised they headed off shore but kept parallel to the coastline. The men thought this was a little odd but thought the locals must know what they were doing. It was not long before the staff sergeant and the six men were below decks organising a meal. When one of them tried to get out of the cabin he found the hatch locked. They were trapped, but they had pistols. The Indonesians had only *parangs* (large knives similar to a machete). Realising they had been tricked, they laid out a strategy for regaining control of the boat. With plenty of food available to them but only a limited amount of ammunition they had to be careful of every round fired. After a day and night of this situation the army men could see that they were still well within sight of land. When the Indonesians felt the last of the ammunition had been expended they opened serious negotiations. Having all the cards in their hands they ended up with the money and the boat. The staff sergeant and his men had to abandon the idea of sailing to Australia.

Another case involved a Cockney driver, Titch, who I got to know very well during the next two years. Just before the fall of Java, Titch had been ordered by one of his officers to drive a three-ton truck to a remote area off the main road in central Java. When they arrived at a map reference the officer ordered Titch to start digging a hole very much like a grave. Titch worked like hell in fairly soft ground and was soon down about 7 or 8 feet. To his surprise he was ordered to drag a large wooden box off the truck and manoeuvre it in the hole. Although he was not told directly what was in the box he gathered that it contained a large amount of money. He was sworn to secrecy as to the location but he could not resist telling us that he would be a rich man after the war. Many of us put pressure on him for even a little indication as to the general area but he was good to his word. He died in far off Haruku two years later without revealing the secret to any of us. We heard that when the money was recovered in 1946 it was shredded in a billion pieces by hungry, and now wealthy, white ants.

There was a strong rumour that a submarine was to surface off the south coast and pick up anyone who could make it there. The area was supposed to be around Tjilatjap but the whole thing was rather vague. We knew now that any attempt to escape must be final, because if caught, the Japanese offered no second chance.

While we were on working parties it was not unusual for the Japanese to remind us that they were taught by their officers that the war would last "one hundred years and all prisoners will die." This theme "all prisoners will die" seemed to be ingrained in their psyche. It was repeated so often and with such determination that we could not ignore it. On parade one day our senior Medical Officer addressed us. He gave a long talk about the hardships the human body could stand, how with the right attitude one could survive anything. We thought this a little odd, as surely he knew we would be liberated in a few months. How right he was, and how effective this little address was to us in the years to follow. Thank you, Doc. The older and more knowledgeable of our camp knew only too well what lay ahead for us. Little did we know? Thank God.

The 11th May brought orders for a move. The whole camp was to be housed in a school in Sourabaya. We were to parade on the runway at noon. This came as a terrible blow, as many of the men were making contact with the local Dutch residents and having a fairly easy life. There were enough volunteers to go out on the working parties, as these had expanded to include work in the town area where there was an opportunity to scrounge a great variety of goodies. People like me who had entered camp with absolutely nothing could pick up a variety of things in the warehouses where we worked, and trade these with the natives for fruit and vegetables. When we found ourselves in a warehouse the goods were in transit and belonged to no one, so we felt quite justified in taking what we could. Just a few weeks before they had been Dutch or Indonesian goods and now they were Japanese goods. So if we diverted some to our own pockets, from whom were we stealing? Besides it was not just a case of taking the stuff - there was considerable risk involved. If caught the punishment was a good beating and confiscation of the loot. The game was on and the stakes were serious for all of us.

Tasik Malaja had been a regular RAF base for the short period of the Far East war. With the fall of Java many of the men had started POW life with a full complement of clothes, presents to be sent home, money, and contacts in the local town. It was only the unfortunate few who had been ambushed on the train and then suffered the bridge disaster who had nothing. We had a long way to go just to get ourselves kitted out and find some source of income.

Noon found us on the runway with our kit. I had managed over the two months in this camp to accumulate a little kit and most importantly, a mosquito net. I had my patent leather shoes and was not the least bit worried about how long they should last as I knew for sure that the Yanks would be landing on Java in about three months and we would be free men.

Our Gilbert and Sullivan training experience of a few weeks ago was now put to the test for real. Before we could be moved a count had to be taken of all those on parade. We had been numbering in Japanese for all our work daily parties so most of us were familiar with the routine. This parade however, entailed the whole camp, so there were the makings of some real entertainment here. Not only were we just catching on to the Japanese numbers but the guards were not the most intelligent people in the world. Once numbers increased beyond the fingers and toes level there were problems beyond recognition. Added to this was the missing person in the middle rank of the last row. If the parade had one hundred men in the front rank it was relatively easy to multiply this by four to get the number in the four ranks on parade. However, there was seldom an even number on parade, which meant that a Japanese soldier had to physically check the last row to determine if one or two or three men were missing. The number of times we were counted was remarkable. May be it reflected the value they had placed on us as a labour force, or was it due to the mathematical capabilities of the average soldier? The Japanese officer called the parade to attention, right turn and quick march. This sounds as if it might have been carried out with military precision. On the contrary it was a shambles. Most of us could not hear the commands, and would not have understood them in any case. We had no idea in which direction we were supposed to turn and march off. It was quite normal for us to be facing each other in our ranks with a hurried discussion as to who was facing the right direction. This of course occasioned the slapping, shouting harangue that accompanied every move. At this stage we were like untrained ants doing our own thing at the sound of some peculiar intonations.

We marched to the railway station through the town of Tasik Malaja. Somehow the word had got to the civilian population and they lined the streets to cheer us on our way. Most of them were women and children as the men had been in the forces. The women and children were good to us. They would dash out to the marching ranks and shove something into your hand as quickly as they could - a handkerchief, bar of soap, papaya or a lime. I was fortunate in this march, as I must have looked like one of the youngest in the group for I had many little gifts given to me. I was most grateful but felt totally inadequate in trying to express my gratitude. How can you thank someone for a gift that meant far more in the giving than the token that is given? And then to do this in the fleeting moment that hands touch. We were shocked to see the attitude of our guards to the women and children who were being kind and generous to us. They were soon shut up by the Japanese, who would hit and slap the women with the same impunity they used with us.

When we arrived at the station in Sourabaya we went through the farcical numbering game again while standing in the pouring rain. A good tropical downpour can get you soaked in seconds. It was only the lucky amongst us who had ground sheets. Once again we marched through town but this time it was evening and without crowds to wish us on our way. Tasik Malaja, having been an operational station at the time of surrender, housed many men who had all their kit. There was a great contrast in camp of the "haves" and the "have nots."

The Lyceum school was already a prison camp and crowded. As soon as we arrived at the gate we were made to put our kit down and then marched off to one side, clear of our belongings. A surprise search was carried out with the result that many men were thoroughly beaten. A few bayonets and large knives were found, plus many souvenirs taken from the sabotaged aircraft at Tasik Malaja. The guards stole a variety of personal possessions that appealed to them. Luckily I had worn my watch around my ankle and, covered by my socks, it was not detected. Soaking wet, we were herded into small classrooms, ninety men to a room. There was not enough room for all of us to lie down at the same time. Those who were in the middle of the room lay on the bare floor while the rest of us squatted with our backs to the wall, where we spent the night. Our kit was left outside in the tropical downpour. We retrieved it the following day. There was a guard posted outside each classroom with the result that we had to get permission to go to the toilet. This was our only way of relieving congestion in the room and getting a chance to stretch our legs. Each time a prisoner left the room he bowed to the guard who in return bowed back. I am sure we had the guards with the stiffest necks in the entire Japanese army. In this situation, where there were no officers around, and the soldiers were as wet as we were, they were able to accept a nod of the head as a bow. It behove them to do this as we spent the whole uncomfortable night sitting, standing or walking to the toilet.

The next day we found that this was our introduction to a drastically new way of life. Strictly confined in a small room, we were reduced to pap, which is basically rice cooked in a lot of water with nothing in it, twice a day. The third meal was dry rice with a thin green soup. Taffy's prediction of rice three times a day had hit us with a vengeance - and so quickly.

The work parties here were on the extensive docks of Sourabaya port. Our job was to load bombs and gas barrels on to the ships at the dock, unload the trucks that delivered them to the docks, and handle all of the captured war materials that the Japanese wanted delivered to the appropriate advance locations. We now refined scrounging into a fine art with high stakes. All the usual methods of hiding everything were used to great effect - material wrapped around the body, cooking oil in water bottles, a wide variety of goodies tied to ones thighs or arms. A favourite trick was to develop a sudden bout of malaria, start shaking like mad and of course have to wear all kinds of clothes to keep warm. The more clothes one had on, the more hiding places were available. This often signified that a malaria patient had a good profitable day on the docks. One could nearly always get away from the main work party long enough to enter another godown and look for food or medicines. Not only were items stolen for individual benefit but also for the hospital. We were all aware of the conditions under which the wounded and the sick were living.

Fortunately for us we were not in this camp too long. It was early in June that Wing Commander Gregson volunteered our unit for a work party at Semarang, a town on the north coast of Java some one hundred and fifty miles to the west. Two hundred RAF men and one hundred Dutch soldiers were to go by train to repair the sabotaged runway, extend it, and to work on the heavily damaged docks.

1   My father was told, by a mutual friend, after he boarded a ship for Freemantle, that I had left a note for him at the Hotel Des Indes. He told me later that he had visited the hotel but was in such a disheveled condition that he did not make any enquiries at the desk.

2   *The Empress of Asia, The City of Canterbury* and the *Ile de France* were bombed for two hours while they disembarked troops. Many of the air force personnel departed for Batavia (Jakarta) on these same ships the following day. { Blackie and Penny were with this group.}

3   We were to learn after the war Churchill's famous words 'In war time, truth is so precious that she should always be attended by a bodyguard of lies'.

4   *Pacific War*— Saburo Ienaga p173. "Japanese forces arrested more than 70,000 overseas Chinese suspected of subversive activities. In a short period of time, too short for their guilt to have been established, several thousand persons were slaughtered in a vengeful massacre". Estimates in Singapore after the war ranged up to 100,000 Chinese massacred. Col Tsuji, Yamashita's chief of staff, was responsible for this massacre. He evaded the war crimes and eventually was elected to the Diet.

5   In actual fact the Japanese landing on the North Coast of Java had only been lightly opposed. The troops attacking us were the advance guard of this landing in the area of central Java. The 48th Infantry Division and the Sakaguchi Detachment of the 56th Regimental Group. (Willmott -*Empires in Balance* p341). Their objective was to race across Java and capture the port of Tjilatjap on the south coast. A few days later we were to meet the hurricane pilots who had tried their best to prevent the landing.

6   The official history of the war against Japan by General Woodburn Kirby does not mention this incident. Many men must have been killed by the explosion, many more trapped in the steel wreckage and some drowned in the river.

7   *High Flight* -John Gillespie Magee.

8   The loyalty and true friendship of the majority of Chinese people during these extraordinary times was heart warming. Under constant threat of death they were steadfast in recognising a common and terrible enemy. The Japanese did try to operate the estate and process tea. Their method of firing up the big single cylinder diesel was to heat coconut oil prior to injection. This method worked for a short period but soon resulted in the factory burning to the ground.

9   The Greater East Asia Co-Prosperity sphere did not mean co-prosperity or equality for the nations dominated by the Japanese. Japans belief in *hakko ichiu* (world dominance) put them in a position of advising *Quisling* governments and directing the flow of resources and manpower for their national security. Indonesians soon changed this slogan to read "The Greater East Asia Co-poverty sphere" as the whole population suffered from a shortage of food and clothing.

10   There was a small resistance movement in Java. It consisted of British and Dutch military personnel. When the Japs discovered some of these groups the individuals were confined to pig baskets, driven to the coast in open trucks and cast into the sea as shark bait. The amazing story by Charles McCormac DCM. *"You'll die in Singapore,"* confirms the existence of a resistance movement in Sumatra and Java. This courageous escape from Singapore ends with the author being flown from the South coast of Java to Australia. If only we had known!

11   In the Philippines this was announced standard practice. All prisoners in many camps were grouped into 10 individuals. Any escape by one of the group guaranteed the beheading of the remaining nine.

12   On joining the RAF I was told there were two basic rules that must be adhered to: Our dog tags (identification tags worn around the neck usually on a piece of string) must be worn at all times and one must always have his paybook available.

3

SEMARANG

INTRO' TO SLAVERY — A GIRL NO LESS

*Non co-operation with evil is as
much a duty as is co-operation with good.*

MOHANDAS GANDHI

It was about the 3rd of June we were loaded onto a train and started our journey. Our last train ride in Java as a group of highly trained technical tradesmen was in cattle cars. Now as a bunch of lowly prisoners we were transported in third class passenger cars complete with seats and windows - - all windows must remain closed. The snag was that the rules were enforced with cold steel by two guards with fixed bayonets in each car.

We were to be used as guinea pigs in a test of strength in the Army Engineers first railroad re-construction project. This turned out to be the first run of loaded railroad cars over a re-built war damaged bridge. Our guards made a great fuss about the mighty, industrious, and incredibly clever Nipponese army. This was an ominous journey for many of us as the last time we had been on a railroad bridge it had been blown up by the Dutch army. The train stopped just as the engine was about to roll onto the recently completed bridge. There were several groups of civilians standing around and a lot of excited discussion taking place. As they pointed to various sections of the mostly bamboo structure it looked to us as if the engineers did not have a great deal of faith in their recent creation. There was a lot of shouting between one group and the train engineer. Sitting in our hot carriages, many of us offered a silent prayer to the Great One to get us across this ravine without trouble. All the windows and the two end doors had been closed with the guards on the outside of the compartments when the train initially came to a stop. Why had this extra precaution been taken for a casual stop? What were they anticipating at this crossing? Eventually the order was given and slowly, oh, so slowly, the train moved onto the bamboo structure. As if to help lighten the train we all, quite independently, held our breath, as each car floated over the ravine and on to solid ground on the other side. When the entire length of the train had passed the danger point the engineer picked up speed and we went on our merry way.

At Semarang station we went through the inevitable drawn out counting procedure - with much slapping and a great deal of yelling. The Nips finally decided that no one had escaped and we were marched off. We were greeted at 3:00 pm on our march through the streets with a most wonderful welcome. How the civilians knew we were coming I have no idea. It was a great and pleasant surprise to us. Once again we received all kinds of little trinkets that the thoughtful residents gave to us. They knew better than we did the situation in the outside world, which made their generosity more sincere and heart warming. One of the Japanese soldiers beat the hell out of a young boy who showed too much exuberance at seeing both RAF and Dutch soldiers marching down the street. The boy was only about 12 and of light build. A few minutes later, as the soldier rode his bike to the front of the marching column proud of what he had done and yelling at the crowd to keep quiet, he turned too fast and fell, sprawling all over the road. There was so much laughter he could not face the crowd and sheepishly picked up his bike and walked along with head bowed as the column marched in muffled snickers behind him.

At Tasik Malaja there had been contact via radio receiver with the world beyond the camp. In Sourabaya we had only heard rumours of what was developing on the war front. There were rumours of a clandestine radio in the camp. This may well have been the case but at this stage we were picking up news on our outside work parties and not concerned with the source of it, as long as the news was good. Most of us had our own idea that it would not take long for the Yankees to rescue us. I continued to think in the terms of three months. I stuck to this idea for over three and a half years. It worked. We were marched to a small factory building and issued mattresses. Of the two hundred men in our group about half got a mattress. I was not one of the lucky ones. We stayed at this building for a short while, marching to the airstrip each day. We unloaded and spread sand from a never ending line of trucks - a boring job with a break of 10 minutes in each two hour period. Japs, or as we now called them Nips, ran around yelling *"Kura, Kura, Speedo, Speedo,"* as if the entire job had to be finished that day. With a continual line of trucks waiting to be unloaded, we were working at the point of a bayonet and subject to many beatings. Unwilling workers ALL. This was to be the first of many jobs where we contributed to the Nipponese war effort. In fact the Japanese used prisoners from this time on almost exclusively to improve their war aims. The huge labour force that we collectively represented was used by the Japanese in the most callous manner with out regard to humanitarian feelings. The Geneva Convention which they had signed, but not ratified, and soon after the collapse of opposition in the Far East, had promised to respect, was not even a consideration worthy of discussion. Red Cross parcels, correspondence and other facets of civilised life were deliberately warehoused and kept from distribution to prisoners.[1]

On June 15th we were marched to the airfield where we were billeted in two Nissen type huts on the very perimeter of the field. A few of the sand trucks were detailed to carry our kit and the cook-house equipment. When we arrived at our new quarters we were divided into two groups with one hundred men going to each hut. A slightly smaller hut housed the one hundred Dutch men. Off to one side was the cook house and outside the barbed wire enclosure was the Nip guard room. There was enough room to make a cricket pitch inside the wire and to establish a couple of tables between the huts for any occasion that might arise. Sgt. Ghent took over one table for religious services and someone managed to scrounge a record player complete with three or four records to go on the other table. Outside one of the huts there were half a dozen spigots that gave us shower facilities. A notice was prominently displayed near the guard house.

NOTICE.

1   All those interned in Camps should obey the following rules:-
1   Everybody has always to give honour to his Imperial Majesty Emperor Hirohito
2   When meeting Nipponese military everybody has to bow the head.
3   The salutation, mentioned under nr.2, when if seated as well as if standing.
4   Sleeping places have to be kept clean and tidy.
5   Men on working-parties outside the camp are not allowed to be noisy and/or talk with women or other persons in the streets.
6   Noisiness is always forbidden.
7   Between the bugle calls "extinguish lamps" and "Reveille" there has to be SILENCE.
8   There is no fixed place where water is boiled, whoever fetches hot water there has to pour into the boiling water drum an equal quantity of cold water. MAKING FIRES IN OTHER PLACES IS FORBIDDEN.
9   Receiving packages etc. from outside and talking with people who are outside the fence is not allowed.
10 It is not allowed to stay on the football field after 20.30 p.m.
11 Prisoners approaching the fence within a distance of 5 meters (5 1/2 yards) will be shot down without previous warning.
12 Playing of card games, chess, etc is not allowed after 22.00 p.m.
13 There is no admittance to the square court behind the Nipponese Guard and the verandahs which stretch along the rooms on both sides of that guard, for persons under the rank of officer (unless in case of special commands to the contrary).

There was no individual choice in where we were to sleep. We were marched into the huts and put our kit down on the bamboo platforms. The result of this was that your marching companion now became your bamboo companion. Curly Pittam was next to me on the bamboo opposite the officers. The huts were identical in size, about forty feet wide and sixty feet long shaped like Nissen huts with corrugated tin roofs, little ovens under the tropical sun. Inside there were bamboo platforms about three feet off the ground that ran one down each side of the huts. Each of these platforms accommodated twenty five men. This left a large centre area that was also constructed of bamboo and three feet off the ground. This centre section was bed space for about fifty prisoners sleeping with their heads towards the middle. There was an aisle running the length of the building around the sleeping centre section. The result was that everybody had access to his sleeping space from the foot of the bamboo. Each person had approximately six foot of length and three feet of width. Not palatial but bearable under the circumstances. Somebody "found" enough string and wire to run the length of the huts so that we could raise our mosquito nets, a real necessity here as the air field was surrounded by a swamp, a paradise for mosquitoes, snakes and other wild life.

The cook-house was a little tin roofed shack with one wall and cooking space for two large *wajangs* (cast iron woks). These were supported by large stones with an opening for the fire wood. It was situated close to No 1 shed where Taffy and I were quartered. Jack, Penny and Blackie were in the other hut. Cooking was done over open fires in huge *wajangs*. The cooks also had a couple of large RAF cooking pots, capable of holding about fifty gallons of liquid. There were also a few smaller pots of about twenty gallon capacity with handles sticking over the top rim. With a long bamboo pole put through the handles they made ideal carrying pots. These were used to bring us water or tea twice a day as we worked on the runway. One of the sought after jobs was to be a tea carrier. This entailed being sent from the sand spreading job to the cook-house and carrying back twenty gallons of tea. It meant that for a short while we were working for the good of our buddies and NOT the Nips. We soon learned on this job that we had to break step. With twenty gallons of hot tea swinging between us if we both put the right foot forward at the same time it would only take a few steps before the momentum literally swung us off our feet. Close to two hundred pounds of hot liquid sloshing between two scrawny prisoners was enough to heighten our sense of self preservation. Any spillage was lost to the workers on the runway because we were only allowed one trip to the cook-house.

We were supposed to be paid ten cents a day for this coolie labour. Sometimes we were lucky and sometimes the money just did not materialise. July the third saw us lining up for our first pay parade. Other ranks were paid 10cents a day,

Sergeants and above received 15 cents a day and I guess the officers got some princely sum commensurate with this general trend of exploitation. There was no explanation for this if the money went astray. When Wing Commander Gregson complained he was beaten. The CO was most upset. He had always had the welfare of his men at heart and now he was ignored by the lowest ranks of the Japanese Army. He protested loud and long to the Nip authorities, but it was a useless exercise. To be in such a helpless position was hard on the CO. The Nips who were the conquering heroes, did not have the capacity to carry off the role with any degree of sophistication. Brute force administered in any way possible was their only way of doing business. The Geneva Convention meant nothing to them.

We heard a great deal now about "the Greater East Asia Co-Prosperity Sphere"— "Asia for the Asiatics" and how the Japanese had ended the European Colonial system. Indonesia and Java in particular had been controlled by several European powers since the arrival of the Portuguese in 1510. Now Asia would soon be free to decide its own future. The Japanese brought Liberation from harsh colonial masters and all Javanese must love them for what they had done. Once again fact and fiction were mixed to such an extent that they were convinced the local population believed the fiction. There is no doubt that the Japanese were welcomed as liberators. The Javanese independence movement under Sukarno saw a definite opportunity to further their aims. The movement did not turn out the way the Japanese led them to believe it would.

We settled down to a routine of working on the airstrip. I became unpopular with my fellow workers because I did not like working for the Japanese. I would spend as much time as possible just leaning on my *chunkal* (a large bladed oriental hoe) or crouched down out of sight of the guards. The men persuaded me that my best course of action was to work along with the rest of them as we were all in this together. Reason prevailed and I started to pull my weight.

We had only been in camp a short while when Sqn/Ldr Carlile was bayoneted in the head by Goldie, a guard. The Sqn/Ldr had been protesting the treatment of one of his men when Goldie decided that it was time for action. Drastic action. He removed the bayonet from his rifle and with a great stabbing motion plunged it into Carlile's head as he was bending down. There was a great deal of blood from this nasty wound. The MO patched him up and got him to hospital the next day. He was soon back with us just as bright and chipper as ever. One of the advantages of this camp was that Doctor Philps could refer the worst medical cases to the local hospital. It was not well equipped by any standards but they had more than a small bag of medicines and a few rudimentary instruments.

This camp was unique for two reasons: We had a black market, and I met Hengie. The black market was a daily affair and consisted of the natives coming to the outside of the barbed wire with all their goods, fruit, *gula malaka* (a locally made brown sugar moulded in the bottom half of a coconut shell), cooked strips of meat, coffee, eggs and anything else they thought they could peddle. This was typical oriental market-bargaining in full swing. We were down on our haunches peering through the barbed wire on a face to face, knock 'em down, no punches barred bargaining session. Our money was hard earned, at one cent an hour, if we were lucky, but they had the experience. We called this a Black Market because the men on the other side of the wire were a couple of shades darker than we were.

Hengie was a Dutch soldier who took a great liking to me. This was also his town. He owned two hotels in Semarang and knew a lot of people. The black market to him was just a convenient way to keep in touch with his interests. He had a couple of runners who posed as the native traders and supplied him with all his needs. In this way Hengie was in touch with his interests in town and pretty well called the shots. He worked on the docks with the other Dutchmen but always kept in touch with his family and friends on the outside. He got advance information of moves, visits to the camp by the local population and, to our amazement, Japanese activities such as a camp visit, celebrating the completion of the runway extension. He insisted that what I needed was a young lady friend to give me some interest in the world at large. This seemed to be a fairly harmless thing to do as the plan was to be pen pals. So he got me in touch with a young Dutch girl using his runner as the go between. We corresponded for the remaining six months we were in this camp.

The Dutch soldiers worked on the docks in town and had a much easier time than we did. They were allowed to have contact with the civilians. Like Hengie many of them had lived here and knew people who were now in a position to make life much easier for them. Dock work was always most welcome as it presented a lot of chances for scrounging and trading. The Nips had allowed some of the Dutch people to stay outside the confines of the camps because they were essential in keeping the country running. In contrast the airstrip was strictly hard labour with no perks. Trainloads of sand were always waiting to be unloaded. Since our arrival the Japanese had extended a spur railroad line to bring the construction materials to the end of the runway. The only selection of jobs was to shovel the sand off the flat cars or to spread it as a foundation for the future runway. The work was sheer hard physical labour. We were allowed to carry fruit and water to the work area on the runway. This gave some of those who had been lucky enough to buy a coconut complete with covering husk an opportunity to bury it in the sand with the hope that at some future date it would start sprouting and break up the runway. A small but hopeful effort at sabotage.

About two months after we arrived on the airstrip I was asked if I would like

My best catch of salmon in the summer of 1940. Qualicum Beach is where Uncle Robbie had a summer cottage, situated on the east coast of Vancouver Island, British Columbia.

Haruku airfield today. Ex POWs visit the field in 1994. Gun emplacements are now growing chili bushes.

The last remnants of Haruku camp cook house. The fireplace where so much rice was cooked.

The shed we lived in at Semarang Camp. The ends were open during our occupation.

POWs (in white hats) and Haruku kids meet on the new dock in Pelau village. The old dock was bombed out of existence by the Americans.

In the uniform of the Singapore Harbour Board Police, 1947

a job in the cook-house. The CO had requested permission to put one more man in the cook-house and I was the lucky one. I would have to work on the night shift. This meant preparing for tea time just before going to bed and then during the night preparing the vegetables for the next day and, of course, cooking the pap breakfast. Breakfast consisted of a bowl of watery rice, and a teaspoonful of sugar, and as much hot tea as you could drink. My job was strictly cook-house helper. Dixie Leigh was my shift boss. He held the rank of Leading Aircaftman (LAC) and was a cook by trade. Sid Hardwick was the corporal in charge. My main job was to cut up the vegetables. The technique here was to go as fast as possible without cutting a finger or hand. Dixie was an expert at this and soon taught me the tricks of the trade. He kept the knives razor sharp so the game was a roulette wheel of time and blood. This was a very nice break for me as it got me off the hard physical labour on the air strip, gave me a lot more to eat and a chance to look around for any other opportunities, however remote, that might present themselves. It was an accepted fact that cook-house personnel would eat more than the outside workers. At this stage of POW life it was an advantage for me but was fatal later on to many aspiring cooks. Once again I was being looked after by a friendly but unknown hand. P/O Hope-Faulkner had been a police officer in Malaya before the Japanese invaded and had known my father. He was one of the five officers we had on camp and had persuaded the CO to give me this job.

One night after we had done the chores, Dixie and I were chatting when I noticed a movement in the ditch, a quiet stirring as an unknown object made a little ripple on the surface of the green jungle water. The perimeter barbed wire for the camp came right beside the cook-house and over the large drainage ditch. Here the job of spanning the ditch with barbed wire had not been too good as the bottom strand of wire was about six inches above the water and the water in the ditch was usually about eighteen inches deep. I could easily get in and out of the camp through the ditch. The movement in the water turned out to be a water snake about four feet long and with a nice round two inch diameter body. Quick as a flash I was into the ditch, under the barbed wire and in hot pursuit of the snake. It took me about a minute to grab it by the tail swing it in a great circular motion and, hopefully, break its neck on the bank of the ditch. Water snakes are harmless, have a nice meaty body, and a finely patterned skin. I brought him into camp and skinned him on the spot. There was no shortage of salt so I rubbed the skin with salt and had my self a nice little prize. I could not get any wood to stretch out the skin to dry so I pegged it into the ground, using twigs from the bushes just outside the wire. I had it stretched and pegged in a sandy spot just behind the cook-house, where it would receive a fair amount of drying sun and be out of the way of any wandering Nips. Every day I would check it and rub in a little more salt or scrape off a little tuft of flesh that had been missed on the initial skinning. I am sure the tanning industry would have looked upon this with a jaundiced eye but souvenirs come in a great variety of quality. This was not intended to be hung on a living room wall. I was not too sure what kind of price this would command on the black market but I knew it was worth something and would get at least a meal or two. A couple of days later one of the Nip guards happened just by chance to walk in the direction of my drying area. Before I could distract him, he spotted the skin and much to my surprise wanted to buy it. He could easily have taken it but was one of the garrison guards rather than the front line troops who considered us beneath contempt. And so started my first little business enterprise, augmenting my ten cents a day with a handsome profit from the guards. This proved to be a nice little business but unfortunately the supply of snakes was not overwhelming. I did put the price up when the snakes in the immediate area became almost impossible to get, but it was too late. My business foundered as the risk of being caught and turned over to the Kempetai (Japanese Gestapo) for torture and a confession of spying, (being outside the wire) countered the lure of profit.

Part of my job was to pick up rations from the depot in town. One day while the black market was still in progress, I was called to the ration truck in a hurry. I had no time to hide the letter I had just received from Jenny, the girl Hengie had put me in touch with. I had not read it yet as this had to be done in the hut out of sight of the Nips. I leapt on to the truck and joined Dixie and Jack as we sped off to the warehouse. When we got to the warehouse the driver was told to go to Kempetai HQ. This, of course, we did not understand and so we continued to stand on the back of the truck enjoying the extra tour through the town. When we got to Kempetai HQ all hell broke loose. Two Kempetai policemen came charging out of the building and made us throw all the empty rice sacks off the truck and open the empty boxes for inspection. I had the letter in my pocket and could only guess that some sort of smuggling was going on and they were out to find the culprit and the goods.

Luckily the letter was only one sheet of paper so it did not take up much room. By the same token, wearing the usual skimpy shorts, I did not have many choices of hiding places. If I slipped it into my mouth they would see me chewing and that would automatically cause a beating. It was too dangerous to drop it. The Kempetai men backed the three of us against the truck and started to search us. I managed to move the letter from my pocket to my waist band and kept my stomach pushed out so as to keep the pressure on it. When they started searching me I pulled out the pockets of my shorts in a great show of innocence and got away without them finding it. We never did find out what all the fuss was about. I had been very close to being arrested by the Kempetai. Not too many prisoners lived to tell us what the inside of the Kempetai barracks was like. Back at the camp the men had been called off the work parties and had a kit search. There is no doubt they were after a radio or parts of one. They were always terrified that we might be operating a radio and listening to the truth. At this time their fortunes had started to change. (Unknown to us the two decisive battles of the Pacific had already been fought - the Coral Sea and Midway.)

On another ration run I found a Nip wallet with sixty guilders in notes in it. It was lying beside the road after we had finished loading the truck. It looked like a plant to me as none of us had noticed it when we arrived. I looked around and picked it up holding it in a conspicuous way as I mounted the truck. I discussed it with the other fellows who came to the conclusion that I was home free. When we got back to camp I told the CO what had happened as it may have been a plant. He arranged to keep the wallet for a few days and if nothing happened he would give it back to me. The sixty guilders put me in the category of "affluent" and made my visits to the Black Market a spectacle to behold. I could now get one of my favourite little acquisitions - *Gula Malacca* - that half coconut shell shaped coarse brown sugar, some Mangosteens, Rambutans, and Durians if the season was right. Jack shared in some of this good fortune as his source of income — washing the officers clothing was not a lucrative business. We had only five officers on camp and the happy days of Tasik Malaja were a distant memory as the ever tightening misery of prison life closed in on us.

Wing Commander Gregson was put into a real quandary when the Nips ordered him to make all the men in camp sign a "No Escape" document. The Geneva Convention recognises that it is the duty of all prisoners to try to escape. Japan had signed the Convention but not ratified it. They were well aware that what they were ordering us to do was against all international accepted forms of behaviour. The CO decided that we were signing under duress and in effect this made the whole affair null and void. We signed. The Nips had made it abundantly clear in the preceding months that escaping was not only a self pronounced death sentence but that the escapee would also be responsible for ten deaths, randomly selected from his buddies. Torture, bayoneting and decapitation were the selected methods of disposing of prisoners. The way of the Samurai Warriors?

July 8th was Visitors' Day. The camp gates were opened to the public and once again the Dutch people showered us with presents. The people of Semarang were most generous. Unfortunately I was down with the most horrible case of Singapore feet. Both feet were close to twice their normal size with puss oozing all around the toes. Needless to say I could not get very far in this condition. The visitors were not allowed in the huts so I had to call on Jack to help me get to the visiting area near the guard house. For the first time I met Jenny, my girl friend pen pal. I had imagined a beautiful dusky maiden fairly tall, lithe and sinewy.

The Jenny of my dreams and the real Jenny were two different Goddesses. She had a most pleasing round face, with large eyes and that most appealing innocent look that is not uncommon amongst the Dutch Eurasians. Under normal conditions I am sure she would be pleasingly plump but was now showing a suppleness that was not natural to her. During our brief encounter I did not tell her of the close escape I had with the Kempetai in case she cut down on the correspondence. There was obviously some danger in this innocent little repartee. Any message found by the Japanese would involve torture until the source of the letters was revealed. She very much wanted to get some medicine for my feet. The next time the Black Market gathered outside the wire Hengie's runner had a package of medicine for me, a native concoction that Dr. Philps would have frowned upon at this stage of our prison existence. It was not long before my feet healed and I was mobile again. Jenny where ever you may be - a thousand thanks. The ladies of Semarang will always be fondly remembered by the prisoners on the aerodrome. They certainly did not have too much food or any other supplies for themselves. Their generosity was in the form of what the land will provide, mainly fruit and vegetables, soap, and sometimes an article of clothing. Their benevolence gave us a most welcome break from our skimpy rations quite apart from the fact that we actually associated with the fairer sex for a few hours.

Blackie had been in the Semarang Hospital with a bout of enteritis about a month before this visiting day. A Dutch girl, Tessie, had taken a great liking to him and now brought him a nice parcel of food and other goodies. For some reason the CO thought this was too much good fortune for one man to have so he divided the parcel amongst those who were in greater need. The senior NCOs not only enjoyed more pay than we had, but also had a supervisory position in conjunction with the guards, which gave them the privilege of a day off the monotony of shoveling sand.

Malnutrition worked its insidious way into our bodies. Little did we realise how many lives this would claim before we were released. Java Balls was a nasty and persistent irritation of the scrotum and the crotch area. We had no idea that this uncomfortable situation was the forerunner of a multitude of progressively worsening symptoms of our prolonged captivity. Insanity, blindness, and death were to overtake so many of our comrades. The only remedy for this is an improved diet. The Japanese were getting a working party every day so they were not worried about the condition of the workers. It never occurred to them that fit men could work much more effectively than sick men. Malaria was now a common occurrence but with quinine available it was fairly easy to get over a bout.

Our evenings were free to play cricket, read or otherwise entertain ourselves with the limited resources available to us. Dr. Philps had some books that he had managed to keep hidden through various searches. He held a reading/listening session before sun set. This was quite popular as he read a selection of short stories or poetry to anyone interested. I was still reading Blackie's textbook on pilot training and telling my self that in three months it would all be over for us. I would "dance the sky on laughter silvered wings." One day both Blackie and another Sgt. Pilot, Munsell, were threatened with death as they refused to reveal some information about pilot training that the Nips wanted. It was rumoured that the Nips blacked out when pulling out of a long vertical dive and that our pilots were most successful in this manoeuvre. The Nips wanted to know how we did it. There were many helpful suggestions, bantered about amongst ourselves, as to just why the White Man was superior in, not only these manoeuvres, but in every other way, but these are best left to the readers' imagination. Such aspects as physique, training, eyesight and attitude and a feeling of innate superiority all played a part. In spite of the fact that we had been thoroughly beaten in battle there was never any doubt as to what the final outcome of the war would be. In actual fact the Navy Zero was mechanically weak in this manoeuvre. There are many recorded cases of the wings folding on the Zero after following a Hurricane in a vertical dive. There is no doubt that the Zero was the best fighter plane in the world at this time and the Japanese pilots the most experienced.

When the Japanese pilots were conducting some extensive dive bomber training from the airstrip we were extending I wandered over to the other hut to visit Jack who was down with malaria. Half way there a Nip guard grabbed me and walked me over to a dive bomber that was beside one of the hangars. He told me to take the crank handle and start winding. Luckily one of our fellows shouted to watch out for the propeller. As I had never done this before his advise was well taken. I cranked and soon the engine burst into power scaring the hell out of me. My immediate reaction, thanks to the shouted warning, was to move under the wing and into safety. If I had moved in the wrong direction then I would have been hacked to pieces by the propeller. Why had they gone to the trouble of getting a young and inexperienced POW to start the engine? There were many Japanese soldiers and airmen in the hangar, most of them standing around and watching my every move. Were they hoping to see a body smashed to a million pieces by the turning prop'?

While I was on duty one night in the cook-house a storm brewed up and seemed to be concentrated right over us. The lightening was striking close to the cook-house and the thunder was so close and loud that the corrugated iron roof would reverberate with each long and extended clap. As the storm increased in violence and the wind picked up Dixie and I secured everything that was liable to blow away. We were so busy with this job in the cook-house that we were surprised when with one almighty whoosh the whole roof disappeared. This put us in a rotten position as we had to keep the fires going for the morning pap and fight the wind and rain at the same time. We stacked wood in the sleeping quarters and had to call on the day time staff for assistance to get the rice under cover. Luckily the main buildings were constructed of stronger materials and stayed intact throughout the storm. I doubt that anyone slept through the episode except Jimmy, who we will meet soon. It is frightening to be at the centre of such powerful forces. The Gods were clapping but we did not know who's side they were on.

The Nips had a "pet" monkey that they kept in their quarters. One day this poor beast escaped and came into our Nissen hut. We tried to make friends with it but it was nervous, keeping a distance and watching every move with intense interest, its head moving continuously from side to side. When a Nip guard came into the hut the monkey defecated all over the place, and raced into the rafters screaming abuse at its tormentor. This was proof to us that there was a lot of truth in the saying "shit scared". We wanted to keep the monkey but were forced to chase him back to his torturers. Even a little caring and more food would not have given this unfortunate creature a new lease on life. Many years after the war I was given an abused monkey for a pet but it remained wary of me and my family in spite of a lot of tender loving care.

We were continually amazed at the inherent cruelty of the Nips. Frequently when they found an insect they would squat around and torment the little creature, pulling off legs or wings or both, one at a time and then watch as it writhed and struggled on the ground. Seldom, if ever, would they think of putting the creature out of its agony by killing it out right. After having their "fun" they would just walk away and leave it to die a slow, painful, death.

We had two celebrations on this camp. The first was Queen Wilhemena's birthday on the 31st August when our rice ration was increased for the day and steak was added to evening meal. This was preceded by cabbage water soup. A nice gesture on the part of our captors. The second had more meaning for us as they announced a special Christmas dispensation ——we would be allowed to write home.

Ten months after being taken prisoners this joyous news was received with great enthusiasm. Our hosts — for they kept telling us we were the "guests of the Emperor" were up to their usual tricks of giving out good news only to modify it in the extreme. We envisioned that we would be given a writing pad and pencil and allowed to go to it. Penny, Blackie and I got ourselves really well organised for this deal. Blackie managed to reserve a spot on one of the eating places outside the huts. This was not a table but more like an upside down barrel. With a little bit of tolerance the three of us could write at the same time. Now came the real message. We were given a average sized post card and told to select three sentences from a list that would be circulated to all prisoners. We were allowed to add twenty words.

My parents did not receive this "letter" until just before the end of the war some two years later. The first sentences are numbered and indicate the three prescribed sentences that I selected. This is followed by my twenty free words. This is what I wrote after approximately a year as a prisoner of war:

2. I am now in a Japanese Prisoner of War camp in Java.
3. My health is excellent.
10. I am constantly thinking of you it will be wonderful when we meet again.

Dearest Mummy.
To day is Christmas. Don't worry about me. Hope all the family are happy. Is Dad safe?   All love
                                                              Tony.

Sending this letter home was done with a considerable amount of scepticism. Not a single letter had been received in camp and not even a hint of a Red Cross parcel. We could only guess that sort of international pressure had been put on the Japanese to try to comply with a basic standard of humane treatment.

Christmas morning did bring another surprise. As I was turning in after a spell of night duty the Welsh men in camp burst into song with some very welcome Christmas carols. Through some tricky manoeuvring they had managed to get a couple of Christmas records into camp which they used as background accompaniment. Several days later the guards were celebrating the 1st of January. They gathered as a group around a large beautifully decorated cake each holding a glass of beer and surrounded by tropical fruit. There was a truly Japanese slant to this whole idealistic situation. The cake was made of cement, the beer was cold tea and the fruit was whisked away as soon as the last picture was taken. A strange celebration for a conquering army!

The job the Dutch had been working on at the docks finished about a month before we had an official aerodrome opening day (October 9th, 1942). Consequently they had been moved back to Sourabaya and were not around to enjoy this celebration with us. This was a big day for the conquering forces. Unlike a similar situation on home territory there was not a large number of civilians included in the celebrations. There were mock air battles over the strip with Zero fighters taking part. Dive bombers made runs onto dummy targets that were not marked on the ground — consequently no one knew how accurate they were. The Nip air force was happy with their new airstrip as it was now operational. We had a holiday and an increase in rations — for this one day — and a bottle of beer shared between two men.

Much to our disgust they started practising dive bombing with live bombs on a target that was approximately 200 yards outside the barbed wire. Many pieces of shrapnel landed in the camp. Luckily the only people in camp were the CO, the doctor, the cooks, medical orderlies, and the sick. The CO's protests were to no avail as this practice carried on for about a week. We were genuinely surprised and happy at the accuracy of their bombing for any misses might have been deadly for us. They did not seem to worry about the native population. There were no warnings that dive bombing with live bombs was to take place in this highly populated area. With the sea so close to hand we thought they would at least tow a target a few hundred yards off shore. We saw natives using the area just prior to the daily bombing practices but did not hear of any casualties. We found out after our next two moves that the welfare of native population was not really a concern of the military.

Christmas day arrived and we were given a small increase in rations for the day. At least the Japanese were recognising a Christian holiday and trying to do something about it. Brutality was rampant but there had been no deaths. In spite of our depraved conditions we were still confident the Yanks would soon be on their way to relieve the situation. Sid combined the extra rations with whatever he had been able to save during the preceding days and came up with a special Christmas treat. *Nasi Goreng* (fried rice) was a favourite. It was an easy meal to cook and nutritious. There were seldom any complaints about this meal as it included the total variety of all the vegetables and meat that came into camp. About a week after Christmas the Nips allowed a truck to come into camp with some presents from the Dutch residents of Semarang. I received a can of meat and a shirt, both very welcome. Dr. Philps took advantage of this new generosity of the Nips and arranged for the camp to have brown bean soup once a week, Mondays. We put great faith in any extra rations the doctor could arrange for us as we felt that his sole concern was our survival. The good doctor assured us that brown bean soup would work wonders for our malnutrition and assist us in our fight against malaria that was now rampant in the camp. We were a pretty demoralised group with no future ahead of us and only a long down hill slide into total degradation. I came down with a temperature of 105 degrees and shook like a leaf for half a day just as an introduction to this killer. It lasted about a week and left me many pounds lighter and a good deal weaker. This was to be my first of many fights against this exterminator.

Semarang camp saw the development of the "Legi line" a ritual that was to stay with us for the rest of our days as prisoners - a ritual that developed in every camp from New Britain to the Burma railroad. Legi is the Malay word for "more" (spelled *lagi*). After the rations were issued at each meal, a line formed to get the leftovers. At this time we were getting the equivalent of about one and a half average sized cups of uncooked rice per day. Breakfast was pap where you could count the number of grains in the water given to you. We always had enough tea. Lunch was a scoop of dried rice with a watery vegetable soup. This had to be carried to the runway in big containers suspended on bamboo poles, a good job helping comrades and not working directly for the Nips. At night we had the meal of the day - this was a repeat of the dried rice but the soup was thicker with vegetables and often meat. I was at a distinct advantage here because the snakes gave me additional meat. Jack was game to join me in these tasty snake dishes. Taffy, Dixie and the others could afford to be fussy at this stage. I could easily fry a four foot length of snake curled up in a *wajang*. The meat was a nice white colour and with a little imagination I could fool myself into the belief that I was enjoying a tasty chicken dinner. Sometimes the rations would be varied enough for us to have a really good *nasi goreng*. Whenever we collected the rations we were always scrounging for an extra sack of anything that might be in the warehouse. This was a tricky business as the Nips did not have a sense of humour, added to which they only had one reaction - physical violence. On many occasions when we were in the ration warehouse I would saunter over to an area liberally stacked with vegetables and try to kick some to our allocation. I got away with it frequently but often the proverbial shit hit the fan. These people could not for the life of them understand that we were continually hungry. It was well beyond their comprehension to turn a blind eye to a few veggies being shuffled across the warehouse floor. If the next day the veggies were rotten it was of no consequence to them.

Jack got himself in trouble on the work party and was beaten unmercifully. After being harangued by a guard for not applying himself in total dedication to the wishes of their God Emperor he responded with a few home truths in a tone of voice that left no doubt as to his meaning. Of course not a word was understood by either side but the meanings were easy to interpret. These little people loved to beat the big fellows. The guard made Jack stand to attention and then punched him in the face at the same time as putting his right foot behind Jack's legs just below the knees. When he took the inevitable step backwards to keep balance as the punch landed on his face he had to fall. Now the guard would be in a position of dominance and would start kicking, and use the butt of his rifle. We recognised a definite pattern to these beatings. The guards would start by shouting and then gradually work themselves into a condition from which there was no return and a beating was the obvious result. If a distraction could be contrived before the moment of no return the poor victim would be saved a senseless beating. Unfortunately this was seldom the case. We had nicknames for all the guards.

Some of them that come to mind are; Goldie, Gummy, Glaxco Kid, Basher Bill, Lantern Jaw, usually named for some physical feature or propensity.

One night as the midnight guard was changed our CO was called off his bamboo platform bed and told to parade every one outside the hut immediately. The whole camp was to be assembled one at a time, coming out of only one exit, with each hut being emptied individually. Guards were posted around both huts and the cook-house to ensure no one moved in or out of the area. The disorganisation of Japanese soldiers running around was astonishing and frightening to us inside the huts trying to guess what was developing. We could hear the CO being shouted at in what appeared to be very coarse and abusive language. It sounded as if the regular guard had been reinforced by troops from the town garrison. It was quite possible that the troops were setting up machine guns as we could hear from the action that we were surrounded - a most unusual development. When we finally emerged from the hut we could see that there were many soldiers from the town garrison helping the guards — something very serious was afoot. Each man was counted as he came out of the hut, and then assembled on the parade ground and guarded by more soldiers. They were obviously looking for an escapee. There were two hundred men in camp and we counted one hundred and ninety nine. All hell broke loose. There was a lot of shouting and waving of weapons - it seemed as if they were encouraging each other in the darkness of the night. A nasty custom as it inevitably led to violence. Now the escaped victim must be identified. One of the senior NCOs was sent into the building to get the nominal roll. As he was coming out of the hut he heard someone turn over on the bamboo. Sure enough there was our missing man, Jimmy, who had slept through the whole procedure. When the runner brought out Jimmy, rubbing his eyes and totally unaware of what had been going on for the last half an hour the Japanese would not believe it. The usual numbering pantomime was started. We spent most of the night counting in Japanese, calling the roll, being paraded past a point for more counting and then finally to bed. The next day was a working day with the guards in an unusually foul mood. For some strange reason Jimmy was not beaten for having slept through most of the proceedings.

On February 7th we were told at 6:30 pm that we would move out of the camp at 2300 hrs. The Japanese camp commander made a big concession as the train would be brought to the camp siding and we would load right there. This gave us in the cook-house enough time to boil some rice and vegetables and make rice balls, about tennis ball size, one for each man. This was a typical move organised by the Japanese. We were crammed into two third class carriages. A normal day coach has seats for about sixty people. As we were two hundred strong this was a very crowded situation in two coaches. The truck with our cook-house equipment was loaded into a boxcar but the cooks were not allowed to stay with it. We thought this would alleviate the crammed situation in the passenger coaches. But this was too obvious a solution. It would also create a counting problem for the guards. An hour after loading we were under way, a most remarkable feat for the Nips. Too remarkable, for we just moved to the Semarang station and stayed there all night. The usual uncomfortable situation of mosquitoes and bugs was accentuated by the surroundings. In Java at that time the train seats were all wood with out any padding. It was a hard, sleepless and uncomfortable night.

We left the station at 0830 the following morning. Our priority rating on the railroad was zero so our train stopped for all other traffic on the way. The optimists who ate their rice ball early during the trip were to regret it later when another meal was not to be had. It was a long, hard, hot, uncomfortable trip. We arrived at Sourabaya at 8:30 that night. A twelve hour journey for a low priority train. It was dark when we arrived and much to our surprise an ambulance showed up for the sick. We had men who could not walk as a result of injuries, malaria, dysentery, and beri beri. The rest of us marched to a camp that we had seen when we were last in Sourabaya, but had not been in. It was much more open than the school we had been housed in and I believe was formerly an army barracks.

All kit had to be left in the main hall for a search to be carried out, and we were individually searched as we entered the camp. A great deal of yelling, shouting and prodding was our introduction to this camp reputed to hold more than four thousand prisoners, mostly British and Dutch with a few Canadian and American prisoners. The Bull, a senior Japanese officer who was responsible for all prisoners in Sourabaya made a lengthy speech to us about the Jaar Markt spirit. So this is where we were! Jaar Markt camp. He told us how the glorious Nipponese army was continuing its victorious progress and would soon have Australia in its grasp. How the war would last a hundred years and the Japanese vision of one world controlled by their God Emperor would be a reality. I had a very welcome surprise as we were served soup by my Semarang friend Hengie. A good thick soup complete with *Katjang idjoe*, a small green bean grown extensively in Java and reputed to be nutritious. Hengie had manoeuvred himself into a cook-house job as soon as his group had arrived from Semarang.

Our CO was severely dressed down when it was found the next day that only 10 men out of the 200 were fit enough to go on working parties. Five of these ten were cook-house men. I considered myself very lucky indeed. It showed us that the rations on this camp were very much better than those we had at Semarang. In all fairness to our CO I must say that the resources available to this large camp were extensive. Money to buy extra rations was somehow arranged. In Semarang there was absolutely no access to any outside assistance. Our Wing

Commander had done everything in his power to create a better situation for us only to be thwarted at every turn by the Japanese camp commander who held us in complete contempt and took advantage of the fact that we were only two hundred prisoners and consequently not a force to be concerned with. It is possible that a certain amount of graft in diverting pay and rations for personal benefit was taking place. We had no evidence of this until we were moved to the islands sometime later in the year when it was clear to all that the sergeant in charge was making a profit from starving prisoners. When we left this camp I did not see Hengie again. I do not know if he survived the hard times ahead of us. I have no doubt that Jenny survived. The Dutch women of Semarang were a very resourceful and determined bunch to say nothing of their generosity and kind hearts.

Semarang proved to be the best prison camp I was in. Tasik Malaja could not be considered a POW camp as it was our place of capture and we were only there until the Japanese determined what use they could make out of this extensive labour force that Churchill had given them. The guards continually told us that they considered us as "Churchill's *trema kassie* (thank you) men." A bonus for their rapid and treacherous victory in the Far East. Jaar Markt (Yarmart) camp was exceptionally good but it did not have the spirit of Semarang. A small camp like this with an outstanding Commanding Officer and relatively good conditions where everyone knew every one else was good for morale and mutual support. In the light of what was to come Semarang was a good camp in as much as we had fairly good rations. Dr. Philps was able to arrange some medical supplies from the town hospital. I believe this was done in a true entrepreneurial spirit. Our main disease here was malaria and quinine is grown in Java so there was some form of supply available. Rumour had it that Dr. Philps was treating many of the Nip guards for syphilis and/or gonorrhoea. It appeared that advanced cases of either one of these diseases were shipped off to the fighting front so that the patient would have the privilege of dying for their God Emperor rather than suffering, not only the ignominy, but the physical pain of treatment. (At this time the accepted treatment for syphilis involved the insertion of an instrument into the penis and was considered excruciating) In return for this treatment the good doctor was bringing into camp medicines that relieved the suffering of our sick and wounded. Wing Commander Gregson was an outstanding leader who did not hesitate to tell the Japanese what he thought of a situation. He was very much respected by all of us. A strong leader with a fair regard for all his men.

200 British Personnel at Semarang Camp, Java, 3 June 1942 to 4 February 1943.
(This list was compiled by Edward McDaniel and sent to me in 1989. It is not complete).
† Indicates this person did not survive POW Camp.
‡ Died since returning home.
Of this random group of 200 prisoners of war 69 did not survive prison life =34.5%

Hut 1

Wing Commander
  Gregson ‡
Flight Lieut.
  Jack Carlyle‡
Flight Lieut. John
  Williamson
Pilot Off.Hope-Faulkner
Dr. Dick Philps
Jock Turbayne
Jock Jarvis
Johnny Johnson
Percy Brown
Roy Mider
Jock Cummins†
Bill Jones
Fred Fleming†
Alf Benson
Penny Penteney†
Blackie Blackmore
Bill Chapman

Sgt. Gent†
Norman Arthur†
Sid Hardwick
Ronnie Hall
Peter Lucani
Lofty Jack Wright
Salmoni
Percy Wood†
Cobbler Keogh
Jimmy Fort
Bert Parkin
Jim Turner†
Curly Pittam
Freddy Bartholemew‡
Tony Cowling
Bernard Yates
Harold Prechner‡
Jock Campbell Petrie‡
Harley Monsell‡

Ginger Francis†
Nobby Hall†
Jim Joch Chalmers
Ginger Noton‡
Brum Marriot,
Jim Anderson‡
Ernie Kidson
Don Peacock
Geordie Robson
Dave Dolby†
Geordie Gascoyne
Gordon Riddle†
Educated Ted Evans†
Gunner Simpson
Taff Hopkins
Jack Marshall,
Jock Pete Lumsden
Dixie Lee ‡
Roy Richardson

L/Bdr. Cannon†
Taff Thorne
Bill Hocken
Jock King†
Paddy Muckle,†
Blondie Thwaites†
Doug Leece
Jackie Ward‡
Arty Harrysman
Jock Beveridge†
Ray Newton
Gunner Grant
"Sheffield" Butlker
Stan Guest†
Mac Edward
  MacDaniel
Ted Gibson†
Bert Neighbour
  Belsham†

Hut # 2.

Ron Thompson
Bob Hewlett
Lofty Orchard†
Jock Bob Currie ‡
Tubby Ragan†
Woodward†
Johnny Johnson
  Joe Maudsley†
Fred Kaye†
Tom McPhillips†
Jim Dyer†
Bill Byron†
Ned Sparks†
Alfred Hickman†
Jack Hart†

Alf Butt†
Jimmy Brackenbury‡
Jacky Beck
Bomber Brown
Titch Harry Brown†
Dick Barnes
Cliff Bastin
Carter
Franck Carty†
Jock Cunningham
Gordon Cursons
Eddie Cooper
Coward
Doc Docherty†
Jack Dudley

Jock Hodge‡
Jack Hollerman
Sid Trader Horne†
Appendix Jones
Barber Jones
Mal John‡
Gordon Jones†
Frank Legig
Eric Legn
Norman Kaye
Abraham Kissin‡
Wilf Parism‡
Yorky Phillip Stokes†
Eric "Flash" Harry
  Mortimer‡

Lofty Logan
Roy Laywood†
Arthur Lepley
Ken Piper†
Lofty Roberts
Titch Robinson
Lol Ramsey†
Henry Rollison†
Titch Rowlands†
Geoff Rowe
Jock Rosine†
Bert Spearman
Joe Symons‡
Smudgere Smith†
Eric Snowell†

Charlie Murcott†	George Dove†	Bill Parker†	Sid Sykes†
Ginger Lonng†	Davies	Jock Thompson†	Scott
Bill Lewis†	Dobbie Dobson†	Reg Maycock†	Taff Phil Smith
Taff Lewis	Ron Davies‡	Winston Piggot	Taff Tucker
Jack Trafford	George Dagmore‡	Reg Macefield†	Bill Tucker†
Tom Gylee	Jock Daziel	McFarlane	Lofty Thompson
Paddy Wilson†	Jock Edwards‡	Jock McAlister†	Charlie Warner†
Paddy McGee	Taff Floyd†	Jock Allan†	Jack Warner
Bill Glovere	Steve Foster‡	Bill Monk†	Lofty Ward‡
Turnbull	Stormy Gale†	Taff Morgan	Arthur Westlake†
Handley	Jack Gilbard‡	Jock McCluskie‡	Harry Warwick†
Rex Lockyer	Alf Grand†	Dai Nettle	Alec "Just Jake"
Paddy O'Donnell‡	Jack Green	Doug Norman	Walker‡
Geoff Bunny Austin†	Billy Green†	Martin Ofield‡	Jock Adam
Arkle	Jim Groom Bridce†	Benny Lynen	Edwards‡
Reuben Alster‡	Eric Hills†	Pritchard	Freddy George
Arthur Bailey	Jack Dobie†		Bartholomew

---

1   During our captivity we saw Red Cross parcels on the docks and knew from general knowledge that the Red Cross would be supplying parcels for our benefit. The only parcels we received were after the bombs dropped.

2   *High Flight* John Gillespie Magee

4

Jaar Markt Camp
THREE SQUARES AND A LITTLE LOOTING

*One should always have their boots on
and be ready to leave.*
MICHEL DE MAETERLINCK   1533 - 1592

Jaar Markt, after the rather unpleasant start, turned out to be a good camp. The first morning we were awakened by a bugle call - most intriguing. This turned into an entertaining time of the day as reveille varied considerably. The Dutch bugler knew many European calls and used these in a most captivating way. Soon after reveille was the "come to the cook-house door, boys", different every day. After breakfast, which consisted of a "pap" rice and sugar mixture, the whole camp, except the hospital patients, was paraded facing the Sun. The Japanese Commander would stand on an elevated platform at the head of the parade and shout out a command. He and his staff would then bow to the rising sun and pray either to or for their God Emperor. We, of course, would have to follow suit. There were guards surrounding the parade also paying respects to their deity. All prisoners had to dutifully murmur something to show they were taking part in this daily routine. What the guards did not know was the filthy abuse that was being heaped upon their God Emperor. In spite of their profane base the expletives were most amusing, especially when one took into account the object of the exercise. The more creative and vocal members of the group had us in stitches. On many occasions it was most difficult to raise one's head after this religious observance with a serious face. Had the Japanese been able to interpret what was going on they would have cut our rations, or perhaps our testicles, off entirely. This was one occasion when the Japanese thought their captured prisoners were being humble and recognising their almighty God Emperor. Little did they know the Western mind? A good example of how they mixed fact, fiction and ignorance.

There was never any doubt on our part as to what the outcome of the war would finally be. It was just a matter of time. The guards were so full of their own victories that they believed everything they were told by their officers. At this particular time, in early 1943, the tide had already started to turn against them, but they did not know it. Nor did we. Most of us in camp knew that the Yankee boys were starting to fight back.

This camp was so well organised that a newssheet, the *Double Cross*, was circulated amongst the prisoners. This was naturally a clandestine operation, with the single sheet of paper being passed around a hut and destroyed as soon as everyone had read it. Who was responsible for the printing and editing was not known to us newcomers. We heard that the Americans had been victorious in a big sea battle (Coral Sea, April 1942)[1] and we also heard that Darwin had been destroyed. The Japanese told us that Sydney had been bombed and a landing had been made in north Australia [2]. Of course we discounted any news that came directly from the Japanese, and we were sometimes a little dubious about the outlandish claims that were circulated in camp. It would all be over in three months, I kept telling myself.

Before we were taken prisoners this camp had been a Dutch army barracks presumably accommodating far less than the current four thousand men, many of them crippled as a result of the fighting prior to our surrender. Dutch, British and a few Americans were the main occupants - Navy survivors of the Java Sea Battle, some American Air Force with British and Dutch from the three services.

The facilities were a real surprise to us. There was a sambal factory, a peanut butter factory, a canteen, and loud speakers to pipe music around. At Semarang we had been allowed to grow our hair to normal length. We were allowed a camp barber, not full time, but available for hair cuts in the evening. Now in the Jaar Markt we were an extraordinary sight. Two hundred men with normal military length hair amongst four thousand fellow prisoners with shaved heads. We felt like outcasts and were soon made to comply with the majority.

The two themes, of a hundred years war and that we represented Churchill's "trema kasie" (thank you) men, kept cropping up. The average Japanese soldier had been thoroughly schooled to believe that we were given to the Emperor by Churchill as a gift to further the ambitions of the Japanese in the Far East. As a disgraced fighting force we were most contemptible and only suitable to labour for the good of their God Emperor. This indoctrination as the Master Race was to influence their attitude towards us for the entire period we were prisoners. I know of no time that they ever considered that they might be asked to justify their behaviour. At no time did they show compassion or sympathy for the vanquished, whether they be military or civilian.

The work parties here were mostly to the docks. There were many good things to scrounge on these working parties, medical supplies for the hospital being one of them. Almost anything one brought into camp could be traded for something to eat. Those who had been here all the time were pretty well off, as they had these opportunities while we were at Semarang spreading sand around. As the major camp of Sourabaya with a large Dutch population it was well equipped and no doubt had extensive contacts with the outside world. The Dutchmen had the 'know how' and the contacts to make life reasonably bearable. None of the British service men had been in the country for more than a few weeks and few, if any, could speak either Dutch or Indonesian.

One day I was approached by Wing Commander Whitic who told me that my Dad had got away from Singapore and had been in Batavia some time before the capitulation. He felt that the Batavia stop was just a forced stop on his way to Australia. He had no doubt made the journey successfully and got away completely. This was the first news in twelve months and most welcome. The wing commander also offered me a job on the sanitary party. I do not remember what this entailed as to actual working conditions but it had the advantage of being a camp job, which meant that I would be out of the way of the guards and the inevitable slapping and beatings. Having had a taste of the dock work and still being very short of clothing, money, and food, I opted for the outside work, but I was very grateful at hearing his cheering news about my father. Working on the docks gave me an opportunity to smuggle a variety of things into camp resulting in trading for more food or money.

I sometimes consider what would have happened if I accepted this offer of work inside the camp, thereby becoming a permanent camp worker and presumably not subject to a move to the outer islands. The officers and men who remained in Java had a much easier time than we experienced. I believe this camp was closed soon after we left and everybody transferred to Batavia (Jakarta). They were housed in permanent buildings and had a more liberal rice, vegetable and fruit allowance. They had spare time in the evenings to organise classes for many different subjects, and occasional entertainment. Some of these men were eventually moved to Singapore as a staging area for the Burma Railroad. This would have given me a chance to put one of my original escape schemes into effect, as the journey from Singapore to Burma, via rail or road, must pass relatively close to the road that leads to the Cameron Highlands and Dad's Blue Valley Tea Estate. At this time we had only heard rumours of senior officers being moved to Japan via Singapore. There was no inkling of work parties leaving Java for other destinations. The course of the next three years would have been drastically changed. Life in a permanent camp in Java was at least bearable in as much as one had three meals a day, surreptitious radio news reports, and time off in the evenings to be sociable and in some cases to participate in educational courses.

We heard that there were still prisoners in the Lyceum (our previous Sourabaya camp) in a most hapless way. Two of them had tried to escape and were now suffering for their attempt. Nobody survived an escape attempt so their chances were not worth betting on. We only heard that they were kept in separate cells and tortured daily - playthings for the Kempetai. The RC padre ran afoul of the guards and was severely beaten.

On our way out of camp one day the Japanese were parading a teenage Indonesian girl with her head shaved to the skull. She had apparently been too enthusiastic in trying to draw the attention of her boy friend as he left the camp on the back of a three ton truck bound for the docks. The guards were making sure that everybody saw her so that she and her boy friend would be mutually mortified. In the 1940s it was unheard of, and incredibly insulting, for a girl to have her head shaved.

On the dock working party we were surprised one day to find a ship with an Italian crew. For us to see other white men working hand in glove with the Japanese was most unexpected. Of course they were allies but we could not figure out why the Italians would be in the Pacific. It was on this particular day that I had the good fortune to be working in a warehouse that had great quantities of small cans of food. Small cans are easily hidden and a most precious commodity. I found some small tins of Vienna sausages and managed to get three or four of them back to camp. They were such a good find that I decided to keep a can for some future celebration. It could be easily tucked away in my backpack or hidden under a jacket. There was an above average chance of my getting it through any future searches.

Apparently the first hut we were put into was only a temporary accommodation as we were soon moved to two bamboo huts with the standard bamboo slats for sleeping on. I shall never forget that night as long as I live. The hut had just been vacated by Dutch native troops and was the home to a billion bed bugs or more, and an equal number of lice and a vast quantity of crabs. Of course we were up all night and complaining like mad the next day. How could we be expected to be tormented all night and work hard all day? The brass finally got the message and we were moved into a hut that had been previously occupied by officers, but not before we were given a day off to kill all the little critters that infested our clothes, blankets, and mosquito nets, and worst of all, our bodies. I soon became proficient at killing the lice in the accepted way - squeezing them between my thumbnails. The lice made just a white mess whereas the bed bugs always exuded quantities of blood — a bloody mess that had the most vile smell.

The Japanese started a new work party that went to the island of Madura. This soon got the reputation of being the best party to be on. To start off, the journey was a long one. The trucks had to cross on a ferry to the island; then there was a long ride to the work area. This meant that we did less work and considerably more riding than the comparatively short trip to the docks. We were crammed seventy men to a truck with Nip drivers that must have had all of two or three months' driving experience — most of this taken up in the training time. We never did feel very confident with them. The only saving grace was their fear of the punishment they would receive if they damaged a vehicle. Since the Japanese vehicles were the biggest and only motorised vehicles on the road we had a feeling that we would come off best in a collision. Apart from a few staff cars that were seldom seen on rural Madura, the only traffic was the local rickshaws, ox carts, pedestrians, and ponies. When we got to the work site we just moved goods around in the warehouses or sometimes worked in a market garden digging the ground for future planting.

Madura is famous for bullock races. Frequently we watched the "bullocks in training" from the back of the truck as it sped along the country road taking us to or from work. The chance of getting on this work detail was strictly a matter of luck. The usual morning routine was for the entire work force to parade in camp and then wait to be selected, on a random basis, for the various projects to be worked on that day.

One day on Madura about six of us were caught on a narrow dirt road when a Japanese truck came by. The driver slowed down to a crawl as we flattened ourselves against a building wall on his left side. On his right side he had an open field and a broad shoulder to the road so that he had plenty of manoeuvring room. The side of the truck caught the first man in line and started to roll him like a cigarette against the wall, the second and third men started to roll along the wall before the driver was yelled to a halt. Another lucky escape for me, as I was next in line. It was a horrifying moment for the three of us who got away without being rolled. Having no room to move away from the oncoming truck we were trapped as observers to our own fate - - being crushed against the wall. The toll: one broken collarbone, a mass of bruises and torn flesh.

One night the loudspeaker announced that the entire camp would assemble for a movie. Our kind conquerors were going to entertain the troops. There was great speculation as to what this would be about. The optimists thought it might be an old Hollywood production. Some even figured that the most recent titles playing in Singapore before the disaster would be shown. So the excitement mounted. There was great speculation as to a completely new attitude towards prisoners in general. No doubt the reversals in the Pacific were having their effect. We sat on the ground with our legs akimbo as the sun sank over the horizon and the short twilight period gave way to semi-darkness. The chatter was at fever pitch when a 16mm projector was rolled into position. As soon as the first flickering light with some unintelligible number flashed onto the screen you could have heard the proverbial pin drop. What was it to be? Was this the first of many movies to be shown? What quality? What subject matter? Would it be in English? Instantly we knew, we should have known our captors better than to be optimistic. The Empire's greatest moment - greatest victory - the Bombing of Pearl Harbour. To the other side the "Day of Infamy," the treachery of undeclared war. The effect on us was subduing to say the least. They reinforced their superior position over us but also reinforced the fact that all this had been gained in a moment of treachery. Their behaviour since taking us prisoners showed that they were totally without principles or respect for human life.

On our work parties to the docks and rural Madura the guards tried to keep us from talking to the Indonesian population. In fact talking to the natives was considered by the Nips to be a crime exceeded only by escaping. A horrendous beating would follow if someone was caught trading with the natives. The Indonesians were well aware of this and usually managed to be a fair distance from the scene as the fan spread its muck all over the place. We were able to find out that the whole attitude of the natives had changed since the "Liberators of Asia" had arrived. The uncertainty of our being helped on an escape attempt in March and April 1942 was founded in the fact that new masters would really be friends to the population in general. A lot of village headmen were naturally being cagey and not enthusiastic to help the conquered white men. Now, a year later, there was no doubt in the minds of the native population as to who was the better master. If they should have a master at all the Japanese were not the ones for them. Already great havoc had been visited on those that did not immediately do as the masters wanted. Beatings and rape were not uncommon[3].

Now came a time of inspections. We were paraded before a variety of senior officers. They gave us long speeches glorifying the Japanese Empire and all that they did for the people of South East Asia. The most prominent of these officers was Lt Col. Anami, known to us as "Whiskers." He had a long scrawny beard which gave rise to his nickname. He claimed to be in charge of all prisoners of war in Java. Amongst other things he said, in reasonably good English, "look at my face, remember me... do not fear for your lives...you are going to a holiday camp where the food will be very good and the work not too strenuous...". A few days later we were to march to the railroad station and then sailed for the island of Haruku. Of the two thousand and seventy one prisoners sent there eighty five percent did not return to their homeland.

During the following days we were issued a pair of shoes and blue shorts. Now we had the most comical medical inspection of our lives. A Japanese doctor, resplendent with Samurai sword dragging on the ground, sat himself at a six foot folding table surrounded by many bowing and scraping followers, all of them dressed for a formal occasion. This entourage was set up at one end of the parade ground where we paid homage daily to their God Emperor. All prisoners had been warned just a short time before this parade that we must have a stool sample to take on parade. There being a great shortage of paper in the camp most of us had to find leaves on which to put this sample, not easy as the camp had few trees. Now we were to take off our shorts hold them in one hand, have the stool sample in the other, and walk past the doctor naked. This would give him an assessment as to our fitness to leave Java for an extended period of hard labour. After we had walked past the doctor there was a big box into which we threw the stool sample. Two thousand and seventy one men were selected, which means that we must have paraded many more. By the time it was over the tropical sun had its effect on the box of stools many of which were either dysentery or diarrhoea. The camp became one huge stinkpot humming with flies.

In this highly sophisticated manner we were selected for what was to become one of the worst working camps in the Japanese Empire. During the POW period it was always difficult to determine exact numbers on a move as the departure figure from a port would be greater than the arrival number at the next port plus the fact that the Japanese changed the numbers of POWs being transported at the very last moment. Deaths and sinkings, plus the Japanese abhorrence for paper work and their attitude of expendability towards us did not make record keeping easy. In fact the searches at the beginning and end of a move had as one of their aims to find and destroy written notes and records[4].

Many of the older men in camp, that is to say the men over about twenty seven or twenty eight years of age, who got the word that this draft was for a work party in the boom docks, put their street wise caps on and procured stool samples from dysentery patients in the hospital. In this way they evaded this work assignment which may have been fortunate. However, little did they know that this was the first of many nasty work parties to be taken to various parts of the Empire to work for the glory of the God Emperor.

During these pre - departure days we saw an ominous figure with the rank of sergeant in the camp. He swaggered around in the most defiant manner and beat the hell out of our new CO, Squadron Leader Pitts. Using both his fists and his sword scabbard he laid into him unmercifully. Little did we realise the significance of this beating. BAMBOO MORI WAS WITH US. Almost immediately after he had finished with the squadron leader he found some excuse to beat a Dutch soldier, called Palm, who was left unconscious on the parade ground as we marched off. We never did hear if he survived.

On the 19th April we were paraded at 4:00 am with all the kit we could carry. We stood on parade for four hours waiting for the order to move. The confusion that takes place when more than two thousand prisoners are kept hanging around for four hours is considerable. The simple procedure of going to the bathroom became an accounting hazard. The guards always had a problem keeping track of the number of men on a work party. Now with more than two thousand men paraded in their camp, having to get into the facilities and onto parade again, presented the ultimate overwhelming problem. Everybody leaving the parade must be accounted for and everybody returning had to be counted. About 8:00 am we got the order to move. This meant counting, recounting, and counting again. The official total of officers and men leaving Java for the island of Haruku was two thousand and seventy one.

We marched to the railroad station and eventually ended up on the docks. We had no idea of our destination or what we would be doing when we got there but we did know "... the food will be very good and the work not too strenuous...". On the docks we paraded again, counted again, and just stood under tight security. We were in front of a small steamer of about four thousand tons. There were three holds, two forward and one aft. This was the AMAGI MARU a thirty seven hundred tons of prison ship[5].

1   American, Australian, and New Zealand navies fought the Coral Sea Battle, 8th May 1942.

2   In actual fact a flight had been made over Sydney by an aircraft launched from a submarine. It was undetected by the Australians.

3   The number of Javanese taken from their homeland to work on the Burma railroad and other projects for the Japanese war effort has never been officially recorded. The native deaths on the Burma railroad are generally believed to be well into the six-figure range.

4   The victor need not justify his treatment of prisoners. It took the Japanese a long time to realise they were not going to conquor the world. Tens of thousands of dead prisoners who had died for the glory of their God Emperor would not be missed while they were supreme. It is interesting to note that the only figures available for either the British, American, Australian or Dutch authorities are those numbers remembered by our own doctors. The Japanese have never volunteered to the Allies the numbers of men they killed deliberately in the construction of their various projects from the Burma RR (27%) to the Sandakan Death March (99.74%) survival rate of the 2,500 Australian and British men sent from Singapore to Borneo. An airstrip building project.

5   The Amagi Maru was a typical Japanese troop transport. Our conditions were more crowded than those of their fighting troops and, of course, the rations were minimal. It was Japanese Government policy to starve prisoners when being transported by sea. (Lord Russell, - "Knights of Bushido").

5

THE BOAT TRIP

BOMBS, GAS, DYSENTERY

The only thing we have to fear on this planet is man.

CARL JUNG

The AMAGI MARU was a prison ship with a vengeance. After we arrived on the dock we were alternately allowed to squat or stand, depending on whom the guards thought was approaching. If an NCO was on his way around the dock area we were allowed to stay squatting. If however, an officer approached us then the parade was brought to attention. After a couple of hours some Nip soldiers, wearing face masks, appeared with garden sprayers attached to canisters on their backs. We were ordered to stand while the soldiers moved through our ranks spraying us with some foul smelling disinfectant. The thought that we were in such diseased condition that we might infect this scruffy non-descript looking freighter was almost laughable. Some considerable time later, after we had squatted on the ground, walked over to the shed to relieve ourselves and generally nullified the effect of the disinfecting spray, we were marched up the gangway to the deck of this transport. There was a large trough on deck which we had to slosh through like cattle being dipped. Carrying all our worldly possessions we were assigned to aft hold and waited on deck while the first in line carefully got on to the vertical ladder and made their way into the depths.

The careful mounting of the vertical ladder did not last long as the guards soon started shouting and bayonet prodding the next in line to make a rapid decent. In order for the hold to accommodate everyone, those already below decks had to take up their position on the "bunks" to allow more prisoners to be crammed below. Little did we realise that this was to be our position — horizontal — for the next three weeks. The sitting or crouching position was equally uncomfortable as the height between layers was three foot. There were no supports to hold onto in rough weather.

The open hold gave a good amount of light below and also allowed us to see what was in store for us. The centre part of the hold was to be kept clear for our baggage. Around the sides were built shelves spaced about three feet high and five and a half feet deep. This was to be our sleeping space. The snag was not immediately apparent as the shelves ran around the entire hold and consequently there appeared to be a lot of room. By the time all men assigned to this hold were below decks and our baggage thrown in a heap in the middle of the hatch we soon found out that the method of travel was sardine can fashion. Each man had the feet of his bunkmates on either side of his head. There was not enough room for us to be accommodated in the normal fashion i.e. sleeping side by side. This was made all the more difficult as the allotted space had been built for Nip troops, whose average height must have been five foot six inches maximum.

There were two wooden structures built over the side of the ship for latrines. These represented our only escape from the stifling heat below decks. These two latrines were not for the exclusive use of the men in the aft holds. They had to be used by all the one thousand plus prisoners on the ship. Each of the four holds were of different sizes with the biggest taking close to four hundred men, but the situation was the same in each hold. The only sleep possible to us was in short snatches as others, close by, on the platform left for a pee. The heat, the crowding, and the nightly rain did not make life easy. The only good thing about the nightly rain was that it drained quickly through the hatch covers under our baggage and we could gather some of it to drink.

We remained tied to the dock for the next three days during which time the hatch remained open. This was cooling during the day but also wet every night as it poured most nights. Those men who had sought to get away from the cramped shelving around the hold and to lie on the baggage in the centre were soon scrambling to get out of the rain. Our second day on the ship there was the most incredible explosion in the harbour area. Everybody on deck was hurried below at bayonet point. Our immediate thoughts were of a bombing raid and that we were in the centre of the target area. However it only took a moment for us to realise that this was a single explosion with much greater force than any bomb in existence. Soon we got the news that a ship had blown up. A ship being loaded with bombs and aviation fuel. Now we found out from the interpreter that we were housed in a ship full of ammunition, high-octane aviation fuel, detonators, and bombs. In fact not six feet below us was a good selection of all of these war materials.

After three days of waiting to hear the engines start we were rewarded with the appropriate sounds and a great deal of vibration. The guards panicked and every one was herded below as the cast off commotion got under way. As soon as we were clear of the harbour the parade to the latrines started again. Our only pleasure during the following three weeks was to get on deck for some excuse and admire the surroundings. The line-up for a pee was a lengthy one, which meant that we had ample time to determine our direction of travel — not that it did us much good. Few, if any, of us were geographically familiar with this area so we only knew that we were traveling in the direction of New Guinea. During the next few days we cruised eastward and kept in sight of the islands that tail off to the east off Java. Bali, Lombok, Sumbawa, Flores, and Wejak. Soon the direction changed to northeast and we left the protection of these islands. It was at this time that a faint unpleasant odour permeated the entire hold. The breeze caused by being under way kept this to bearable proportions. By the time of our first docking it would be unbearable.

Most of us thought this method of travel — hugging the islands and then nipping across the open stretch of water to the island of Ambon was being overly cautious. After the war we found out that Yankee submarines were active in this area at this time. How many would have survived being housed six feet above this super explosive cargo if a sub' had attacked?

During the trip many cases of dysentery developed making life unbearable for the men who had to scramble out of the holds and wait their turn in line to use the boxes. It was not long before these boxes became caked with dysentery and soaked with urine. There was a separate and crude arrangement for peeing but even this entailed a lengthy wait. Salt-water hoses were used to clean the latrines but it was a losing battle from the beginning. As if to prove their superiority over us some of the guards would move to the head of the latrine line and then take an extended time to perform. They knew full well that there were men in desperate condition waiting to use the facilities. It was not always easy to gauge the time delays when shut up in the bowls of the dark, humid, hold. And always it was hot — with the temperature of the water in the eighties, the air temperature in the nineties.

The most enjoyable part of the entire journey was the waiting period during the line up for the latrines. At this time we could admire the exquisite beauty of the jungle fringed shores with their gleaming white beaches. The contrast of the deep green jungle to the reflective white shores gently lapped by the sky blue ocean made us aware that one day we would be real people again.

We arrived in Ambon approximately eleven hundred miles from Sourabaya, in the early evening (Wednesday, April 28th, 1943) with instructions to get the boat unloaded as soon as possible. Once the baggage and bodies were cleared away, and the hatch covers removed we discovered that some optimistic Nip had stored several loading nets full of oranges over the regular cargo. These had just been lowered into the hold and let go so that they had fallen between bamboo, the bombs and the high-octane gas with a small mountain of them in the middle. The tropical heat in the enclosed hold had cooked these nice soft oranges into a slimy mess that was sporting a thick hairy growth of fungus. As the panic to unload started we slithered and slipped our way over this deadly cargo. Trying to pick up a fifty or hundred pound bomb that has been lubricated with rotten oranges requires a skill that we did not have time to develop. The pressure to unload meant that any means of sliding or bouncing the bombs into a net was acceptable. We did not know that we were within the range of American bombers and this was probably the reason for the extreme haste to unload.

The pouring rain, the slimy rotten oranges and the yelling Nips did nothing for our efficiency. Having lived on two watery meals a day, immobile except for the short climb and walk to the latrine and now expected to work full tilt on an empty stomach was just about par for these fanatical little people. After we had worked for several hours without let up our officers asked for some hot tea. The guards said they would arrange this. An hour later one luke warm bucket of water arrived — enough for a sip for half the workers. When the officers complained that this was not the way for men to be treated, especially under tropical conditions, they were told that the water would be taken away if further complaints were heard. This was our first work experience in the Moluccas Islands — "where the food will be good and the work not too strenuous." The unloading continued all night and through the next day. Carrying bamboo to Ambon was the like giving refrigerators to the Eskimos. We did however unload a lot of building materials that were definitely not available locally. Remembering the ship that had exploded while we were tied up in Sourabaya did not make the handling of slimy bombs and barrels of aviation gas any easier. This was probably the first time that most of us became really fatalistic. Our destiny was alien to our control. The only control we had was of our own minds; to be positive, to help others less fortunate, and "Nil carborundum bastardorium" our Latin version of "Don't let the Bastards grind you down."

The most enlightening episode took place while we were unloading the bombs and aviation gas. Some Yankee bombers came over, the first we had seen since being taken prisoners. The Nips scrambled a few Zero fighters to meet them. We did not hear any machine gun fire so I gather the Yanks were well on their way before the Nips arrived on the scene. Many years after the war I read that the Nips scrambled fighters to get them out of the way, not necessarily to attack the bombers. I have no doubt the decision to attack or stay clear depended on the numerical superiority of the moment.

Friday we headed off again with some of the bombs and aviation gas still below us. We did not appreciate in the dark, that we were headed in the direction of New Guinea where the Yankee boys were making good progress and at last beating the hell out of these little zealots. It proved to be an overnight trip as the anchor rumbled out just as the dawn was breaking.

This time we were anchored in a beautiful bay on the west coast of Ceram with the village of Amahai just out of sight. No sooner had the anchor hit the water than the usual alarm, occasioned by a new situation, started. With a great deal of yelling, bayonet prodding and slapping we were to unload more cargo. The scheme was to put all the gas barrels directly into the water and the bombs into small lighters that came alongside. Men went over the sides on nets and some of us spent the next twenty-four hours in the water swimming gas barrels to shore. Others were taken ashore to man handle the bombs into dispersal areas and to receive the gas that we left on the beach. When the aim is to unload at all costs and the labour is cheap then food is not a consideration. One of the fellows, tired and exhausted from swimming and pushing gas barrels all night, grabbed a barrel and just swam with it not paying any attention to the direction he was headed. By the time he grabbed the barrel it had floated free from the ship and he was headed out to sea at the wondrous speed of, maybe, one tenth of a mile per hour, if he had been able to sustain the effort. Soon a hail of bullets was peppering the water around him and no doubt woke him up to the fact that he was escaping. One man with forty gallons of aviation gas on his way to New Guinea? When he finally got to shore with so much activity and confusion going on he just plunged into the water for another barrel—the punishment for this incident was lost in the lack of communication from ship to shore. When we finally came out of the water we were like prunes—dehydrated and literally dying of thirst. Our only thoughts during this period were for the number of barrels remaining in the ship, the next food break and a drink of water. The water was warm and the problem of sharks for some unknown reason did not trouble us. I worked in the water until dawn the next day with only two short breaks for food — can you call a wet rice and watery soup a meal? This was our fare.

There were two other ships at anchor in Amahai Bay, both with similar cargoes — prisoners and war materials. It took us about three days to get the ships unloaded and to leave one thousand Dutchmen (*Godverdommes*)[1] here to work. If a man can walk he can work. This was now to be the immutable law of the Islands.

Then off again to a new destination - Haruku and the infamous Gunso (Sergeant) Mori. This camp was destined to have one of the highest percentage mortality rates of the Japanese Empire. The death rate in European camps was four percent, in the Japanese camps twenty seven percent. The final Haruku death rate was eighty five percent[2]. With the monsoon in full swing we made another short passage between these islands. Leaving Amahai behind we turned westward to Haruku.

During the following months the reason given to us, by the Nips, for the high death rate, lack of medicines, and shortage of food, was the US blockade. Supposedly the supply services were under constant attack by the American air forces and submarines. This we had reason to believe as the occasional bombers were evident from the very first few days on this camp. However, some months after our arrival, the men from Amahai camp joined us - having successfully completed their task of constructing an "unsinkable aircraft carrier." (Apparently the Japanese government was boasting to the Axis powers that they were constructing a series of unsinkable carriers in the South West Pacific. Unknown to us at this time aircraft carriers had eclipsed the battleship as the primary fighting unit of the world's navies. Using POWs, as slave labourers, they were making small Pacific Islands into "unsinkable aircraft carriers.")

Amahai is further from both Ambon, the main supply depot for the Moluccas Islands, and Java the administrative centre for the entire region of Indonesia. The death rate on Amahai if this condition prevailed should have been proportionate to our death rate on Haruku. The one thousand Dutch men that we left on Ceram suffered thirty-one deaths. Three of these were caught in an escape attempt and according to the Bushido code were made to dig their own graves prior to being beheaded. The routine here was for the culprits to dig their own graves, kneel at one end of the grave so that the executioner, whether he severed the neck or not, would knock the body into the grave — dead or alive. The simple task of filling the grave followed without further ceremony.

1   *Godverdomme* was the favourite swearword of the Dutch Army troops. We soon nick named them "The Hot for Dommers".

2   Dr. John Pritchard FRHist, MBIM, University of Kent, UK

6

HARUKU 1

THE CAMEL'S HUMPS

*... in modern war you will die like a dog for
no good reason.*

ERNEST HEMMINGWAY

(Haruku is a small island in the Moluccas Archipelago of Indonesia. Located between Ambon and Ceram it is too small to be named on most maps. Two hundred miles south of the equator, it has an average year round temperature of thirty-eight degrees Celsius (100.degrees F). In 1943 the island had a small population housed in a few villages usually located on the seashore and near a river. (Fish and Fresh water) To the best of my knowledge the Nips did not have a presence on the island until we arrived. By the time we finished working "The Camel's Humps," it was a fighter airstrip with a supporting garrison on the island and a large POW graveyard)

It was 8:00 pm when we heard the anchor chain rumbling through the hawsehole. After three weeks in this Hell Hole with two meals of pap a day and the recent intense labour we expected to arrive in a camp that had some basic facilities. Whiskers had told us the "food will be very being good and the work not too strenuous." "Look at my face...remember me...Do not fear for your lives...Your are going to a holiday camp where the food will be very good and the work not too strenuous." Should we believe a Nip Colonel? This tiny island not far from New Guinea and just south of the equator was to be our home for the next sixteen months. The monsoons were under way which made life difficult under the best of circumstances. We waited in the holds for four hours. Finally the magic signal was received and we were told to get off the ship. It was midnight. Unloading a prison ship is difficult under dockside conditions but now the Nips had to exacerbate our difficulties. There was no indication on shore of where we should land. Unknown to us the Yankee bombers had been visiting this area at night causing the Nips to use extreme caution with the result that lights were out of the question. Choppy seas, monsoon rains, and a pitching sampan did not make the unloading process any easier. With a net slung over the side and barely enough strength to lower ourselves we somehow found the heaving sampan with a yelling complement of Nip guards. Had our peasant guards been told how many men to put in one sampan? Or would this be up to the sampan man? Since the Nip guards could not swim and the weather was inclement they had a good incentive not to overload the vessels. If we had foundered on the way to shore the guards no doubt would have been lost to the deep.

Somehow we got into sampans and soon found ourselves on shore in the devastating rain. The guards had been given candles to guide us up the slope to the camp. Like us, they had no idea where we were supposed to go. A narrow footpath about one hundred yards long led into an area with some half-constructed barrack-like huts scattered around. Some of the huts had roofs. Most of them were bamboo frames waiting to be worked on. A few large trees, coconut palms, canary nuts and nutmeg, were in the camp area. The undergrowth had been cleared with the result that the ground was a quagmire. Some of the huts had been constructed with the idea of saving the coconut palms and the wild life that accompanies them. With the roof built around the tree and not waterproofed we had regular rivulets in the huts. All this we determined as we slithered around in the darkness looking for somewhere to settle for what was left of the night. We were herded into a framed hut with a roof and without walls. Here we could put down the only kit we were allowed to bring off the ship — water bottles and canteens.

One of the men made a dash for the bushes as he had dysentery[1]. Unfortunately he was next to a guard, other wise he would not have been seen. The guards reflex was to hit the fellow, which he did most effectively, but he hit him with the candle. The result was the most horrendous panic situation you could imagine. Now in total darkness the guard thought we were all going to escape or kill him. At the best, with a light, he could see only about six men out of fifty! At this juncture escape was not even remotely on our minds. Totally unprepared, hungry, and exhausted we could not seriously consider this option. I guess he figured he would lose his head to the glory of his God Emperor if one man was not accounted for. After the yelling and screaming died down one of our men, who had been astute enough to keep his lighter through the many searches, produced it, so the guard could light his candle again. The poor dysentery victim had relieved himself in the middle of the jellyfied mud and thus started a trend that was to carry on for several weeks.

We milled about under the protection of a roofed hut deciding just how we would spend the rest of the night. Because there were no drains or gutters around the huts the ground under the roof was wetter, if that was possible, than the open areas. The rain pouring off the roof made nice little rivulets through the hut. The camp was constructed on a slight hill sloping to wards the sea some one hundred yards away.

It was not long before all hell broke loose again. A sampan had arrived at the little dock some distance down the road with some equipment from the ship. This turned out to be some of the cook-house equipment, *wajangs* (woks), drums for boiling water and some other related cook-house materials. We were herded down the road and put to work carrying this equipment to the cook-house. This job lasted all night. As the ship was unloaded and dawn broke we got the full picture of Haruku Prisoner of War Camp.

About a dozen huts in various stages of construction had been erected for us. There were no effective toilet facilities. No dry wood. No dry ground to sleep on. A small stream for drinking water. No fire places in the cook-hut. With the monsoon season in full swing! Half of the cook-house equipment had been off-loaded at Amahai with a lot of personal luggage and was lost to us forever.

Two thousand and seventy one men had arrived on Haruku the fourth day of May 1943. All had been fit when we were paraded naked in Java in front of the Nip MO. After three weeks in the holds of the ship fifty men were suffering from advanced stages of amoebic or bacillary dysentery. We had been fed two meals a day of rice and a watery soup with tea to supplement this. For the last week, after arriving in Ambon, we had worked for periods of twenty four hours non-stop, sometimes in the sea for continuous hours on end - - still on only two meals a day. We discovered much later in our travels that it was Japanese government policy to keep prisoners on the minimum of rations during sea voyages. This policy deliberately kept the prisoners weak and demoralised with the obvious purpose of preventing an uprising.

Our first priority was to get a hospital organised. A hut was allocated for this purpose and a latrine dug right next to it. Several latrines were dug close to the existing huts. Drains were constructed around the huts so that we would eventually have a drier place to sleep. Work parties kept unloading the ship and building the camp. Native Ambonese were allowed in the camp to complete the roofs and attach the *attap* (wall and roof material made from coconut fronds) to the frames of the huts under construction. A few shallow latrines had been dug by the natives but these were useless as they were full of water and overflowing.

Other groups were working on the cook-house and carrying logs from the jungle. The cooks found it impossible to keep the fires going—the best they could do was to get barrels of tepid water, throw in a few handfuls of tea, and call the resulting mixture hot tea. There was absolutely no way to cook rice until enough wood was dried out to boil water. Since rice was our staple diet this became a worry for the whole camp. The work party chaos during these first few days was beyond belief. If by chance a group was dismissed after having worked for twenty four hours it was quite possible that a new set of guards would come into camp and want the same work party for some job that had just come to light. They would pick the only men in camp that appeared to be resting and so the group would be paraded again for a days work. All the protestations in the world would only meet with a beating for the officer in charge of the group. The language barrier was nullified by physical beatings. Some of the most dramatic performances I have ever seen in my life took place at this time.

On the second day in camp, my nineteenth birthday, Taffy, my buddy from the ambushed train, and I opened a can of Vienna sausages, kept especially for this occasion, that I had smuggled into camp from the docks in Sourabaya. I had been separated from my other friends and chummed with Taffy until we each found our own little groups again. This small can contained about ten miniature sausages. The cook-house was still having problems boiling water, so our rice ration that day consisted of rice cooked only on the outside. Because of the long drawn out period of cooking rice in tepid water it never got cooked right through, resulting in a tender outside with a hard core interior. We consoled ourselves that the uncooked portion would swell in our stomachs and we would then feel that we had, indeed, had a good meal. The soup was the usual *katella*[2] leaf type. At this stage we were lucky to receive a few leaves in the soup. I remember that night; my nineteenth birthday, Taffy and I had rice and green water for our supper supplemented only by five Vienna sausages each. The ration of meat had not arrived. It was a fact of life on Haruku that the rations were not constant, every item that came into the cook-house was subject to wide fluctuations. Whether this was graft or just plain greed on the part of the Japanese, stealing our food, I have not been able to determine.

Once the ship was unloaded and the basic camp organised, latrines and drains dug, etc. the conditions we were to live in for the duration of the monsoon became apparent. We had been issued with a thin form of grass matting about six feet long and two feet wide. This marked our sleeping area on the ground in the huts. Of course we did not have two feet of sleeping space so there was a big overlap of our mats. With the uneven mud floor trenched with streams of water and the roots of coconut palms the mats lasted about a week. The sodden mess had absolutely no use and had to be discarded. This was a shock to us as we made some use of everything. These mats would normally have been turned into fuel for our fires, but it was impossible to dry them out. Having trees situated in the huts not only cut down the available space but meant that we had a lot of insects of all types sharing our quarters. We thought the situation would settle into some sort of routine. Had not Whiskers said "...the food will be very good and the work not too strenuous? ... do not fear for your lives..."?

Because the officers and the sick had to have separate quarters this meant a lot of crowding on our part. The original hut set aside for the fifty dysentery cases soon expanded to three huts accommodating dysentery, starvation, beriberi, and malaria patients. The sick personnel were developing at such a rate that those admitted to the hospital had to be accommodated in the aisles on the wet ground between rows of other men who were too weak to move to the latrines. The resulting mess of excreta and urine only contributed to the overall death rate. Our doctors were frustrated at every move by the Nips who refused to acknowledge the situation. Within one month there were more than one hundred deaths. The general population of the camp were starting to look like scarecrows. Our working reserves of flesh were coming into use. My weight had probably dropped from one hundred and twenty to ninety pounds at this early stage.

Dysentery was so severe that some men were defecating one hundred times a day and more. This meant that they could not possibly reach a latrine and so they made a mess in the mire of mud that was the camp. The situation was compounded as the sick men who were not admitted to hospital struggled to get to the latrines on all fours. They had little chance of making it, as they were extremely weak and sick. The whole camp was a mixture of mud and dysentery. With the monsoon in full swing, giving us about six inches of rain every day, the ground was a mixture of mud, blood, slime and shit. The death rate climbed.

Our officers knew that we could soon make this place into a camp fit to live in if only we were to do some of the basic work that would, in the long run, save lives and consequently give the Nips a larger work force. The Nips had other ideas. There was other work to be done that was of importance to their God Emperor. However, after our CO made repeated efforts to save the situation, a couple of days were set aside for a few men to work in the camp.

The first requirement was to dig one hell of a big hole about fifteen feet long and two feet wide and many feet deep, the latrine, commonly known as "The HOLE." Once we got past the root layer, for there were a few really big trees in the camp, the ground was easy digging. Again after the five foot level the digging was difficult.

A continuous problem with the Nip guards was the fact that they thought more men meant more work would be done. It is a pity the camp administration did not think in this manner as it seemed that they were quite content to let people die. A good healthy work force would be capable of the coming hard labour and no doubt would have finished the air strip in short order. The administration was hell bent on annihilation by starvation.

In a confined area such as this elongated grave only five men could work effectively during the initial few feet. Then more room was required to throw out the diggings, but the Nips insisted that the original five men continue to dig at a depth that meant two men had to stand idle - not an easy thing to do with a fanatic standing over one's head. After completing the digging the finishing touch to "The Hole" was to put short lengths of bamboo across the top with spaces about one foot apart and one foot wide. The end result was a big crapper that could accommodate many men at a time. And so "The Hole" was born. Here you could hunker down on your haunches and try to fill it. Toilet paper was a thing of the past. We had long since learned the Dutch method of using a bottle of water in lieu of toilet paper. The bottle method soon proved to be a luxury as the bottles were lost into the depths of many feet of maggots by people too weak to hold them. Better to lose the bottle than fall to certain death amidst the quiet hum of a maggot's paradise. There were also urinals constructed of split bamboo leading into huge soak-away pits. In this fashion the camp was worked on for the next few days.

None of the work was easy as we were still in the monsoon season and never in a position to get dry. The death rate mounted daily. The hospital was expanding in leaps and bounds, not in the true sense of the word, as the expansion meant a reduction of the fit men's quarters. We were on the camp less than a week when the Nips gave the order that camp work would cease and regular work parties of six hundred men must construct an airstrip near by. They wanted two parties of six hundred men each. One to parade at 0600 hours each morning and work until 1230 and the other to parade at 1200 and work through to 1800 hours. This sounded very liberal on the surface as one gets the impression that prisoners are scheduled to work only six hours per day. This of course was hogwash; as the "off" group would be working at some other military task i.e. moving bombs, petrol, etc.

The first day this system was to be carried out—May 10th 1943, I was in the morning work party and marched off to see why we had been brought here to "...the holiday camp where the food will be very good and the work not too strenuous..." as Whiskers, the Nip Colonel, had promised us. After about forty minutes of marching, during which time we passed through the beautiful, tiny village of Pelau, where the minuscule population peeped out of their *attap* huts to watch us as we passed, we arrived at the top of a small hill. This hill faced a valley and was confronted by another hill of about equal size four hundred to five hundred yards away. These we nicknamed 'the camel's humps'. A nice view, but where was the land that we were to make into an airstrip? Surely this would be something like Amahai where the foreshore was a flat area that only needed trimming and clearing. A Dutch English Japanese interpreter had been sent with us to relay orders as to exactly what our job would be. You could have bowled the whole six hundred over with a blade of cooch grass when the Nips produced three hundred household hammers and chisels and ordered us to cut the tops off the hills and carry the debris into the valley. This was how to build an airstrip Japanese style?

A truck arrived with hundreds of little baskets. These little wicker baskets were about twenty-four inches wide, eighteen inches from back to front, and had a carrying handle on either side. Their load capacity must have been all of twenty - five to thirty pounds. These were unloaded and the men without hammers and chisels started carrying baskets full of our scrapings to dump in the valley.

In the fashion of prisoners we thought the best way to organise this situation was for us to work in buddy pairs. The man handling the hammer and chisel would have a regular carrier taking all his work to the valley floor. In this way we would be able to control the amount of work each individual had to do. By keeping an eye on your buddy you could judge the size of the pile you made and be ready to keep him waiting an appropriate length of time for both to have an acceptable rest. This system did not get to base one for it meant that the carrier might have to wait a few minutes while his hammer man, engaged by a particularly tough piece of coral, worked up enough material for a basket load. The guards had different ideas. The carrier was moved to a load or combined two or three piles to make a load. Our system came to naught.

The Nips had brought us all this way in a hell ship to work like coolies constructing an airstrip in the most primitive manner conceivable. We were obviously an expendable commodity. Their contempt for us was obvious. It was clear that they were going to get the maximum work for the minimum expenditure.

I realised that my life was at stake. Our captors did not have a conscience. This was truly survival of the fittest or even more primitive — straight survival — for who amongst us was fit?

That night our "dinner" consisted of twenty one pound cans of meat, a few vegetables and some rice to be shared by nearly two thousand and seventy one hungry, half starved, working male adults. The rice, half cooked, measured out to half a billy can each. The hell of Haruku had started.

Back at camp we heard the sorry news that the six hundred men who had replaced us included many who had been given a medical excuse not to work for some reason or other. These reasons included such common local hazards as cut feet and legs, ulcers, and general debility (starvation/weakness). In the jungle there were many bushes with long sharp thorns, some of them up to three and four inches long. At night, especially, it was impossible to avoid these, and most painful when you stepped on one. A foot or leg injury was particularly hazardous as the Nips would not recognise this as a disability. Most scratches or skin punctures developed quickly into full blown, painful ulcers. In their simplistic way of thinking, once you were on the airstrip you were quite capable of working. How one arrived there was not their concern.

Malaria is a disease that gives you a terrible fever for a day or so only to be followed by a day of comparative calm. This is most deceiving. The doctors recommend that this day must be a rest day in preparation for tomorrow's onslaught of more fever and the shakes. When the Nips saw a person on this alternate day he was invariably beaten and forced to work. The fact that yesterday he had a temperature well over a hundred degrees and tomorrow would have this temperature again was of no consequence to them. Today's work was more important than tomorrow's life.

The temperature was in the thirties (nineties Fahrenheit) and the rain continued unabated. We worked for two hours at a stretch and then got a ten-minute break. During the break we stood around or squatted native style on our haunches. The ground was much too wet for sitting. There were many smokers in the group who were now reduced to smoking all kinds of dried leaves wrapped in pages of the Bible. In fact the Bible pages were only used by the affluent. The most usual wrapping for a cigarette was a dried leaf scrounged off the jungle floor. The few Bibles in camp took on a great new value as each page was sought after with unbounded enthusiasm.

As a stroke of luck one of the fellows next to us in the hut was a "Hot for Dommer" man who had been in the tropics all his life. Born in Indonesia and with mostly Indonesian blood in his veins he knew the flora and fauna of the tropics better than we could dream of. He claimed to know all about plants and those that were edible. He was one of the sick in camp and had an opportunity to cook up some roots and leaves if we brought him the right stuff. We had no idea what was edible so we gathered whatever we could and brought this to the hut every night. Three days of supplemented rations was most encouraging for us. We did not have a lot to eat but it was satisfying to get a little extra and we were learning about edible roots and leaves. Our learning was of the most elementary type — it consisted of recognition only. We were not the least interested in names or types of plants. Our sole purpose was to eat them.

The fourth day we brought in a great haul of leaves and a few roots. Since Marcel was working in camp he was in a position to protect any of this surplus that we may want to keep for the next day. This only happened when pickings had been particularly good. Being on the early shift we would be back for lunch so Marcel would try to cook up some soup for us. He was suffering from a deep cut on the sole of his right foot. It was almost impossible for him to walk as dirt and dysentery slime had been ground into his foot from the time of the initial cut. We had brought him a five-foot long branch from the jungle to use as a crutch. This meant that he could get to The Hole without having to crawl on all fours or hop through the mud, shit and slime. When we came back to the hut on this day Marcel was not there, but the fire was smouldering with a billy can of our leaves and a root cooking. One of the other sick fellows shouted a warning that Marcel had been taken away with violent stomach cramps. Penny raced over to the hospital to see what was wrong. Disaster had struck. Marcel was in critical condition and not expected to live.

With such hunger gnawing at our bellies we schemed around saving this soup but it was impossible. It seemed that Marcel had helped himself to a blick (billy can) full of it when tragedy had struck. Which ingredient was the poison? This left us in an immediate quandary but it also made us a little more cautious during subsequent foraging escapades. It meant not only the loss of this immediate meal but a friend in camp who could be counted on to produce something for us when we brought in the goods. We now had a rudimentary idea of what was edible, but could we trust ourselves after such a dramatic demonstration of what one mistake could mean?

We ate our lunch from the cook-house. This consisted of half cooked rice, and a billy can of *katella* soup. *Katella* is the leaf of a potato like root; it grew to a height of approximately ten feet when left to develop on its own. At this height it would have such well developed roots that they were too tough and stringy to be of any use and the leaves too bitter. Under our conditions of extreme hunger if we were lucky enough to find these plants in the jungle they would be up rooted regardless of the height. *Katella* was one of the reliable plants. We knew this plant well and always felt safe in eating the roots and leaves no matter how tough. The ideal find was a plant about four feet tall which could be uprooted easily and quickly and had reasonably well developed roots and large but tender leaves. We discovered that the trunk of a banana palm could be boiled and eaten without too much trouble. These palms are ninety nine per cent water and not nourishing but they did fill a gap. It was not unusual to see a couple carrying a ten-foot banana palm shorn of its leaves to the cookhouse.

Sickness was rampant. The hospital had been expanded to take over nearly half the huts. Dysentery was epidemic. The men with uncontrollable dysentery could not get to The Hole in time to relieve themselves. The result of this was that there was excreta all over the camp. Usually a trail of blood and slime from the hut door to The Hole mixed with the horrible four or five inches of mud did not give us fit fellows much of a chance to avoid being infected. The camp work party, made up of hospital inmates, dug more "holes" so that the trip could be made in less time. This was accompanied by a radical increase in the severity of the dysentery and the numbers with the disease. Like a rolling ball it seemed to have no end. When it rained just a slight bit more than usual the holes filled and overflowed with the resulting mess all over the camp. It was like living in effluent of a watery grave.

Exactly one week after we had started constructing the airstrip with twelve hundred fit men this number was knocked down to eight hundred men officially. Officially meaning that the Nips recognised that it was impossible to make sick men work with out killing them before the project was completed. On May 17th when this number was paraded it was found that only seven hundred and seventy five men were actually fit for work. Over seven hundred were in hospital, which meant that they were so sick they had difficulty walking. The remainder were men who were either officers, excused duty people, or camp workers: cooks, medical orderlies, and those like our late, deceased, friend Marcel who had severe cuts and other injuries. New bandages were non-existent, the original supply had long ago been used up and washed and reused many times. Clothing from the deceased was torn for use as bandages. These invariable stank. The smell of rotting puss cooked in a tropical sun is not appealing. This was another fact of life in our stinking surroundings.

The routine on returning to camp was to form a burial party and put to rest those who had died the previous night and that day. Initially the carpenter was kept busy making bamboo coffins but as time went by this proved to be too expensive for the Nips to keep up with so we buried our dead in rice sacks. We carried them, shoulder high, from the hospital morgue to the swamp that was our cemetery, in a coffin and then opened the coffin and took out the rice sack covered bodies. The graves were shallow as slightly below the swampy surface was the coral rock. It invariably fell on the sick in camp to dig the graves. Normally only one man can dig a coral grave at a time as this involved swinging a pick axe, so it becomes a drawn out difficult task. It was absolutely impossible for a sick man to dig six feet down in coral in one day. It was imperative to bury the dead the same day as the heat, flies, and rotten condition of their bodies meant that deterioration had already set in when they were hoisted shoulder high. Many of us on the burial parties had the experience of a liquid flowing slowly out of the coffin and over our carrying shoulder. The gravediggers could not keep up with demand for new graves so a common grave became the accepted way to lay to rest those that had succumbed during the last twenty-four hours. A grave for ten, twelve, or fourteen was to be expected at the height of the dysentery epidemic.

Normally a Nip guard would attend the burial ceremony - not out of respect for the dead but to guard the burial party as the cemetery was outside the camp barbed wire. Many times when we had been kept working until after dark it was the guard's job to light the way to the cemetery with a candle in one hand and rifle in the other. Occasionally Sgt Mori would come to the cemetery, sometimes solemn, sometimes drunk. On these occasions he was a menace as he would brandish his sword, yelling at the top of his guttural, syphilitic voice at all within earshot. His actions confirmed the persistent rumours that he had syphilis. The doctors confirmed that his behaviour was entirely in keeping with the advanced stages of syphilis. On one occasion he was so drunk that he vomited into the grave as the body was lowered to its final resting place.

Blood was the nickname that one of the camp wags had given Sergeant Mori. His cruel and inhuman treatment of all the prisoners he thought were not co-operating with the aims of the Nip war effort was to get him hung for war crimes in Singapore soon after the bombs were dropped. Slime was the name given to the Japanese interpreter, Kasiyama, who followed Blood around like a puppy. Slime was a horrible little man who loved to misinterpret if he thought the end result would be a severe beating. Blood and Slime are the symptoms of dysentery. There will be some more detail of this interesting and brutal couple in the next chapter.

The Nips had discovered that, unlike them, we had many skilled tradesmen in camp. Not only did the R.A.F. have mechanics, fitters, armourers, pilots, etc., but also tailors from civilian life, jewellers, cobblers, and almost any trade you can think of. As far as we could make out the Nip army was comprised solely of uneducated peasants. The more skilled of their population must have been employed in the other services. A hut was constructed at one side of the camp to house: 1. A tailor, 2. A jeweller, 3. A cobbler, 4. A carpenter (to make coffins), 5. An operating room, (to clean ulcers), 6. A shop, 7. Dispensary, 8. Out patients treatment. This was done on the pretext of catering to the prisoners but of course the Nips wanted some use of these facilities for themselves. After working on the coral at the airstrip or in the jungle our clothes, such as they were, got badly torn. Shoes and boots were chewed up. Any clothing that was beyond repair and torn up for bandages had the stitching removed first. In this way the tailor was kept in business repairing Nip clothes and the doctors could use the stitching. The Jeweller was used almost exclusively by the Nips as few prisoners, except the officers, had watches. The cobbler's main job was to repair our wooden "clompers." These were wooden platforms with a canvas strap over the toes. They made a characteristic clopping noise when walking on a hard surface. The carpenter's job was to make coffins for the deceased prisoners and a variety of "things" for the Nips

The carpenter was probably the fattest man in he camp as he curried favour with the Nips and was well fed as a result. When the situation changed during the coming months he quickly fell by the wayside and was buried on Haruku. There were only one or two other men who sought the Nip favour for their own immediate gain. I do not know if they survived but it is highly unlikely as conditions were so changeable and their aim was to get more food, which proved to be disastrous in the long run. When the extra food was denied to these people because they lost their privileged position, the sudden drop to camp rations was too severe. Consequently they died usually within a matter of weeks. Needless to say the rest of us despised these men.

Ulcers were becoming a real threat to our everyday life. A small coral cut would soon fester and without any treatment grew to be a major medical problem. Ulcers down to the shinbone and an inch across were most painful and lead to what was to become a dreaded quotation "on der tarble." Our Dutch doctor Springer, a man of incredible courage, would say this to an unfortunate prisoner who had decided to report his condition to the medical staff. This was usually because he could hardly walk or the pain was too intense. The good doctor would inspect the ulcer and then say "on der tarble" at which time two or three orderlies would grab the unsuspecting victim and hold him down while the doctor would scrape the puss out of the ulcer with some home made instrument, get down to nice clean flesh, and then sprinkle it with powder. It was most painful. I had this done with three ulcers - one on my right leg that was deep enough to expose the shin bone, one on my right foot behind the ankle over the Achilles tendon and the other on my right foot near the little toe. You could drop a quarter into any one of these ulcers and watch it being swallowed up as the puss enveloped it. Oh, to have had a quarter!

Todd Slaughter was one of the fellows who took life easy. A good buddy who was always willing to help in any situation he never seemed to be perturbed. He used to hum his favourite tune, one I had not heard, as he wandered around the camp after returning from a day's work on the potential airstrip. "We shall surely meet again, my lovely Russian Rose" or words similar to this. One day he climbed the large canary nut tree in camp to relieve the ever-present pangs of hunger. This was strictly against the rules for some unexplained reason. Soon after he had got himself hidden in the leafy branches who should make his appearance on the scene but Blood with his little tailpiece, Slime. Todd was all set to send down a good selection of nuts when as if by magic he spotted what was going on down below. The deathly silence that followed was a heart stopper for all of us. Anyone caught in the tree would receive an unmerciful beating. We all dutifully bowed and bowed oh so low so that the great one would have no reason to dilly dally on the spot. Blood and Slime had only been out of sight and sound for a moment when a thundering crack announced the arrival of Todd in double quick time. The branch supporting him had given way. We grabbed him quickly and had him through the barbed wire to the hospital section for a rapid check over. He was on the work party the next day. I think he was the last man to get into the upper branches of that magnificent tree. Just a couple of weeks after this Todd went into hospital with dysentery and left the island on the first sick draft some time later. His fate was sealed. I never saw him again. Before he left the island we made arrangements that if ever we should be parted we would meet at the British Car show held in London every year. Our meeting place would be the Morgan four tour display on the first Monday of the show. It was an excellent idea but I heard of his death on our return to Java some two hungry years later.

The death rate continued to climb. After only one month on Haruku one hundred had died and at the end of two months two hundred had died. Our two thousand-man work force was dwindling at an alarming rate. While distressing to us there were many indications that the Nips were not the least concerned. Kasiyama's remarks about "hurry up and die" and other references to our practising cannibalism did not fall on deaf ears. He suggested that rather than burying our dead we should eat them. Of course this suggestion was held in the contempt it deserves. What we did not know was that the practice of cannibalism was frequently encouraged by senior Japanese officers and widely practiced in New Guinea. Rations did not improve. In fact the Nip camp policy was that those men who did not work were to receive half rations. Since our camp staff was responsible for the distribution of the rations I do not believe this was adhered to. There was some difference in the rations for the workers and those in hospital but I do not think it was reduced to half for them. Our administrative staff was far more concerned with survival of the men than obeying the orders of a demented sergeant.

1   Dysentery is a disease of the intestines that comprises: Diarrhoe, blood and the mucus lining of the intestines. This mucus was known to us as slime. Dysentery represented Blood and Slime to us. This became a significant appellation during our incarceration on Haruku.
2   Katella is a potato like plant. Normally the root is eaten. The leaves grow on an upright stem and are edible if picked before ageing.

7

HARUKU 2

BEATINGS AND BOMBINGS

War would end if the dead could return.
STANLEY BALDWIN

The Japanese were bragging, in their inimical style, that we were constructing an unsinkable aircraft carrier. Apparently their propaganda machine was boasting to the Axis powers that the Japanese Pacific Empire was to become invulnerable with a whole series of unsinkable aircraft carriers. Haruku, and Amahai on the island of Ceram, were part of this plan to fortify their empire. Little did we know the significance of aircraft carriers in the war that was raging around us?

We figured the Americans were advancing up the east coast of New Guinea, about a thousand miles to the east of us, because of the bomber night flights over Haruku. Some of our fellow prisoners had seen a flashing light to the west of the camp when bombers were heard overhead. It was rumoured that the natives were in contact with these flights and that our close proximity to New Guinea meant that an espionage system was certainly aware that prison of war labour was being used to construct the airstrip.

By May 19th 1943, of the two thousand and seventy one fit men that had arrived in Haruku only two weeks earlier only five hundred and fifty were "fit" to work on the airstrip. This figure should be taken with scepticism as the classification of "fit" included anyone who could walk upright. The only people in camp who might conceivably weigh in at their Java weight were the cooks. Even this is unlikely as the bulk of our diet was rice and this was seldom cooked through. We had been on starvation rations for over six weeks, worked to the bone day and night and lived under the constant threat of torture and beatings. "Tiny" Mason had lost more than one hundred and twenty pounds. This was more than I weighed when I joined up.

Around the middle of May because of a declining number of airstrip workers the officers were paraded and lectured about "poor spirit" and its relation to sickness. This was the reason for the terrible state of sickness on the camp.

Food, or the lack of it, and disease were not to be taken too seriously. Our commanding officer Squadron Leader Pitts kept telling Captain Kurishima that a lot of the sickness would vanish if the camp was made at least habitable. This included building a latrine over the sea where the tide would flush the effluent away. This suggestion was waved aside with the comment that their God Emperor's sea would be spoiled if we treated it in such a lowly fashion. A few days later, with the continual low turnout for the airstrip and the fact that the Japanese finally understood that the job would not be completed if the prisoners kept dying before any substantial progress had been made, permission was given for the work on the airstrip to halt while all prisoners worked on the camp and the officers built the sea latrine.

A symptom of dysentery is diarrhoe made up of blood and mucus (slime) from the large intestine. As I mentioned before, "Blood and Slime" were the nicknames for our two main tormentors, the couple that terrorised our lives— the Japanese Sergeant "Bamboo" Mori, or Blood to us, who had made himself a hero in the China war. Blood was known to his fellow soldiers as Bamboo Mori. During the early part of the China war he had filled sections of bamboo with dynamite and used these as hand grenades. Being a naturally aggressive and ingenious individual he had made a great reputation for himself, no doubt well deserved, as a fighter and disciplinarian. Kasiyama was his little Korean interpreter and known to us as Slime. These two were inseparable. Blood wanted a toady and Slime a champion. Blood was later to beat a prisoner to death in front of the whole camp paraded for this purpose,

Blood stood about five foot five inches, had an extremely powerful body, long arms and short legs, a round face with high cheek bones, no neck, and a determined, aggressive look. When he walked he thrust his head forward and looked down, animal fashion. He was most aggressive and dangerous when the moon was high. He had a sense of humour, albeit warped, and would occasionally laugh, displaying a mouthful of gold teeth. He could enjoy a joke, providing he had initiated it. Slime was small beside Blood, subservient, sneaky and treacherous. Skulking around the camp at night he would listen to conversations in the huts with the simplistic idea of hearing something anti-Nipponese. Usually someone would spot him hiding near a hut with the result that the conversation glorified their God Emperor and the Rising Sun. He loved it. He thought we were typical cowards who surrendered without a fight and did not have the "good spirit" to die for our cause. He had no sense of humour and believed what we were expressing was our honest assessment of our feelings. He would lie when interpreting and go out of his way to have Blood beat a prisoner.

On the work parties we maintained our meagre rations but the sick continued dying of starvation. Malaria, dysentery, beri-beri, dengue fever, ulcers, and starvation were all a fact of everyday life. We were told there was no malaria on Haruku, but many of us had picked up the malady in Java and brought it with us. It was so debilitating that it contributed to the rising death toll. To go into hospital was most often a one-way trip. Few men came out alive. Number One ward was the death ward.

I only know of one man who lived to tell of the horrors of being in No 1 ward. Dave Harries, a stalwart Welshman, was in this ward and soon fought his way back to the Mad Monk's party. A man of incredible determination and "good spirit," not only did he fight his way out of the infamous No 1 ward but managed to live to see his loved ones again, after many hazards and some narrow escapes at the hands of the Japanese. He was the only man I know of to have plunged a bayonet into one of our captors, while a prisoner, and lived to tell the tale. He was instrumental at a later date of "procuring" medical supplies from the guards store hut. An incredible action of guts and daring, where the end must be either death by torture if he was caught, or the relief for his own suffering and that of the dying patients in the camp hospital. Dave will be telling this story at some later date I hope.

Briefly this is what happened, after he had recovered from No 1 ward and joined the work force many months later: Dave was in a group of five or six people all working for the common cause—survival. One of his group was a "loveable" rascal, a character who has no scruples but a great deal of personality and a lot of street smarts. He had grown up on the tough side of the tracks and knew how to survive even in depression years. Let us call him Joe.

Dave and Joe were working on the Mad Monk's party when they found an opportunity to get away into the jungle and look for the staff of life —roots and leaves. While they were scrounging around, off the beaten track, but on a pathway to a village, a couple of natives came along with some fruit they were carrying home. The immediate response was to bargain for the fruit. I do not know what they had to bargain with but the process was well under way when a Japanese, unknown to them, came down this seldom used path. He must have been one of the men recently arrived to support the air force that would one day operate from the airstrip. Realising that they had been caught red handed, Joe's reaction was to get rid of the witness. He grabbed the man around the neck and tried to throttle him to death. However his emaciated condition had left him weaker than he imagined. Dave was up to the situation and grabbed his bayonet. With one mighty plunge he skewered the man's heart and put and end to a most embarrassing and certainly life-threatening situation.

Now the only problem was to dispose of the body. After dragging the corpse into the jungle they used the bayonet to dig a grave and dispose of the evidence. Luckily for them the natives had disappeared at the first approach of the Japanese, so there were no witnesses. After returning to the Mad Monk's party they waited for some sign that a soldier was missing. Days passed and nothing was said. I did not hear of this little episode until I met Dave 1986, for the first time since the end of the war. Needless to say not a word of this was ever mentioned in camp by the two involved.

Great quantities of sand were carried from the beach up the side of the hill and placed in the camp area, spread and stamped down, to make a passable parade ground. A barbed wire fence was strung between the fit quarters and the hospital with strict orders that no men were to cross between the two, in the hope that this would cut down the spread of disease. Pilot Officer Mason with a crew of men worked in the stream creating a dam near the cook-house so that water would be more readily available. The dam was only about two feet high but it did allow the cooks to fill a bucket in one fell swoop instead of filling by the cup. It also acted as a bath if one could get away with it. The cook-house, a grand name for a shed that had no sides, only a roof, was moved bodily from the hilltop site of the camp to the streamside. Some sort of stone structures were put together to make fire places so that the cooks could more effectively do their job. We were most fortunate on Haruku that the island was so sparsely populated and that there were no villages up stream from us. It is the common practice in Indonesia to dispose of all effluent by using the simplest and most practical facilities at hand, the nearest stream or river. The huts were completed, giving us more protection from the weather as the sides were put on. Also the huts had sleeping platforms built in them. This meant that for the first time since arriving on the island many of us would be off the soggy ground and at least dry for what sleep we could get. Conditions were so crowded that when someone went for a pee in the night his place on the bamboo was immediately lost. This resulted in disturbing all one's neighbours on either side of the space just to regain a position on the *bali bali*, as The Dutch called this type of bamboo bed structure.

With the luxury of being off the ground we found that we had to find a place between two split bamboos to place our hipbones. The bamboos were placed running the length of the hut not the length of the "bed." Consequently we soon found that hipbones were red raw and quite painful. The scrawnier we got the redder our hipbones. Later on this became a feature of one's sartorial splendour as the only garment we wore was a loincloth.

In the huts where we had been so crowded, space was now available for individuals to spread out. On one of my night excursions to "the hole" I was squatting down to relieve myself when I realised that for the first time in months I was alone. The camp was deathly silent. The only disturbance was the hum of billions of maggots beneath me eating their way through many feet of the most colourful shit you have ever seen. The moon was bright, and the palm trees down by the beach were swaying gently in the breeze. Suddenly I realised what a beautiful spot this world could be if only we all treated each other with a little respect.

I had not allowed myself to think of home. I must only think of 'today' and in three months the Americans would be here. I was seized with a strong realisation that this was no longer just a case of being a hungry prisoner, but that the Japanese were definitely out to get rid of as many of us as they possibly could.

What could I do to survive this situation? Apart from dysentery, beriberi was the big killer and this was brought about by eating too much rice in relation to the other vegetables or fruit. I resolved that night to only eat extra rice when I had an equivalent amount of "something" to offset it. Although it was not easy to get any extra rice I must hold true to my resolve. We were so hungry every day that it was natural to eat any thing one could put one's hands on. Usually the only thing available was rice, roots or leaves. Occasionally rice, on the pain of death, could be stolen from the storage depot. I determined to learn more about roots and leaves and take more chances in slipping away from work to forage in the jungle. With death stalking us every day what did it matter how the end came! We discussed amongst ourselves if it was better to die now rather than continue this existence of degradation, for the prospects of any relief from this unremitting hunger, disease and degeneracy seemed so distant. It was obvious that the guards were not going make the conditions of daily living any better for us and we had no idea how the war was progressing. Some men did release their souls to a better existence and quite willingly, given the circumstances.

It was most noticeable now that our only topic of conversation was food. The stories around the cooking fire at night, where we mixed a few roots and leaves, were totally concerned with food. Women had taken a back seat to our hunger. Now the stories were of what we had eaten; the wonderful meals we had and the places where we had them. Seldom had any of the macho types, now lucky if they topped the scales at eighty or ninety pounds, taken a woman to dinner, or so it seemed. But they had eaten mountains of food, gourmet food of every description. What was the first thing to do when we were released? "Eat!" Our all-consuming interest in life - nay - life itself was food; perhaps only roots and leaves but food nevertheless. As we gained confidence in the jungle pickings we augmented the daily rations of rice and *katella* soup. It was never easy to get food into camp as we underwent a routine search every time we entered. What the guards thought we were stealing on an isolated island where there was only jungle and coral I don't know! Maybe this was all part of the final solution Japanese style?

Originally our guards were Japanese front line fighting troops. Now they were mostly Koreans and of peasant stock. Few of them could read. Occasionally a note would be sent to a guard which meant that we could stop labouring for a moment as we watched him trying to fathom out which way was up. Literally he would turn the piece of paper around and around not knowing where to start. Becoming aware that the whole work party was watching him he would then understand that we knew he could not read. In spite of this he was master of the situation and soon had us working like hell again, getting over his embarrassment by yelling and asserting his authority, eventually to sneak off to find someone who could interpret the hieroglyphics.

When we marched back to camp after a day of hard labour in the pouring rain, scrawny, hungry, half naked, cold, wet, and carrying a *chunkel* over our shoulder for the anticipated work in camp, we invariably sang, "Colonel Bogey," "I've Got Sixpence," or some other Air Force favourite, to keep up our spirits. The guards could not understand this and tried desperately to stop us. They, too, would be soaking wet and uncomfortable in spite of their good boots and rain gear, but they were on their way to a dry comfortable hut and a good meal. They were well aware of this so there was little incentive for them to make too much of a fuss about our singing. I believe they were also a little nervous, as there were many more prisoners on the island than guards. They had no idea what we were singing about. After the initial fear that we might be singing some sort of revolutionary song they seemed to accept the fact that white men liked singing to keep up their spirits. They may even have enjoyed it, for their lives were little better than ours. One of the guards committed suicide rather than live under their conditions. In spite of their propaganda they knew as well as we did that the Americans were flying over every now and again. On many occasions we would hear the guards singing their own favourite song. It came to be known by all of us as "Get your hair cut" and had quite a catchy tune.

We graduated from household hammers and ordinary coal chisels to pick axes and chunkels, two-man carrying baskets rather than the one-man one basket system, then to bombs and even tractors and small construction rail cars. The labour force had been shrinking every day as the death rate mounted, and the enemy was advancing with increasing speed. The tempo picked up as the Japanese realised that to get the work done they must find an alternative to strictly manual labour. In fact the hills shrank under our constant attention. As the months went by we found ourselves going to work on a sheet of glaring white coral.

After we had been on Haruku several weeks, the monsoon season ended and brought with it new problems. When one is living, should I say existing, so close to nature, a change in the season is a change in life style. From being constantly cold and wet, and to a certain degree clean, one becomes like parchment, totally dried out, thirsty and dirty. The thirty-eight degree Celsius temperature (one hundred Fahrenheit) was bearable for me as I love to be warm or even hot, but it was a hardship for those who are alien to the tropics and the seemingly erratic change in weather systems. Red Mac had a particularly hard time of it as his red hair coalesced so naturally with his exceedingly fair skin. In the year or so that I knew him in the islands he did not pick up a suntan and suffered terribly as a result.

It was about this time that we noticed a four engine flying boat frequently flying over the camp on its descent for a landing in the huge bay of Ambon Island. If Whiskers had any concern for our "holiday camp" situation he could have arranged for a small package of medicine to be flown into Ambon where Capt. Shimada[1] could have arranged for its forward passage to our camp. The wonder medicine of this time was M & B 693. If the Japanese had any concern for the labour force that was building their airstrip, an average size bottle of this drug could have done an inestimable amount of good for the dying of Haruku. Even a ten-pound package of quinine, which grows in Java, would have been a godsend. Instead they kept repeating that these medications were not available. In fact there was no shortage of these supplies in Java. Some months later we found a great variety of medical supplies on the docks in Ambon. Needless to say there was a slow and steady transfer of ownership as the work parties smuggled them back into camp, where they were put to immediate use.

One day a truck load of fifty and one hundred pound bombs appeared on the work site. Now we were ordered to dig slit trenches four foot deep and strategically placed on the hill sides, put the bombs in them, fuse them, and then run like hell for the surrounding grassed area. The idea of course was to blow the tops off the camel's humps. It worked well and progress improved. The Japanese even brought in a small hand truck railway. The rail lines were laid down one side of the airstrip and the small tip wagons mounted on the lines. After we completed laying this strip and detonating a few bombs the valley began to fill at an appreciable rate. The bombing was always a risky business as they continually tried to cut back on the amount of fuse we used to detonate the bombs. The longer the fuse the better our chance of reaching a safe distance before the explosions. There were no shelters to run to. We just ran as fast as we could and threw ourselves into the long grass, hopefully at a safe distance from the bombs and before they exploded.

I kept relatively fit on Haruku, if you can call a nineteen year old at seventy pounds fit, but one day I came down with a most preposterous toothache. Knowing that it was dangerous to stay in camp because Blood was always on the prowl I hesitated to report sick. After two days of this I finally succumbed and saw the camp dentist. He had a few dental instruments and wasted no time in telling me that the only solution to the pain was an extraction. He did not have any painkillers and would have to pull the tooth immediately. There seemed to be no alternative so out it came as I sat on a seat on the edge of the parade square, clutching my fists as the doctor unmercifully levered the tooth back and forth. I could feel every motion magnified a thousand times. As the struggle went on I tried to watch the bright blue sky but I am afraid my eyes were shut most of the time. Eventually relief came as the pressure of the dentists free hand on my forehead eased and the tooth slowly came into view. The whole procedure had only taken a few moments after breakfast so I was back on the work parade still swallowing my own blood.

With the death rate mounting in camp a Japanese doctor (Shimada) from the Ambon garrison was brought into camp to perform several autopsies to determine the cause of death. He was assisted by Drs. Phelps and Springer who later informed us that the stomachs of the deceased were the equivalent size of a three-year-old child. This startling evidence did not convince the Japanese to improve our rations or our living conditions. Dr. Phelps told Doctor Shimada that he knew why our men were dying and that if he really wanted to help the men he would examine the living and prescribe the necessary rations to maintain life. They did insist on weighing a small random sample of the men in camp. I had returned from work on the airstrip and was detailed for the burial party that evening. As we approached the hospital to pick up the coffins we were ordered to stand beside the small weight scale that had been brought into camp. Apparently the Japanese doctor wanted to get the average weight of the workingman. This selection was made on a casual basis such as those who happened to be on one end of the column when we were halted for the search before entering camp. My weight at this time was seventy-two pounds. I could count every rib and see the minuscule muscles hanging from the bones in my legs and arms. My eyes had recessed so that my head was just that of a walking skull.

Penny, who was just a few days short of his twenty first birthday, was taken down with a chronic bout of dysentery and transferred to the hospital. The hospital had been segregated from the rest of the camp by a barbed wire fence. Those in the hospital were kept separate from the working party. It was forbidden for us to go into the hospital. If caught, the result was a horrendous beating, with Blood doing the honours.

The work parties had been expanded to several other areas on the island. One that was avoided at all costs was the Mad Monk's party. We had a nickname for all the guards and this particular individual was especially dense. If one did not respond to his shouts immediately one was beaten and then told again, in Japanese of course, what should be done. This process could be repeated many times before the idea was a reality. The Mad Monk's work party was sometimes in the same direction as the air strip, so we seldom knew if we were on his party until we left the camp and marched down the road. On other occasions he would make a great fuss about the men that he wanted for a particularly hard job. He always got his way, as most of the guards did not care who worked for them.

One day, just after Penny had gone into hospital, I was marching back from a day with Horse Face in a group of about fifty prisoners. Luckily Horse Face was leading and I was close to being one of the last in line. There had been a slight drizzle and the guards were wearing their rain capes, when there was the unmistakable sound of a falling coconut just off to my right. Out of the corner of my eye I saw approximately where it landed, some fifty feet into the bush, and bounded off without a moment's hesitation. I grabbed it by the tail, as all ripe coconuts fall with that wisp of a stalk on them, and headed back to the marching column. There was a guard with his rifle levelled to his eye and about six feet away from me yelling his head off and pointing the rifle right at my head. In my starving, scrawny condition I really had nothing to lose so I yelled back "Shoot you Bastard, shoot," knowing damn well that a Korean guard with a rifle to his eye and marching at the same time had not a hope in hell of hitting me or my coconut. I joined the ranks and this miscreant put his rifle back on his shoulder. We both had our jollies!

Now I had the equivalent of two days' supplementary rations. One coconut represented a fifty per cent increase in rations for two days. Its value was exorbitant and meant that if I could get any additional rice I would not be breaking my resolve to only eat extra rice when I had a supplement to go with it. That night the search, on entering camp, was casual as the rain had started in earnest. As we passed into camp I manoeuvred myself in to the middle rank and was not searched. The guard that accosted me was not on search duty that night or he would have relieved me of my valued coconut. Since Penny was in hospital I decided to share the nut with him. It might give him that little extra boost and will to live. After eating my half which I mixed with my evening meal, I squeezed through the barbed wire that separated the hospital from the workers' camp and found where he had been the previous evening when I had visited him. His spot on the bamboo platform was empty. My first thought was that they had moved him to the recovery section, but the fellows there told me he had died that afternoon and was now in the morgue.

This was a sad blow as Penny was my best friend and being a pilot, had accomplished one of my own ambitions. Penny could fly a Hurricane with great ease and considerable amount of skill, but could not drive a car, whereas I could drive a car with great ease but could not fly a Hurricane. The next day I gave Blackie the half coconut and he shared a can of meat that he had successfully kept until this time. That day when we both volunteered for the burial party, Blackie wore his battle dress complete with wings in honour of our mutual friend.

It was a sad day for us.

The hospital was now accommodating thirteen hundred and seventy five prisoners. With over one hundred dead this amounted to a seventy-six per cent casualty rate in a period of a few weeks. Hospital conditions were aggravated by the continual tussle for supremacy between Kurashima and Blood, always at the expense of the prisoners. Kurashima was a weak Captain and Blood was an aggressive Sergeant. Under normal military circumstances this would come to light fairly quickly and Blood would lose out. Under the prevailing conditions, where the only troops on the island were our guards and consequently Kurashima was the senior officer, he had no one to call on to help him control Blood. Kurashima would give orders and Blood would intercept them and put his own interpretation on them or cancel them completely. Blood in his turn would issue orders only to find Kurashima had intercepted them and changed them to his liking. Generally speaking Kurashima was not interested in the camp or the welfare of the prisoners. I believe he chose to annoy Blood on occasion just for the hell of it, and of course we suffered. The officers who on occasion were summoned to see Kurishima told us that his main occupation in life was to spar with an invisible sword against an invisible enemy. Since this whole exercise seemed to be imaginary we speculated that Blood was the one being decimated by Kurishima's magic sword.

With the hospital becoming a closed compound, in theory a fairly good idea, the side effects were contributing to the increasing death rate. The walking patients were not allowed outside the barbed wire, which meant that they could not get water to wash either their dishes or themselves. Those patients who could walk were so weak that they were lucky to make 'the hole'. There were cases of patients going to the bathroom a hundred times a day and more. The orderlies had to use tin plates as bedpans - a messy business at the best of times. The water that was carried to the hospital every day was used to wash the eating plates and billy cans which meant that eventually it became a soup like mixture itself. Under these primitive conditions there was just no way to beat the spread of disease.

The whole camp was chronically short of clothing. The patients in hospital who had been carefully covered with a blanket during the shivering bouts of malaria frequently had dysentery at the same time. The end result was that the precious few blankets available were soiled with dysentery. The guards only allowed enough water into the hospital for immediate washing and drinking purposes. This meant that soiled blankets were put to one side for washing later. Later had to be within a few hours in the tropics. The guards would not allow the blankets to be taken to the stream to be washed immediately they were soiled. The blankets could not be washed in the hospital because there was not enough water so the end result was that they had to be burned. This also applied to the valuable clothing. A devastating waste for people who had nothing and no hope of renewing lost supplies. Basically the guards were terrified of the conditions in the hospital. They had no idea how to handle a situation like this. None of them would enter the hospital after the first few days on the camp. This condition produced much speculation as to the escape possibilities. They had no idea how many men had died in any given period. They were too frightened to look into dysentery-infected coffins so they had to accept our word for the casualty rate. The other side of this coin was that they had terrorised the local population to such an extent that a POW seen outside the camp, un-escorted, represented a bounty. We were brown over ninety nine per cent of our bodies but the natives were black and herein lay the difference.

A canteen of sorts was created. The Japanese had promised to pay us ten cents per day but we never saw this. However, a system of tickets was started for the workers. If you were on the work party continuously for a week you would be rewarded with a ticket at the end of this time. This meant that you could go to the canteen and either exchange your ticket for some bananas, papaya, tobacco or a coconut. The canteen was supplied from local produce so the selection was limited. The bananas came in quite variety - green bananas that were ripe, red bananas, finger bananas and the ordinary yellow bananas. Occasionally we saw rambutans, plantains, dried fish, and other types of local produce.

This ticket system was introduced by our own officers as I believe they kept all monies earned by the work parties. This was done in an effort to counteract the Japanese effort to kill everyone in the hospital by denying them food. It also meant that the sick men tried desperately to go on a work party - even if this hastened their death. One of the fellows mentioned that he would rather die eating the rice we were served on work parties than the pap the hospital patients were forced to eat. If a full ration was not enough to live on how could anyone survive on half a ration? With the accumulated camp money the officers tried to equalise the benefits for all men - sick, dying, working. But accumulated money meant there was room for a little graft even on our pitiful pay scale.

Blood was a hero to his fellow countrymen but also a greedy peasant at heart. Now that he was in a position to wield a little power why not gather a little money at the same time? Our commanding officer and his officers soon became aware that the coconuts that cost the camp three cents each were being purchased by Blood for two cents each, the hapless native trader not having a choice in the situation. This was a simple transactional profit on the surface but one that cost starving men thirty three per cent of their supplementary diet. Did Blood really think he would get rich on this scheme? May be he was saving up for some new gold teeth! This seemed to be one of his weaknesses. We discovered some time later that gold teeth was a neat way for the peasants to get money back to the homeland in a legitimate fashion.

At this time Kurashima or Blood restricted all the food going into the hospital to three bowls of rice pap mixed with a weak solution of vegetable water for each patient each day. Kasiyama would shout to the patients in hospital, from well clear of the barbed wire, so he would not be infected - "Why don't you hurry up and die?" Surely there could be no mistake of their intentions. Kurishima had suggested to the doctors that we eat the dead patients. Cannibalism was not a rare experience for the Samurai warriors of Japan[2].

This was not the only mystery that haunted us at this time. At night after the official "lights out" and close to midnight, the drums at a village nearby would start to pound a regular rhythm. This continued for several weeks and was the object of a great deal of speculation. Did the Ambonese play drums for an extended period like this to celebrate a wedding or a funeral? And why only at night? And so late at night? Were the natives planning some kind of uprising? Was this an accommodation to the circumstances that now held all of us in its grip? An appeasement to the Empire that proclaimed freedom from colonial domination? Whose highly advertised slogan "Asia for the Asiatics" was proving to be more myth than reality? It would have been so nice to have visited this village and learned something of the culture of these remote people. This was to be another unanswered question from our stay on Haruku.

Flight Lieutenant Audus was a biology professor in civilian life and now put his considerable talents to work in creating a supplement to our diet. He devised a process of cultivating yeast from some of our precious rice ration. There were many cases of men going blind as a result of malnutrition and the overall conditions. These cases were halted with the addition of vitamin B in the yeast and then, with the success shown by these individuals, the rest of us were able to benefit from this ingenious addition to our meagre fare. We had all suffered from "Java Balls" at an earlier stage and now our skin in spite of a burnt hue showed some beautiful shades of purple - a symptom of pellagra caused by advanced malnutrition. We must have been an unusual sight - scrawny, ulcerated and colourful. Pellagra makes the skin most colourful with the mouth and throat developing gaping sores. It is an advanced symptom of malnutrition. Our skin having a dark brown background with purples and blues imposed on it outshone any clothing we would have been brave enough to wear.

Another innovation of the camp officers appeared about this time. *Tempeh* was a small cake issued to us when the rations permitted. Sometimes the ration issue included *kadele* beans and *kadjang idjoe* (mong bean), a small green bean grown prolifically in the Far East. These were processed into small tasteless patties and issued to us for their nutritional value. If the rations included oil these were occasionally fried which made them a little more palatable. Usually our only indication that meat had been issued to camp was minuscule beads of fat floating on the surface of the green leaf soup.

The strip, now, at last, was starting to look like an airstrip, with a small rail line down one side and trucks driving over the level areas and pure white coral surprisingly smooth where the steam rollers had done their job. At work one day we were taking our lunch break at noon, with the temperature in the high thirties, (hovering around 100 degrees F) when one of the Dutch prisoners decided to take advantage of the shade under a truck. Because of the angle of the sun he lay down with his legs astride the right rear wheel and his head towards the front of the truck. No sooner was he down than he fell fast asleep, knowing full well that as soon as activity started again he would not be left in that enviable position for more than a second or two. Without warning a Japanese driver hopped into the truck and drove off. Feeling some resistance he just gunned it and drove right over the sleeping prisoner from his crotch to the top of his head. A ghastly death for a man who was so successfully avoiding the hospital and all the deadly diseases that we constantly lived with! He was the only prisoner of war on Haruku Island given a decent, crude, burial. The next day a funeral party was formed and escorted by a few guards, including Blood and Slime, to the cemetery. Instead of being buried in rice sacks he was afforded a bamboo coffin. The cross at the head of his grave was made with a local wood rather than two pieces of split bamboo. This was the guards' idea of a good burial for a POW. Everything is relative.

One night, well after dark, we heard the now familiar sounds of Flying Fortresses in the distance. It was not unusual to hear the drone of these aeroplanes as they went on their way to some target far distant from us. This particular night the drone took on ominous overtones as it became louder and louder. Our camp was the largest facility on the island and looked exactly like the barracks that it was. We now had a large white sand parade square that must have stood out like a jewel under the bright tropical moon. Surely they were not after us? We had convinced ourselves that the Americans knew we were here. Our location and close proximity to New Guinea must be within their sphere of intelligence. The faith was strong that night but not strong enough to keep us on the bamboo as we heard the whistle of falling bombs. Not many of us knew of a Japanese camp that been built to house their growing presence on the island. This was the target for the night, but sadly a thorough demolition job was done of the native village.

The next day we were paraded in the usual fashion for work but with more beatings than was normal. Their revenge procedure had started. We marched to the now non-existent village of Pelau. The first one hundred men were detailed to a different destination. I was in this group and soon found myself clearing up the demolished village. This was a really rotten job as revenge was uppermost in the guards' minds. They had cleared away all their own dead bodies by the time we got there and claimed emphatically that no Japanese had been killed. However, I found a scalp in the debris. It looked almost exactly like a skullcap and was without doubt the scalp of a Japanese soldier for it was close shaved. Only the Japanese soldiers had their heads shaved in this fashion. Bomb blast is a most peculiar thing. In this case it scalped a soldier. In Singapore I had heard of an airman having his head severed from his body and the body remaining upright in the chair he had been sitting in before the bombs fell. There were many native bodies in the debris which we were ordered to pile just clear of the destroyed buildings. After clearing the destruction of the village we marched on to the airstrip for a day's work.

Later we heard that the camp doctors had offered their services for the wounded of the village. After two or three days delay three of the camp doctors were allowed to see the wounded. We heard from them that in some cases shrapnel was still sticking out of wounds and the treatment given by the Japanese was of the crudest kind. Once again the treatment of the natives was questioned. Was this deliberate torture of the most bizarre type, just complete ignorance or policy of the Japanese government? If ignorance, was Major Shimada really a doctor or just a soldier given this title? Did they think the natives really believed their slogans —"Asia for the Asiatics" and "The Greater East Asia **Co-prosperity** sphere?"

In July our CO tried, and succeeded, in getting us a half-day off work. This was the first day, or rather half day, of rest we had since arriving on Haruku just prior to my birthday on the 6th May. Initially the hours had been at the whim of whoever wanted a work party, and frequently meant that we worked for up to twenty-four hours or more, without a break. Now we had a whole half-day to ourselves! We indulged in such profitable little tasks as cleaning our black billycans, repairing clompers (wood shoes) and even getting our heads shaved or killing lice. Our hair had to be kept at less than an eighth of an inch in length. This was very much to our advantage as it cut out the problem of lice in this area.

It was on this momentous half day that I experienced another great revelation. We had just finished our evening meal and I was walking down the slope from the main camp to the river to wash my billy can when I became aware of two guards behind me. They always talked in a loud manner so there was no mistaking their presence. I hastened my steps as one never knew what they might do next. To avoid any incidents I wanted to have as much room as possible between them and myself. Just as I was distancing myself from them they put down the wooden bucket they were carrying between them and shouted *Makan* the Indonesian word for food. Without a moments hesitation I turned around and was helping myself to the dregs of a bucket of soup. Being the closest to the guards when they put down the bucket I was first on the scene and had a good chance of scooping up at least half a billy can of soup and enjoying it at my leisure. What a dreamer! No sooner had I bent over the bucket than there were a dozen hungry prisoners fighting for every last drop. I suddenly realised that I was acting like a dog. In these fleeting moments I had left the dignity of mankind behind me and had the potential for acting out the animal in me. I hurriedly withdrew from the fighting mob without more than a mouthful of the precious soup and regained my composure as Kitchi Cowling. I was not going to be reduced to animal status in spite of the terrible hunger that we lived with. What a price to pay for principle. I continued my hungry journey to the river to wash out the empty billy can. Kitchi was my nickname in camp. It is the Malay word for small but it was given to me to represent youth.

As the year wore on the work progressed, not only with our efforts but boosted by the Japanese realisation that they were suffering severe military setbacks. If they really wanted this airstrip finished then they had to get serious about it. Just as the bombs had appeared one day, now a couple of tractors appeared. Imagine my surprise as a reddish Bucyrus Erie tractor complete with red spots all over it hove into sight. All the way from Singapore. I wanted to give it a friendly kick, a nudge of recognition, a portend of better days around the corner, but by this time I was without shoes. My feet were tough but not that tough. Dare I think back to those days in Singapore when I was the supervisor on the aerodrome and the big boss's son? No, no I must not for a moment think of that, only that the Americans will be here in three months. I had to settle with a few thoughts of how to put it out of action, rapidly, if the occasion arose.

Not only had tractors arrived but some steam rollers as well. The valley was getting full as the hills were getting low. We were still exploding bombs on the strip. Now we were also cutting firewood for the steamrollers and stacking the cord wood in the grass a couple of hundred feet to one side of the runway, the seaward side. On a bright and dry afternoon as we set light to the fuses and ran for our lives into the grass I heard a native shouting in Ambonese that "The ships are coming, — the ships are coming." He was pointing seaward and greatly excited. This conjured visions of American warships cruising down the passage between the islands to make a landing and our imminent rescue. I signalled the man to hide in the long grass, so that I could go over to him and find out more about this momentous happening. He crouched in the grass as I wiggled my way towards him flat on my belly. As I got closer I again signalled him to join me behind one of the cord woodpiles. We just got hunkered down for a good, albeit, fast chat when the air was rent with an almighty "*Kura Kura—Baggero*" the guards favourite way of telling us they wanted our attention. Unknown to me a guard was on the other side of the woodpile. He had been crouching down on the wrong side of the woodpile to get protection from the bomb blast. Or was he curious and just wanted to see what the demolition looked like? Well! One of the strictest rules in camp was not to talk to the natives. If Blood got hold of a culprit doing this, his chances would be slim indeed.

I was called to attention, luckily by the private who discovered me, and the process started. First was the shouting and the unintelligible harangue that went with it. The purpose of this was to work the guard up to a frenzy so that he would have no hesitation in carrying through with a sound beating. He followed all the rules and finally put his right foot behind my left leg and punched me in the face. Naturally when I stumbled back I fell over his booted foot. Now with me sprawled on the ground he was the dominant figure. I naturally took the fetal position to try and protect myself as much as possible. He started kicking me, with most of the blows landing on my left kidney, as I was lying on my left. After his legs tired of this he used his rifle butt to smash my head and shoulders. Most of the men had gathered around and were shouting at the guard to lay off. After several minutes of this one of the senior guards — a *gocho* (corporal) — came over and stopped the proceedings. Because of the rigid structure of the army it would not be good for a private to best a corporal. This may well have happened if the beating had gone on much longer. The private may have a heap of flesh and bones to show for his afternoon's work. What would the corporal have to show? For an army that glorified physical torture and a rigid rank structure this could not be tolerated.

I limped lamely back to work and was screened by my fellow workers for the rest of the afternoon. They were considerate of my condition and allowed me to squat out of sight while they did all the work. After we got back to camp Dr. Phelps gave me some of his precious supply of morphine and confined me to quarters for the next few days. I was lucky to get away with it. I had survived a major beating from a minor minion[3].

When the first *"Kura Kura"* had rent the air the native ran like mad and was not seen again. He was far too fleet of foot for the guards to worry about. Apart from that they had a victim on the spot. I never did discover what he was talking about as there were no ships in sight then or for the remaining months we were on Haruku.

We saw a magnificent display of American technology one day as we were working on the airstrip. It was a puzzle even to the most highly trained of our work party who were all air force types. Somebody's attention was drawn to the beautiful deep blue sky above and in a northerly direction. It looked as if there was a bomber with a fighter escort at about two or three thousand feet. The bomber appeared to be almost stationary and was at such an angle to us that the wing was in line with the fuselage making it appear as a flying fuselage. Without any warning the bomber suddenly sent out sprays of what we thought were ignited incendiary ammunition, or even small cluster bombs. It looked to us like a controlled explosion. We watched fascinated and thought that the Americans were experimenting with some new type of weapon. After the smoke from the incendiaries had dissipated there was nothing to be seen. Now we were really confused and hoped the bomber in question had not exploded in mid flight. The odd part about it was no sound to the explosion. In fact during the whole episode there had not been any sound of aircraft engines. *"Kura-Kura, Speedo Speedo"* and back to work we toiled. Now nearly fifty years later it is fascinating to speculate that what we saw may have been a UFO. The whole sighting is certainly in keeping with this thought.

On the march back from the airstrip we had to pass through the now sparsely populated remains of the village of Pelau. We seldom saw anyone there but we did see the occasional dog running around. We managed to catch the odd hairless dog now and then. One dog butchered in the soup for several hundred men did not make a noticeable difference to the taste or the nutritional value. We consoled ourselves that the protein was there even if we could not taste a change in the meal. To actually get a piece of meat was to score and also gave us a sign that the cooks had put the hapless beast into the soup. Cats were not as a popular as dogs on Haruku. I do not remember ever hearing of, or eating, cat soup.

My look out for snakes on Haruku was not rewarded. Perhaps I was not still long enough to notice one or possibly they do not thrive on the island. I was able to capture several iguanas which were both tasty and smelled heavenly when opened up after baking. We had three ways of cooking anything that we might scrounge out of the jungle: boiling, frying and baking. Normally we boiled our jungle findings. Not only was this the easiest and quickest way of getting the goodies into us, it was the most practical. Frying depended on a lucky "find" of coconut oil or some crafty bargaining. This seldom happened. Roasting or baking was kept for the special finds such as iguana or a particularly fine specimen of *katella*, sweet potato or some other kind of root. Baking or roasting was accomplished by wrapping the iguana, in this case, in a neat blanket of mud and sand and burying it under the fire. This method took a lot longer and demanded a constant watch on the fire to make sure it did not go out and that no one else would have time to relieve us of the prized meal. After dark, the aroma would waft through the huts and raise many covetous feelings in our hungry neighbours. These tasty little morsels would only make one meal so there was no problem attached to keeping the remains safe for the following day. I had absolutely no resources to dry the skins and repeat my successful enterprise of Semarang camp. It is doubtful that a market existed for this type of refinement. Our whole existence had changed so radically from the relative civilisation of Java to this camp run by a mad man who seemed most concerned with our demise.

The question of the disposition of personal effects was raised by the guards as they insisted that these should be returned to the UK via the Red Cross. This appeared on the surface to be a most concerned attitude; our captors respecting in some small way the mores of a civilised society. However, it was odd that they were deliberately starving us to death while being concerned for the belongings of the deceased. Having encouraged us verbally to "hurry up and die" and on other occasions to resort to cannibalism, they now wanted to look after the few personal trinkets of the deceased. Unbelievable! And so it was. They went so far as to insist that documents must be initiated listing the possessions of the deceased. These documents and the possessions must then be kept for onward transmission to the Red Cross. When the last draft of prisoners left Haruku in 1944 the box containing the documents and, supposedly, the possessions was still in the guardhouse. Was there somebody in the Japanese organisation that had a streak of decency but not the will or the power to back it up? We will never know. This is the kind of thing that the guard we called the Emperor may have done, for we knew him as a "good" Japanese, but he was only a private and this meant nothing in the overall picture. By now the only personal effects for those lucky enough to have any, consisted of letters, photos and other keepsakes of personal intrinsic value. All clothing, if any, was given to those who were working in only a *jawat* or loincloth. This included most of the people in camp.

Once we were well over the monsoon season and sweating like pigs on the various work parties outside the camp it became necessary to have some form of bathing at the end of the day and the time to do it. Sometimes this was granted and we were allowed to the stream for a wash or into the sea for a swim. The sea swim was most welcome in spite of the location being next to the latrine. On occasion a guard would shoot into the water if he thought a prisoner was too far from the crowd. The river had the advantage of being cooler than the sea but was shallow. There being no villages above this point, the cool freshness of water gave us a moment of relaxation and cleanliness, two feelings in such contrast to our surroundings.

The dry weather brought another problem, first for the hospital patients and for the whole camp. The Japanese never thought conditions in the camp were caused by the appalling lack of normal, basic living necessities. Such rudimentary prerequisites as basic sanitary facilities for the latrines and clean cooking conditions were foreign to them. The cause of all our problems was twofold; flies and bad spirit. The bad spirit theme we looked after by either pairing off with a buddy or in small groups. It is easier to survive under these primitive conditions with shared responsibilities. The bad spirit from the guard's point of view referred to the fact that we were not totally committed to helping their God Emperor win his war.

Flies soon became the aim of the guards focus for our survival. It cost them nothing and introduced another reason for beatings and slappings. All hospital patients were now required to kill twenty flies before receiving their bowl of pap three times a day. Many times this ration was cut to twice a day and on occasion withheld altogether. The dying patients were hardly able to move let alone chase energetic flies. If the hunting was good then the other men would look after their buddies but it frequently resulted in the restriction of rations for the day. The guards were terrified of entering the hospital huts which meant that sick men, or the duty orderly, had to carry their flies on a plate or half coconut shell to the hut entrance for the guard to inspect the catch before another billy can of pap was allowed into the hut. The flies had to be destroyed in the presence of the guard so that they could not be reused for the next meal. This was the best method of stopping the spread of disease, they told us. With a lack of washing facilities, the handling of hospital flies in a dysentery hut just prior to a meal left something to be desired. The first morning after this new routine was introduced we watched as the hospital patients walked past the serving drum with a billy can in one hand and the flies in the other hand. It was only a matter of days before the whole camp was involved in this "life saving measure." For us on the work party it meant that as soon as we got back to camp we had to rush around and catch fifty flies before getting our meagre meal.

I only once had a conversation on a face to face basis with Blood. I happened to be visiting in another hut when the signal was received that Blood and Slime were on the warpath. One never knew what this mad man was up to so evasive action was the immediate response. It was wise to be in ones own hut when he was on the prowl. I was making a rapid exit from the hut when I came face to syphilitic face with this ominous specimen. Due to poor timing on my part we met at the entrance, the narrowest part of the hut and almost bumped into each other. I stepped back smartly to one side, made a rigid forty five degree angle bow and let him go unhindered on his way. He stopped and stared at me for a long moment. Was he identifying me in his sick mind with some unhealthy prank or horrendous deed? Stealing something or smuggling food into the camp? Was I to be the next victim for a public "beating to death" on the camp square? Eventually his guttural voice roared "Umor Baruppah?" his Indonesian version of "How old?" I replied "Sappulah blass" (nineteen) "Tida bagus" (not good) he commented and continued on his way through the hut without another word.

---

1   Dr. Shimada when questioned by our doctors about the conditions in camp admitted that they were deplorable but as a military officer he could do nothing about it. His attitude is summed

up as military obedience takes precedence over human considerations.

2   It was an accepted belief that eating one's enemy gave them strength over that enemy. See *The Knights of Bushido, Japanese War Crimes*, Lord Russell of Liverpool. Also *"Hidden Horrors Japanese war crimes of World War 11"*. Yuli Tanaka, Westview Press, 1996.

3   After the war and my return to England my left kidney was removed as a result of this beating. I spent a considerable time in hospital recovering from the effects of our existence in POW camp.

8

HARUKU 3

WHORES AND HAM

There is no possible line of conduct which
has at some time and place been condemned,
and which has not at some other time and place
been enjoined as a duty.

WILLIAM LECKY

In November of 1943, the Japanese were concerned with our welfare! Three hundred and ninety eight men had died during the first three months and now some six months after our arrival the hospital had over seven hundred patients[1]. Many of the men considered to be fit could hardly walk and weighed an average of approximately seventy-five pounds (thirty four kg). They told us a draft of the worst cases in hospital would be shipped to Java for medical treatment. The next day seven hundred patients from the hospital were carried or hobbled down to the jetty and loaded on the ship. Most of these individuals could not walk. They were human skeletons just capable of sustaining souls. How could they survive the hazards of prison ship transportation? My two good friends Jack and Todd were on this draft. We felt it was a good thing that they were being released from this living hell. Taffy, who had shared my Vienna sausages on my nineteenth birthday, was now in the graveyard not far from Penny. He had been moved from our hut with relatively mild bout of dysentery so I did not keep in touch with him for many sunsets. It was pure coincidence that one day after work as we reported for the evening burial party I asked one of the orderlies how Taffy was doing. To my terrible surprise and sorrow he was amongst the dead that we were carrying to the cemetery that night. Taffy and I had shared all our jungle gatherings since arriving on Haruku. Penny and Jack were always part of our group but due to the exigencies of our conditions there were periods when we were allocated different huts and frequently toiled on different work parties. This was the case on my birthday when only Taffy and I shared my sausages. All four of us, however, had enjoyed the iguana delicacy.

The chances of survival on Haruku were looking pretty slim when the hospital draft was announced. Provided the majority of patients could survive the horrors of a prison ship we felt that conditions at the other end must be better than this. Little more than six months previously we had arrived on this beautiful tropical island in a disastrous condition after setting out as a labour force of "fit" men. A trip that normally takes three days had taken close to three weeks. Now with the increasing American air activity, this trip would take longer as they would probably hide each day and travel by night.

The seven hundred men were never heard of again. Some say the ship, the *Suez Maru*, was torpedoed, others that it was sunk by bombing. Who knows? All the lives were lost. The news spread around the camp like wild fire but we were so sceptical that most of us did not believe it. It could very well be another little trick of the Japanese to belittle us and show their contempt for us. The guards would not talk about it. One rumour was that the whole ship, crew, guards, and prisoners had been lost. We heard later from our guards on Haruku that the ship had been torpedoed without survivors. In Java at the end of the war we heard that some of the guards survived and had continued their duties at the big camp in Batavia. This remains an unsolved mystery but we do know that no prisoners survived[2].

The camp now had a slightly different configuration as the narrow stretch of jungle between the camp and the Japanese quarters had been cleared away. This left us with the river on the west side, the sea on the north side and the guards quarters on the east side, and jungle on the south across the road that was adjacent to the camp. Now permission was given to start a vegetable garden, to be worked only by those in hospital and the "sick in quarters." The jungle would be cleared and mostly *katella* and sweet potato planted. The whole project was to be run by the prisoners for the benefit of the prisoners.

The garden development worked quite well, with good results showing after a fairly short time. Maize and tomatoes, chillies and lombok were all growing as we watched them daily on our march to the airstrip. The fast growing conditions of the tropics were a delight to behold and a saviour for us at this particular time. Eagerly, we watched the development of these future succulent meals. How nice it would be to have a few tomatoes, lombok and chillies in the soup. We realised that the sick would have first crack at these goodies but our turn would come eventually. When the time arrived for the first fruits to be gathered from this great garden development imagine our astonishment and outrage when the guards took it all and gave us the *katella* leaves. As usual the Japanese helped themselves to whatever they wanted. The main drawback to the garden was that whenever Blood saw prisoners working there he figured they were capable of working on the airstrip and beat them for "bad spirit." Slime was always there with a sickly grin on his face, kow-towing to his all-powerful master.

It was not uncommon for the camp canteen funds to buy fruit in large quantities from the local vendors. All deals had to be supervised by the guards. This always meant Blood was involved. On most occasions the amount of fruit received in camp did not tally with the amount paid for. The RAF officer in charge would buy five hundred kilos of bananas and receive only three hundred and fifty kilos. The native trader, paid by the Nipponese, would be paid for three hundred and fifty kilos. The guards kept the cash difference of one hundred and fifty kilos of bananas. To add insult to contempt the guards then took the best of our bananas for themselves. The camp would be lucky to receive three hundred kilos. It almost seemed a challenge to find new ways to kill off prisoners.

We were told that as guests of their God Emperor we would receive a bar of soap each. This did not excite us too much as we were able to wash fairly effectively in the sea or the stream. We usually wore whatever clothes we had, so they got a regular washing on our bodies. A bar of food would have been divinely inspired and accepted as a worthy gift from such a magnificent being. Even this "gift" from their God Emperor cost us five cents each. Many like myself, who did not have the five cents, were allowed to keep the soap. Now that there was so much of it in camp, its trading value for food was non-existent and the possibility of keeping it for trading later was negligible as the rats also had a liking for it.

The God Emperor's birthday on 29th April 1944 was declared a holiday. We were actually allowed to stay in camp and rest. I do not remember what had occurred on Christmas day 1943. I am sure it was not a holiday. The last holiday I remember was the half-day in July 1943. It should be mentioned here that the guards were always concerned that somebody might have a written record of what had occurred in camp. All the searches on leaving a camp and entering a new one were aimed at recovering written records. Occasionally we arrived in camp after the normal working party to find that all the prisoners in a specific hut were denied their evening meal for some trumped up charge - a fire left smouldering in the sand, untidy conditions, not enough flies caught, or too many sick in one barrack. The fires were the individual cooking type, less than six inches in diameter with three stones to hold a small pot and surrounded by sand — not a danger to the camp.

The majority of us were reduced to wearing a *jawat*. This is a piece of string about eighteen to twenty two inches long with a piece of cloth attached to the centre of it also about eighteen inches long. First the string was tied around the waist with the cloth hanging over one's buttocks. Then you reached between your legs and brought the cloth up to the front string and tucked it in. Voila - a *jawat*. These are commonly worn by the peasants in India. No need for a tailor to maintain these sartorial goodies.

The author leads in one of his Dad's winners in Penang 1948.

№. 2928.65
IDENTITY CARD
(Population Census)
SINGAPORE

Name ....
姓名
Address ....
住址

Race ....
何屬
Age ....
年歲

RAFFLES HOTEL

Census Officer

A   B   C   D

My ID card before I boosted my age to join the RAF.

Part of the checklist I found after the A-bombs were dropped. I made copious notes on this checker's list and in a 1941 diary that was given to me in September 1945. Probably one of the best used diaries as it had entries covering the 4 year period 1942-1945.

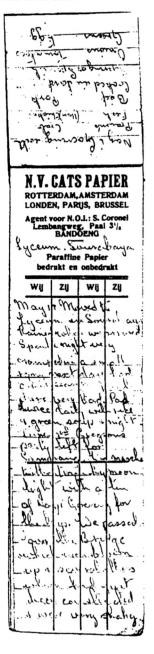

N.V. CATS PAPIER
ROTTERDAM, AMSTERDAM
LONDEN, PARIJS, BRUSSEL

Agent voor N.O.I.: S. Coronel
Lembangweg, Paal 3½
BANDOENG

Lyceum. Soerabaya
Paraffine Papier
bedrukt en onbedrukt

Wij	Zij	Wij	Zij

Identification tag number 6029 discarded by a happy ex-POW as soon as the news of the atomic bomb reached us. This is typical of the ID tags worn by prisoners who remained in Java for the duration of the war. The death rate in the islands was so rapid and the conditions so primitive that this form of ID was not considered as far as we know.

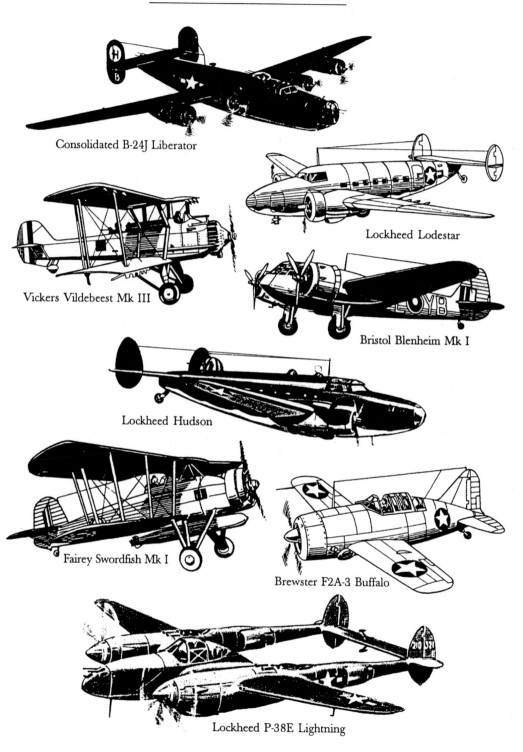

Consolidated B-24J Liberator

Lockheed Lodestar

Vickers Vildebeest Mk III

Bristol Blenheim Mk I

Lockheed Hudson

Fairey Swordfish Mk I

Brewster F2A-3 Buffalo

Lockheed P-38E Lightning

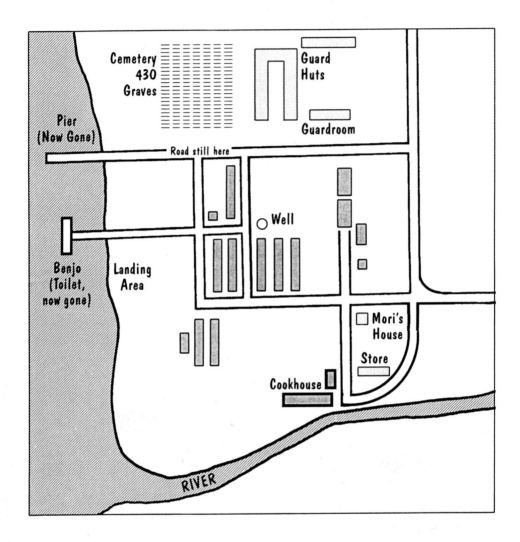

Haruku (Dutch spelling Haroekoe) camp as we left it in 1944. A far cry from the unfinished huts that greeted us in the May monsoon of 1943 when we found coconut palms growing through the roofs with boundless numbers of insects journeying up and down the trunks. It was devastating to see the amount of water that was collected by the fronds and channelled into our sleeping quarters.

It was about this time that the doctors in camp procured a good quantity of coconut oil and some sulphur powder. After getting back to camp one night and attending the routine work of the camp such as the burial parties (imagine a daily routine that includes such diverse activities as burying your buddies and carrying wood for the cook-house) we were ordered to attend what must be the most unusual parade in the history of the RAF. After supper we were paraded naked under the light of the moon in two columns with our elbows at our sides and hands outstretched, in front of us, palms up. Now two medical orderlies walked in front of each column. One poured a little coconut oil onto one palm while the other shook out some sulphur powder on the other palm. Thus equipped, individuals in the two ranks then clapped their hands together and applied the resulting mixture to their scrotum and crotch.

Now to make sure that all scabies were attacked, the distribution process was repeated to the men in the rear rank only. After mixing the oil and sulphur powder they applied the mixture to the buttocks of the man in the front row. About turn, repeat the process, and everybody is parasite-free. A most unconventional parade, but effective. This must be the most unusual and bizarre parade ever officially sanctioned in the RAF.

Both scabies and Java Balls[3] were rampant throughout the camp, but for most of us lice and bed bugs were not big a problem. We all suffered from lice but some how we had developed an accepting attitude towards them. They were uncomfortable to have around but then they were inevitable. They were part of our daily routine - when you had a moment you would take off your *jawat* and hunt for lice. What could be more natural? The sulphur/oil mixture was intended to combat scabies. This unusual buttock rubbing parade was so successful that a repeat performance was carried out the following night. It proved to be a great relief to our constant scratching and cut down, at least temporarily, on the spread of scabies.

We were surprised to see a group of Dutch prisoners arrive on the camp. They seemed to be in good physical condition and reasonably clothed. Imagine our surprise when we found that these men were the group we had left at Amahai on the neighbouring island of Ceram. They had been on the island all this time with the loss of only thirty-one men out of one thousand[4]. Three men had been beheaded for trying to escape. Only twenty-eight men had been lost to disease. Having finished the airstrip on Ceram they were now brought to Haruku to help us complete this strip. Needless to say they were most unhappy with this strange turn in events. Their continued existence was now in the hands of Blood and Slime — a real gamble with the odds stacked clearly in favour of our captors.

New huts were built in camp to accommodate the Dutch men and for some unknown reason {American advances in the Pacific?} new huts for the hospital were built. Of course they were needed. Leaking roofs that are home to a great variety of insects do not make the best hospital accommodation. Of course there were no sprays or nets to reduce the hazard of falling or flying insects. A road-building programme was initiated and for a short while it looked as if Blood was not about to beat the living daylights out of the next person to cross his fancy. With the arrival of nine hundred and sixty nine men fit and well clothed, it seemed that life on Haruku might be taking a turn for the better.

With the temperature hovering around thirty-eight degrees Celsius (over 100 degrees Fahrenheit) we were working as usual on the airstrip, now in its more advanced stage of construction. There were various jobs such as: digging holes for the bombs, loading the already bombed and loosened material into the miniature rail road cars, pushing the cars to the dump sight and then spreading the dumped coral.

My particular group was assigned to pushing the cars back and forth to move the coral— two men to a car. I was on the airstrip side and under the eye of the guards. They were shouting in a particularly aggressive and obnoxious way so I shouted back speculating as to their probable illegitimate origins. The reaction of one was immediate. He was carrying a pickaxe handle and moved in for the kill. With one swift blow he caught me on the back of my neck and put me out of action for the time being. I lay on the coral runway in a stunned heap until I regained my senses. Eventually, in a dazed fashion, I found my way back to the rail car and kept my mouth shut. It was a painful lesson re-learned. It was not always easy to keep one's mouth shut.

Since the end of the monsoon season and the onset of the hot dry conditions in which we worked every day, the guards usually allowed us to have a drum of water on the airstrip near the main work area. Every day we carried a coconut shell or billy can and a spoon to work so that we would have something from which to eat when the mid-day meal arrived. This consisted of dried rice, full of weevils, which we looked upon as protein, and predictably the watery *katella* soup. Occasionally (may be two or three times) we had the remains of a water buffalo. On one momentous occasion the guards had two cows tied to the trees outside the fenced area of the cookhouse. We hoped and prayed these would end in our soup and sure enough some of the intestines and bones did just that. But for the majority of us the only enjoyment of this episode was the aroma that wafted across the parade square into our pinched nostrils. We were past the stage of thinking that the Japanese would bring anything in the way of good and substantial food to us. We were expendable labour. There could be no doubt about that. The primitive conditions of living on Haruku represented to us a deadly situation. For the Japanese and Korean guards the food situation was normal fare. Certainly for them there was no shortage of food and very little sickness. As far as we could observe none of them lost weight - just their tempers. One guard had committed suicide. We never did find out the reason.

I was walking over to the barrel of water, situated on the jungle side of our work party, when there was a great commotion and some of the fellows started running parallel to the jungle. Looking up to see what was happening I spotted a beautiful wild black pig of great proportions. Food, running around so close to us— so near, so big, so fast, so fat. Like a school of fish we reacted without hesitation. With tool in hand the chase was on. However, the smarter fellows shouted for us to stop running and for the guards to shoot it. Everyone froze in his tracks and started yelling for the guards to shoot the pig. They just stood there and watched as a fantastic meal disappeared into the jungle. There was great excitement and the basis of much imaginative speculation as to just how and what would have been done if the lucky creature had been unlucky.

It was not long after this that I found a three quarter square inch piece of water buffalo hide. It was about half an inch thick and made a most welcome and unique piece of chewing gum. It lasted me for many days and was unfortunately stolen by the rats one night. My first suspicion was that the rat may have been two legged so I watched carefully to see who, that bunked close by, would spend the day chewing my special piece of gum. It turned out that the Japanese had given our cooks the remains of a water buffalo that had been their rations; no doubt it was on the verge of going rotten. I was lucky enough to be walking past the cookhouse when I spied this morsel in the sand.

We experienced a rather amusing incident about midnight when all was quiet in camp. A large rat surfaced at one end of the hut on a level with everybody's head. It apparently had a destination at the other end of the hut in a straight line from where it started. The result was that it ran over every head, about fifty of them, in that section of the hut. This awakened most of us so that every one sat up to see what had happened. But is was too late to do anything about it. The lucky devil escaped with his life and no doubt my gum. One just speculated as to what was on those clammy wet feet before it started on its face-lifting journey. At this time rats were being sold for fifty cents each and mice for twenty-five cents. This one was extremely lucky to get away with his life. To give you some idea of just how valuable these little creatures were a whole hand of bananas could be bought for ten cents or less.

We were allowed to have fires in the camp close to our huts. This made life easier as we could cook the leaves and roots that we found. Everybody experimented with anything that looked edible. We were in the jungle one day on Flat Face's party when we came across a swampy area with what looked like bull rushes growing quite profusely. The only difference was that the knob at the top of this bull rush, instead of being a dark brown colour, was bright red and consisted of dozens of tiny berries. One of the braver men took a great bite of the berries. He was still alive in two minutes so the whole area was picked clean in a flash. I never did find out what these plants were but they were edible for sure. We saw them only once.

Now with more Japanese troops on the island we could see the reason for our next surprise. On the routine march to the airstrip one morning we were really surprised to see, squatting on the roadside, six Japanese or Korean women chatting away to their hearts' content and gazing at us in stunned bewilderment. We were obviously the first White men they had ever seen, and what a scrawny bunch at that. They must have wondered what kind of an enemy their God Emperor had chosen to fight. Scrawny, near naked white men staggering down the road hardly represented a worthwhile target for their fanatical army. We asked the Emperor, the most civilised of our guards, if he had visited the newly established brothel. He shook his head in a most definite manner and told us this was not good. The Emperor allowed us to bow by nodding the head rather than the full formal bow. The Emperor was our favourite guard. I am sure he disapproved of the terrible business that he was caught up in. He did his duty as he saw it. He was distant from the degradation that surrounded him. He was fair and civilised, which is all that we expected of any of our captors.

Bowing was probably the reason most prisoners were slapped about. Every guard was in a position to say your bow was not correct and then stand back and make you bow several times while he enjoyed the prestige of being momentarily more than a peasant. Sometimes when they hauled one of our officers over the coals for incorrect bowing they felt that they should at least return the bow. Now we would watch as these two bowed to each other in quick succession. The British officer, having been made to bow, did not know when to stop and the Nip peasant was not quite sure why the officer was giving him more than one bow. A novel form of entertainment!

The Japanese have looked down on the Koreans for many centuries. The Koreans are, to the Japanese way of thinking, a people to be subjugated to every whim and wish of their God Emperor. Now in this wartime situation they could be used as camp guards and for other menial tasks, but not for fighting. This was the prerogative of the noble warrior class, the Samurai, who ruled over a dependable, fanatical, highly indoctrinated, peasant population ready and able to sacrifice life for their Sun-God Emperor. Men who had left nail and hair clippings at home so their wives or parents would have a remembrance of them. Men who expected to die in the noble cause their God Emperor had chosen for them. Our guards were mostly Koreans, and unknown to us harboured this inbred hatred of the Japanese. We were always looking for ways to make trouble between the guards but this information would have been of little use to us, as the Koreans were terrified of the Japanese, and especially Blood whom they saw in action every day.

A cage was constructed at the edge of camp, and close to the guardhouse. Most native buildings are constructed of bamboo and *atap*. In this case the *atap* was closely woven and assembled in a tight fashion, almost as if the aim was to have an airtight enclosure. The result was a dark and almost airless cage about three to four feet wide and six feet long. In the tropics the roof is usually placed at least a foot above the walls to allow for a circulation of air. But not in this case. Soon after the cage was finished, but with one end hinged open, two natives were dragged down to the hut and thrown in. They had obviously suffered terrible beatings and were only just conscious. The end wall was put into position and secured with rope. How long they were in there before they received a meal I don't know. Eventually our camp staff saw a plate being pushed under the bottom row of *atap*. There were no sanitary facilities, with the result that the whole camp soon became aware of just what was going on. When the smell got to be totally unbearable and the poor devils had suffered enough to satisfy Blood's lust for discipline, they were dragged away - never to be seen again. As Blood was making money on all the purchases that came into camp there was no doubt, in our minds, that these poor devils had crossed him in some way. "Asia for the Asiatics."

One night soon after the monsoons had finished and we were all thoroughly dried out I was not sleeping well, and figured I could get down to the beach and enjoy a moment of solitude without having to pass the guard and consequently be under scrutiny. It was easy to get in and out of camp for the barbed wire was not effective and the guards knew we had nowhere to go. They patrolled their assigned paths and no doubt dreamed of better times. The path to the toilet built over the sea was on a gradual slope from the camp huts to the beach and off to one side of the camp. I decided not to go past the guard but to slip under the wire half way down the slope. I determined that the guard was at the top end of his run and so I would have only to worry about getting into camp again. Slipping under the wire I walked quickly down to the beach and then headed in the direction of the stream that supplied the camp. The nice bright tropical night with clear white sand under foot was a real pleasure. This was the first time I had been alone since that night on the hole, months ago, when I had made the momentous decision to not eat extra rice unless I had a supplement to go with it - - a life saving decision.

Lying on the beach with the breeze gently wafting over my *jawat* clad body was so relaxing, yet I dare not shut my eyes. If I had gone to sleep outside the camp wire Blood would have another victim to boast about. I would have to satisfy myself with this brief sojourn into a life that was not to be ours. On my feet again I walked along the beach and crouched in the bushes beside the pathway waiting to hear the guard on his patrol. I must have waited twice as long as it takes for the guard to do this one patrol and nothing had happened. In spite of being on the path to the toilet I did not want to come in contact with the guard as he might well remember that no one had recently been to the latrine. They always made a fuss about bowing so it would not be difficult, even for one of these peasants, to remember who had passed them during the last hour, at this time of night.

Fearing that something had developed while I was lying on the beach I started to walk up the path which was on the outside of the wire when I heard the foot steps of the guard coming down the path. Too far along the path to beat a retreat, I had only one way to go and that was under the bottom strand of wire. I figured the guard was so close that if I tried to separate the strands of wire to climb through he would see me. However if I crawled under the bottom strand the bushes would shield me for that extra life-giving moment. There were bushes on the inside of the wire so it would be easy enough to hide if only I could get my body past that low strand. Much to my surprise it was quite tight, being the lowest strand, and only about six inches off the ground I guess that it had been the easiest to tighten. I eased under, but had to let go of the wire to hide my body as the guard was now too close for comfort. In letting go of the wire one barb pierced the calf of my right leg which was still on the wrong side of the wire. I had no alternative but to drag my leg under the wire with the barb sticking into it. A razor makes a nice clean cut but this galvanised barb left a jagged six-inch tear in my muscle and an enormous amount of pain. This was all the more distressing as cuts turned to ulcers. I lay frozen to the ground with my back towards the pathway. Unable to see the guard I had no idea if he was even remotely aware of my presence. Slowly he paced on his way down the path and I quietly lifted the wire barb out of the calf and moved back to the hut. If the guard had been fully awake I would not have had a chance. What price solitude?

Nightly bombing excursions were being carried out by the Americans. Ambon was a major military base and only a hundred kilometres from us. The town itself was little more than a glorified village, but one with a four hundred year history that involved the great European trading powers of past centuries. The day came when, as we arrived back at camp, there was great excitement. George Barnes had seen a twin fuselage fighter plane skimming at sea level in the direction of Ambon. This was soon identified as a P 38 Lockheed Lightening. The really great news for us was the fact that we were now within fighter range of the closest American base. Since the time of our arrival in May 1943, we had been well within bomber range but now the Americans must have made great advances in New Guinea to put us in fighter range. George was one of the men in camp who kow-towed to the Japanese. He received extra rations for doing their menial tasks; consequently he was not regarded very well by the rest of us.

This awareness that the Americans were closing in and the fact that the death rate had dropped drastically made life on camp more of a routine work world. The fact remained that we were expendable, but the process had slowed down considerably. Did this coincide with the turn of the tide? Or was it a fact that those surviving were the especially hardy types who are, by nature, survivors?

This new turn of events created a new and heavy-duty work party for us. Like all Japanese outposts this would be defended to the last man, and that meant building shelters and pillboxes for the defenders. Most of the coconut palms grew at sea level but the defences were to be constructed on the slopes above the beaches and around the airstrip. Our job was to carry coconut trees from the sea to the upper levels of the island. About fifteen men were assigned to a tree. Coconut palms are dense and heavy. Just getting a tree as awkward as this on our shoulders was quite a skill but one we learned in a hurry. The palm tree would be carried on alternating shoulders. In this fashion half the men had their heads on one side of the tree and the others on the other side. To get a tree up the slope of a coral hill on a narrow and treacherous path is not easy. You start off with the weight being fairly evenly distributed between the all the men, a heavy task at the best of times. Now to proceed up a hill where the path is at various stages up or down means that the weight of the entire tree rests on two or three or four people depending on the terrain. This is murder, as the tendency is to cave in under the weight or to jettison the tree. To jettison the tree may be death to the others who happen to be on the wrong side of it at the crucial moment. Sometimes the tree would be as much as three feet above you as the ends were on high points in the path. Alternatively those in the middle of the tree would be carrying the monster as the men on the ends walked free. Added to all this, many of the trees were home to a variety of ants and other insect life. Most insects when disturbed want to find a nice hole out of the sunlight in which to hide. Ears, nose and an open mouth make an ideal homing area when the panic to get out of the way is paramount. Panting hot breath in the tropics is not a deterrent to a colony of frightened red ants. When holding on to a tree, for the safety of all is more important than the comfort of the individual, and consequently an intolerable situation faced each individual quite frequently. Apart from a variety of insects wanting to hide, the red ants have a nasty bite.

The saving grace of this particular work party was "millionaires' salad." The heart of the palm is snuggled away in the centre of the fronds, a tasty dish that can be eaten on the spot. We would hack off the fronds and get to the tasty centre of the living area. When the guards saw that we were eating part of the tree they wanted to know what was so good about it. They could not understand why we liked it so much. They never did catch on to the fact that we had fed them the bitter outside sections, which looked exactly the same as the tender centre area.

On this job our lunch break would be called while we were on the beach chopping down coconut trees or cutting the tops off before carrying them to their bunker site. A new hazard developed as we moved into a site that had old ripe coconuts still in the fronds high above. Sitting under the palm casually slurping *katella* soup, one of the fellows was shocked out of his wits as a ripe coconut fell like a bomb from fifty feet above him. Luckily it missed his thigh by a few inches and supplemented his meals for two days.

While we were building these bunkers for the defence of Haruku we were ordered to another job site in so much of a hurry that they put us on the back of a three ton truck and drove off along a beach side road. We were all facing the front of the truck and traveling at about twenty miles per hour when there was the incredible roar of a P38 just above tree top height with guns blazing — we were the target. Our reaction was the immediate evacuation of this moving truck. Bodies were flying in all directions as the bullets pock-marked the side of the road, fortunately for us a safe distance behind us. The truck stopped and the driver dashed for cover but it was too late as the fighter was well on its way to the real target for the day. This was just a bit of target practice. We all survived without anything worse than a good shake up, in spite of being the target. We loved every moment of it — irrevocable testimony to the fact that the Americans were on the way. After an episode of this nature we would discuss at great length what the pilot would have for lunch when he got to base, lucky devil. If on his next sortie he would drop the garbage cans from their cookhouse we would live like kings for a day.

One night, long after 'lights out' there was the most colossal disturbance. Guards were running around to each hut getting people off the *bali-bali* as some huts were paraded at the foot of their respective *bali-bali* beds. When Slime arrived at each hut all men were ordered to lie on the bamboo with their feet over the edge so that a Korean guard could walk past and feel the feet of each man. Funny people these Koreans. Apparently, after a few huts had been inspected in this manner they thought up an alternative method of finding out what they wanted to know. Again Slime gave the order to each hut that all men must stand at the end of the *bali-bali*. This time the guards put their ear to each mans chest— listening to the heartbeat. Nothing much came of this disturbing night but there was a great deal of speculation.

It appeared that three or four men had tried to get to a motorised sampan that had been seen that evening at anchor a short distance from shore and within easy swimming distance of camp. Something went wrong with the plan and the fellows had to abort the effort and return to camp. One of the guards had spotted the returning men and immediately raised the alarm. The one place in camp that all the guards were afraid of was No.1 ward, the death ward; the ward with the worst of the dysentery cases, the ward that fed tomorrow's burial party. No.1 ward was also closest to the beach. Quickly the men decided to hide in this safe haven. This gave them enough time to get into camp, dry themselves, and pretend to be asleep or to stay hidden in the ward. The only clothes they had were the shorts or *jawat* they stood in. These were easily disposed of as they either kept wearing the *jawat* or lay naked on the bali-bali. I heard of this story from my good friend Tom Coles but I was not in one of the huts involved in the searching that night. Was this a genuine escape attempt? No one was talking. Never again was a boat left at anchor near the camp.

In spite of our enthusiasm, and considerable art for stealing, we confined this practice to stealing from outside the camp. During these hard times I am sure the natives did not mind our taking the coconuts that fell. Most of the roots and leaves that we gathered were growing wild. We respected the obviously cultivated plots of land, as they must be owned by someone little better off than we were. The Japanese did not recognise that the coconut palms belonged to anyone. On a small island like Haruku the harvesting rights of coconut palms were allocated to individuals even if they were in a public area. As soon as the Americans were within threatening distance the palm trees were felled. We had noticed this total disregard for other peoples' property in Java. We had been ordered on many occasions to knock down a wall or smash a connecting hole through some property on the whim of a corporal or sergeant in charge of a work party.

This respect for the possessions of fellow prisoners meant that discipline in camp was not an issue. The most common disciplinary problems in the services are concerned with fighting and stealing. With a common and sadistic enemy there seemed to be a collective realisation that one must not step out of line. Fighting was out of the question, for there was enough brutality in our daily lives without our contributing to an already ghastly situation. Our own officers would be reluctant to discipline anyone under these terrible circumstances and reporting a culprit to the guards was out of the question. Generally speaking, the harshness of the daily actions of the Japanese put enough fear in all of us to obviate internal discipline. Living so close to death and watching our mates die on a daily basis inculcated a respect for individuals and the group as a whole. This created a unique situation where discipline was not a problem because there was group concern for the group itself and for the individuals comprising that group.

1   In fact 650 of the worst sick cases left the camp bound for Java. The Suez Maru was sunk in the Java Sea a short time later with the loss of 548 men (the other official figure obtained from the Dutch records state 539 were lost). This large discrepancy gives the reader some idea of just how difficult it was to maintain important records. I have not been able to determine what happened to the missing men. Given a death rate of 10-12 men a day and knowing the delays between boarding a craft and the departure time anything is possible. There may have been a transfer of men to another boat before leaving Ambon. I took part in a commemorative service conducted by Air Chief Marshall Sir Michael Armitage KCB CBE RAF (Rtd) in December 1994, on the spot where the Suez Maru was sunk. My very good friend Tom Coles of the Muna sinking experience was with me. Courtesy the Caledonia Star.

2   When the seven hundred men arrived in Ambon it coincided with the arrival of Japanese wounded soldiers from New Guinea. Many of our men were taken off the transport and the Japanese put on board. By the grace of God my good friend George Crowsley was one of the men taken off the ship and moved to Liang camp, Ambon.

3   Scabies is a skin rash and intensely itchy - caused in part by malnutrition. Java Balls, a form of scrotal dermatitis, was caused entirely by malnutrition. A most uncomfortable disease involving a weeping suppurating scrotum that forces one to walk with legs wide apart.

4   New information has come to light since the first printing of my book. Thirty-one men died on Ceram. Twenty-eight from disease and three beheaded. These three were left behind with the assurance of the major in charge of the camp that an investigation would be conducted into their escape attempt. Immediately the camp was vacated the major and Col. Anami ("...where the food will be very good...") watched the men being beheaded.

9

HARUKU & AMBON

DEAD NATIVES. WE ARE ALL TRASH

And our hearts ...like muffled drums,
are beating funeral marches to the grave.
H.W. Longfellow 1807-1882

We arrived on the airstrip and the jobs were being allocated for the day. My particular group was assigned to pushing the railroad cars back and forth to move the coral — two men to a car. I was on the airstrip side of my car and therefore under the eye of the guards. On the other side of the cars the open field, long grass, and a slope down to the palm shrouded shore. We had a beautiful view across the deep blue water to the island of Ceram, though we were not in a position to enjoy this ideal setting. Our hunger dictated that we concentrate on the jungle and scheme some way of gathering roots and leaves. There was a great deal of shouting back and forth as we vented our frustration on the Japanese and they yelled back for us to keep quiet and work harder. It was not always easy to keep one's mouth shut. A feeling shared by most of us was to the effect that we actually had little to lose as it seemed that life was closely related to time. Men were dying every day and conditions remained the same. How long could one survive under these conditions? There was nothing to live for. Our daily work was for the advantage of the enemy, in contravention of the Geneva Convention and against all civilised moral standards. Continual hunger, beriberi, malaria, dengue fever, starvation, and beatings made our existence drag from one day to the next. We did not know the day of the week, the date of the month or even the month of the year. If we suspected a birthday was on the horizon we could find out the date from the officers who were trying to keep some record of the situation. We had not seen a piece of paper since arriving on Haruku, let alone a printed-paper. The normal amenities of life had long ago been given up as the Japanese considered us to be totally unworthy. We buried our dead every evening when we got back to camp. Our life was like a roulette wheel. Every morning the roulette wheel was spun. We worked through the day to find at night that the little ball had hit the wrong hole for another group of men. Our gamble was to keep the little ball rolling. Surely when the last day's work was done the last man would die. What a perfect job — for them — totally expendable labour! This appeared to be what they were working towards. Blood would get a medal and more gold teeth. Another hero for their God Emperor. Another Master for The Greater East Asia Co-prosperity Sphere.

My notes (written in camp after the bombs dropped) for this period tell me that our daily routine was to be awakened at 6:00am, paraded and counted at 6:05am. This usually took the best part of half an hour, as, for the life of them, these little martinets couldn't count. Breakfast of pap was at 6:35 am and work parade at 6:45 am. We were now counted again and had to be marched to a designated work area at 7:00 am. It is interesting to note that the fifteen minute breakfast did not give us enough time to wash our billy cans as this meant running to the stream to wash them out. This was out of the question so licking was the answer. If, by chance, one iota of pap was missed, which was highly unlikely, then the ants would clean the billycan, plate or coconut shell, when we started work.

When we arrived at the strip our marching column was halted and allocated the different work projects for the day. We worked continuously for two hours and then had a ten-minute break. During this time any perceived infraction of the nebulous rules, or perhaps laziness, was punished. This could be anything from talking too loudly to stopping for a minor injury, such as cuts, bruises, stumbling on the coral, being hit by flying coral sent up by a glancing blow of a pickaxe. Most of these little delays were punished. The ignorance of our guards caused the punishment to make more delays. A favourite trick of the guards was to make a man stand with two big lumps of coral, one in each hand, and the hands raised sideways and level with the shoulders. Now the guard would stand with his rifle and bayonet placed about two inches beneath an outstretched hand. As you tired, your hand lowered with the weight of the coral rock and would naturally impale it self on the bayonet. Of course we tried to avoid this, with the result that this little torture was set up again after a good whack across the head. After the guard had succeeded in drawing blood he sent you back to work. However if he was feeling miserable then the process would be repeated with the other hand. Holding heavy chunks of coral over your head was another favoured trick. This time the guard would try to ensure that the rock fell on one's head after getting tired.

One hour was allowed for lunch. It was brought to the strip by truck and consisted of two barrels, one full of rice and one full of soup. The soup was watery with a few *katella* leaves on the bottom. This meant that the soup had to be continually stirred so that each man would get his fair share of leaves. It took nearly an hour to serve lunch as there was only one server and usually at least two hundred men to be served. Hundreds of starving men will watch carefully that no one gets more than his fair share. Here we are talking about half dozen grains of rice. It is not easy to be that precise. Two or three hundred pairs of hungry eyes watching the cook's every move makes him - oh, so careful. The trick was to be first in line and then drink your soup while forming another line to have what was left in the barrel. This was called the "Leggi" line. It had started for us in Semarang and was a fact of life until "the atomic bombs" were dropped. If your particular work party was at the other end of the strip or at some other location then most of your hour was taken up in marching to the lunch area. We were never formed up to march anywhere without counting, not a simple matter for the guards.

The utensils for serving both the rice and the soup had been made especially for the purpose. The rice ladle was made like the bottom quarter of any ordinary vegetable tin except it was about four inches in diameter and an inch and a half high. The cook would hold this in one hand and a flat piece of wood in the other hand. Dipping the ladle into the barrel of rice he would scoop out a ladle full and then compress it into the ladle, with a piece of wood in his other hand, smooth off the top so that the amount in the ladle would be the same for each prisoner. Simple. This should be a fair method of serving a meal. However when you have extremely hungry men watching this process there are many accusations of putting too much pressure on the ladle and therefore favouring friends. Of course this was a possibility but most of us went along with the system. The server had the most favourable job in camp and could not afford to lose it. In most cases when a move took place and a cook lost his job in the new camp the shock of reduced rations was too severe for survival. On some of the longer boat moves the cooks did not survive the journey. In all our camps the cooks were always the men with the most flesh on their bones. Maybe I was lucky in doing this job only once, and that before the conditions really deteriorated.

After lunch we carried on with our work until 6:00pm when we were formed up to march back to camp. During the five-hour afternoons we had two ten minute breaks. The only concession the Japanese made to us was to allow a man to boil water for drinking. There was a scramble every day to get the job of "hot water" man. In this position one could wander off to the jungle and pick up wood to keep the fire going. This also meant that one had the opportunity of gathering roots and leaves - a most advantageous situation. If one proved to be good at this job he kept it until falling out with the guard over some disagreement, or for staying in the jungle too long for the amount of wood collected. In spite of the effort to boil water to purify it, it was seldom successful. It took a very big fire to get 60 gallons boiling. This would be emptied after our mid day time break by hundreds of thirsty prisoners, and the whole process started again.

During the dry season the water was boiled, on rare occasions, but this was seldom, if ever, accomplished during the monsoons.

Back at camp there were a variety of jobs waiting for us. The burial party varied in number depending on how many had died in the past twenty-four hours. During the height of the dysentery epidemic we buried thirteen men in a single day in a common grave. A well was constructed in camp for the use of the guards. This involved a party of men having to carry stones from the river to the well site. These stones were about eighteen inches in diameter and seemed to weigh fifty pounds each. It was a long uphill haul and a heavy task at the end of a scorching day under the sun. Wood had to be carried from a jungle site to the cookhouse. Here again we were forced to carry as much as possible and for a far greater distance, but it seemed to be a better job than carrying the well stones. Frequently bamboo has very fine hairs growing along its stem. To shoulder this and then find you have an ear full of these itchy little hairs was another of the little annoyances. Smaller stones were carried for a road project that was going on adjacent to the camp. Sometimes as we marched back to camp from the strip we were diverted to the village dock. Here each man had to carry six or eight bamboo poles, each twelve foot long back to camp or to the new Japanese quarters that were being built near the strip. Stores had to be carried from one place to another. There were always jobs to be done after we finished a day's work. Since the dry season had arrived we had been working every day for some months.

Squadron Leader Pitts complained to Kurashima that many men were exhausted. He wanted Captain Kurashima to give us a day totally free of all work. As the Commanding Officer of the camp I believe he would have authorised this without hesitation. Kurashima had been in charge of a camp in Java and our men said he had been reasonable at that time. That was before Blood came on the scene. It must have taken a great deal of courage for our officers to approach the Japanese as their usual reaction was one of violence. His courage and good intentions resulted in our doing more work for longer hours as Blood reaped his revenge for this audacious move. This situation was most unusual and only pertained because of the personalities involved and the extreme isolation of the camp. A beating was a natural reaction to any request that involved the slightest degree of humanity, compassion, or civilised behaviour.

One afternoon we were returned to camp early, we could only speculate as to the reason. Rumours buzzed. Maybe we would get a few hours to ourselves?

By this time the camp was in good shape. The parade ground was a large glaring patch of white sand clearly visible from the air. Every grain had been carried up the hill from the beach by both sick and fit officers and men at different times during the past few months.

On arrival in camp we were ordered to the parade ground in single file so

Blood and Slime

that each man had an uninterrupted view of the square. We waited in the late afternoon sun. A fellow Canadian prisoner was brought into the centre of the square and stood to attention under the uneasy watch of every man in camp. Our worst fears were confirmed when Blood, with his usual psychotic demeanour, appeared dressed in his finery - - jack boots, sword dragging at his side. Slime a few pace behind him. He walked up to the poor devil and started his frightening harangue. The 'trial' had begun. Slime told us the man had stolen a can of food from the Japanese storehouse. Blood, with lightening speed, struck the man in the face. He quietly stood his ground and of course was not allowed to strike back. The blows now came with such alarming speed that the Canadian was knocked off his feet. He was felled, staggered to his feet only to be felled again and again. I lost count of how many times this happened. The image of Blood kicking the life out of a fellow prisoner was vividly impressed on the whole camp. The beating continued until the man could no longer raise himself to his feet. He lay there unconscious - a heap of bloody flesh. We, the unwilling "spectators", felt enormous sympathy for this man. His sheer guts at rising to be beaten again and again showed us that even in our starved and demoralised state we had something these belligerent individuals could not take away from us.

Blood left the scene with his tailpiece, Slime, shuffling a few paces behind him. We got the message about stealing from the glorious saviours of the Greater East Asia Co-Prosperity Sphere.

As soon as Blood was off the parade ground the orderlies carried the broken mass of flesh and blood to the hospital where he died a short time later. A brutal beating to satisfy the lust of a syphilitic mad man who appointed himself judge, jury and executioner for a can of food.

A few hours to our selves? When would we learn the true nature of our captors?

"Lights out" in camp was at 9:00 pm. This is a very grand title for the few coconut oil lamps or candles that existed. For the vast majority of us the lights were out when the sun went down. As we left the strip at 6:00 pm this in theory gave us three hours to ourselves. The march back to camp could quite easily take an hour or more, depending on the extra jobs to be done on the way back. If there were none, then there were the fatigues to do in camp. The end result was that we were lucky to be finished with the day at 7:00pm. For those of us who had a jungle job during the day, now was the time to cook up the hunting and gathering proceeds of that day. During this half hour we might be able to go to the stream or the beach with its latrine built close to the low tide mark. Here we could clean our filthy, discoloured, ulcerated bodies.

The lights in camp were all oil lamps. Most of them used coconut oil. Coconut oil is useful for cooking so we seldom had a light in camp. We did discover that a fairly creditable light can be made by putting some coconut oil in a half coconut shell and then using an old dried out coconut seed cover as a wick. This gave about one candlepower and served the purpose for any of the things that we might have to do after dark. Since we had absolutely nothing except a few simple necessities the only jobs to do after dark were to find a lost clomper, piece of clothing or some other article of our meagre possessions. Those who were lucky enough to have started prisoner life with full kit were now down to bare necessities.

The birds on Haruku were some of the most beautiful to be found anywhere in the world. We tried desperately to catch them but only on rare occasions did this happen. Iguanas were caught every now and then and what a delight for the lucky person who could boast of iguana meat for supper. Strangely enough there were no monkeys on the island.

The strip was now so far advanced that it was a common sight to see a truck being driven the length of it. Haruku, the island of the camel's humps was now an unsinkable aircraft carrier. A landing strip that had cost many hundreds of R.A.F. and Dutch army lives. A landing strip that could have been built in a few short weeks with the right equipment had taken more than fifteen months of hard labour. It was now time for the planning staff to visit. A few senior Japanese officers, with the attendant yelling and screaming on the part of our guards, now came to inspect our handy work. Apparently they were satisfied for a few days later as we were working on the jungle side of the strip a Navy Zero circled the runway and much to our surprise attempted to land. It soon became evident to us that he had no way of judging the height of his approach. A pure white coral landing strip beneath a tropical sun gives off a tremendous heat haze. The first pass seemed to be normal but he started landing about fifteen feet off the ground and cautiously lowered the fighter until he was about three feet off the ground by this time he had used up the length of the runway and had to gun it for another attempt. He used much the same procedure the second time around. The third time he changed tactics by flying low and lowering his tail until it touched the runway. Here was a pilot with considerable skill. We watched with intense excitement as he kept nudging his tail down, down a little more, down again, until he felt the good earth under him. By this time he had used up the length of the runway and circled out to sea for another attempt. On his fourth try he managed to gauge the height of the shimmering heat haze. It was an unconventional landing but a successful one.

This new strip now presented them with a new and probably unforeseen problem. Heat haze was not an easy problem to combat. Whether they counteracted this successfully or not I do not know. I doubt it, as the Americans were making frequent flights over the area and the Japanese time and resources were limited. We knew that the Yanks were getting close because we were now in the range of P 38 Lightnings. It seemed most unlikely that the Americans would allow a new operational field to be set up when they had control of the air.[1]

Soon after this I was asked by Dr. Philps if I would like to become a medical orderly and work in the hospital. I leaped at this opportunity because it would give me a chance to help my fellow prisoners rather than working directly for the Japanese. We had over three hundred and fifty deaths by this time and the draft of six hundred and fifty sick men transferred to Java. There was now room in the camp to house everybody. Instead of fourteen inches of bed space on the bamboo slats we now had about twenty-four inches for the workers and the sick hospital patients had more than this. I moved my meagre possessions to the orderlies' hut and was instructed to wash my hands in permanganate potash every time I touched the patients. An enamel basin was kept at the entrance of each hut for this purpose. This was my orderlies' training for there was nothing much in the way of medicines with which to treat the patients.

My first day in these new surroundings coincided with my first attack of malaria since leaving Java. I felt that this might jeopardise my job as medical orderly, with the result that I would soon be back on the strip. One of the Dutch doctors took my temperature. I watched him closely as he shook his head and put the thermometer under my tongue again. He could not believe the reading which I found out later to be over 108 degrees. Needless to say I was totally out of it. I wanted to curl up and sweat myself to death. After a day of sweating and shivering came a day of comparative rest followed by another day of uncontrolled sweating and violent shaking. I do not know how many days I was out of action but thanked my lucky stars when I was strong enough to get on my feet again. One is so totally helpless under these conditions. Knowing that the Nips are on the prowl all the time contributes to the utter hopelessness of the situation.

I was soon going around the wards and having a totally new world opened up to me. The worst of the dysentery epidemic was long past, but now the hospital was full of those who had advanced beri-beri, numerous ulcers, bouts of malaria and a few men who had lost their sight as a result of malnutrition and the strong glare of the white coral as we worked on the strip. Dr. Springer performed a successful appendix operation under the crudest of conditions.

Having spent all my time on the various outside working parties I had no idea what life in the hospital was like. My first visit to No 1 ward was a shocker. I walked down the centre aisle with scrawny lifeless bodies on either side of me. Men who were only skin and bone with puny little bits of flesh hanging where muscles should be. I was devastated. Had I made the right decision to work for my buddies? I soon realised that it was far more important for me to be in here, regardless of the conditions, rather than out in the sun and rain working for an enemy that wanted to starve me to death. When I had finished taking in my new surroundings I mentioned to the doctor that one of the men had a scrotum swollen and heaving. I asked him what this condition was. The poor devil had been given up for dead in an effort to save other more promising lives. Flies had laid eggs in the cut on his scrotum and now maggots were developing inside this man. Other men, who by shear willpower had overcome fantastic odds, had been in the ward for a long time, lying curled up in the fetal position for the lack of space. Now the ligaments behind their knees shortened so that they were incapable of walking. In fact they could not straighten their legs, which were permanently bent at the knees. The doctors had arranged for orderlies to get some rocks from the beach, string from an old rice sack and assemble a weight tied to a patient's leg and strung over a bar at the foot of the bamboo. The constant weight of the rock would supposedly stretch the ligaments towards their normal position. I do not remember a single case of successful recovery. This little trip through No 1 ward made me aware that there is always someone worse off than you are!

When the Americans bombed the air strip, the doctors, Forbes and Philps, wanted to get there immediately, but were frustrated by the Japanese not allowing them to leave camp. As the result of the delay of many hours, one of the fellows died. The Japanese doctor was not the least concerned with the native casualties and went as far as delaying until the next day all the efforts of Forbes and Philps to assist these bombed victims. "Asia for the Asiatics" was again proved to be a myth. Asia for the Japanese was the reality. The British and Dutch colonial systems were heavenly compared to this immoral disregard for humanity. The Indonesians had changed the Japanese slogan to; "The Greater East Asia Co-Poverty Sphere".

I was introduced to the placebo system of relieving pain. The Japanese brought a few hundred tablets of soda bicarbonate onto the camp. These were large tablets and under orders of the camp doctors the chemist, Joch Bowman, broke them into four pieces. They then became M & B 693, the miracle drug of the day, aspirin, and a host of other confidence-inspiring cures. They usually had the desired effect. I learnt how to inject sterilised water into the arm of a suffering patient letting him know that the doctor had prescribed something precious recently received on camp. This proved to be most helpful as all the patients wanted was the fighting chance that this kind of treatment provided.

Soon after a work party returned from the "Yasume Barracks," (this was a new work detail that had sprung up when the Japanese presence on the island was increased to activate the operational aspects of an advanced fighter aeroplane base) I ran into Blackie, who was wearing a most contented smile. He had obviously accomplished some worthy deed during the day. This was his story. When his work party arrived at the Japanese barracks he had been assigned clean up duties at the rear of one of the huts. When he got to the scene he found a ladder propped up against the barrack wall with a piece of board placed from one of the rungs to the wall. On this board was a crude sort of nest for a chicken that one of the Japanese sergeants owned. While Blackie was cleaning up around the ladder the chicken laid an egg. With a quick check on every side of the building he determined all was clear and promptly ate this heaven-sent missile. He managed to get rid of most of the shell just before the sergeant appeared. The sergeant immediately spied some fragments of broken shell on the ground and accused Blackie of eating the egg. The quick thinking Blackie pointed to the chicken and made believe he had seen the chicken eat the egg. Without a moment's hesitation the sergeant drew his sword and sliced off the chicken's head. No more eggs for this bright one! And a smile on Blackie's face that lasted all day.

To convince the sergeant that the chicken had eaten the egg Blackie had to perform some dramatic, determined and life-saving gesticulations. All the time making believe that the chicken was the culprit. A performance he will never forget. Just imagine, for a moment, if Blackie had not been able to convince the sergeant that the chicken had eaten the egg. Would the sergeant have sliced off Blackie's head? We knew from long experience that violence was their immediate reaction to a situation they did not like or understand.

I was only in the position of medical orderly for a short time when the order came for the camp to be closed and the prisoners moved. We had an extremely short time to prepare for the move. We did not know if it would take one day or one month. We had no idea of the destination. The only real information we had was that we would move to the small jetty in the village. Fortunately for us it was still standing. We marched, carried and dragged our sick with us to the dock at Pelau. Stretchers were made with two rice sacks and two bamboo poles. There was absolutely no way that these people could walk. They were unable to stand and had to be carried the entire distance to the dock. The parade started first thing in the morning with the inevitable counting procedures. The sick had to be taken out of the hospital and put on the ground as if on parade.

After arriving at the small wooden dock at Pelau Village we waited under the tropical sun for a boat to arrive. The beach was used as a latrine. This meant that we had to carry the sick to the beach every time they had a bowel movement. The main problem was fresh drinking water. We knew there was a stream on the other side of the village as we marched through it every day on the way to work. After much cajoling we talked the guards into letting a few men walk under guard to the stream with some pots. With this basic necessity satisfied, we sat and waited for a boat to arrive. This sounds easy but it was not in the nature of our guards to remain silent for long. They soon found something to yell about and had a small group collecting stones from the beach area and creating a pile beside the road.

Late that afternoon a small boat arrived and some of the sick were loaded into the hold, with a party of fit men to look after them. Shortly after this another boat arrived, approximately the same size - about sixty feet long. It had a hold half full of empty fuel barrels. These were not neatly stacked as one would normally find on a seagoing boat but thrown in a random fashion. This hold was for our group. About seventy-five of us were ordered at bayonet point below decks. The place stank of petrol fumes and did not have a flat area anywhere for anyone to sit or lie. The result was that preference was given to the sick, with the rest of us finding any spot that would accommodate our scrawny soulful bodies. The hatch covers were in place, making this an oven filled with gas fumes. The preferred areas were those that allowed one to have his buttocks on a barrel with his back against another barrel. These were few in number. We spent the night tied to the dock, with an occasional glimpse of the stars. We took it in turns, more or less, to go on deck to relieve ourselves and get away from the stench below. It was almost impossible to get the sick men on deck in time to avoid having them making a mess of the place. It was not long before the concentration of petrol fumes was mixed with the stench of dysentery and diarrhoe. If the Japanese had any consideration for us we could have easily spent the night on the dock, in the fresh air. The fresh sea air caressed the beach and made the palms rustle gently. It could have been a night of relative comfort. It was always a source of wonderment just to watch the perfectly clear heavens with a million twinkling lights and wonder what happens up there. What would it be like to be here as a free man, to really enjoy this beauty and the people that lived here?

The next day about noon we were cast off for an unknown destination. With seventy-five men in a small boat hold half full of gas barrels, our chances looked pretty slim. The Americans were making frequent flights in this area. We had seen P38 Lightnings flying over the sea in the direction of Ambon. This is where the military targets were located. Ambon, the former large Dutch Naval Base, was now doing the same job for the Japanese. The island is not large but still much larger than Haruku. It is the supply base for the Moluccas Archipelago with a large well-protected bay almost dividing the island in two.

On Haruku there were only the two targets - the Japanese barracks and the airstrip. If we were headed for Ambon then the chances of our being in the target area were exceptionally good. After all were we not expendable labour used on military targets? It would have taken only one incendiary shell out of the hundreds per minute that a Lightning fires and our little fish boat would explode into a thousand pieces.

The motion of the boat soon made many of us vomit. Since there was only one exit and that was up a bulkhead ladder there was no chance to be sick over the side. Only one person could exit at a time. The guard on deck would only allow one person to be above at one time so the stinking mess below became increasingly unbearable. By this time we had organised ourselves enough to have a small area set aside for such an emergency. It had already been used by the dysentery patients and was contributing to the general discomfort of all of us but at least it was a confined space. As the heat of the day increased and the hold became insufferable we started asking for water. To request was to ensure a denial. There was no accommodation to feed us and it was becoming apparent that they had no intention of giving us any water. After we brought an unconscious body on deck the skipper appreciated that the situation below was a torment for all concerned. Generally speaking, we had found in Java that the navy personnel were more civilised than the army and particularly the army guards. About an hour later a large pot was brought on to the aft deck with tea in it — so they said. We shared this out as evenly as possible only to find it was half seawater. Many of the sick found this unpalatable and suffered the consequences. With ulcerated mouths and/or throats it was too painful to swallow. I had long since learned that survival meant making the best of a rotten situation. I drank the mixture, slaked my thirst and survived for another day.

Pelau on Haruku is less than sixty-five miles by sea from the large bay on which the town of Ambon is situated. Unknown to us this was our destination. Sometime during the night there was a resounding crack, which shook the barrels and knocked people all over each other. Our first thought was an American attack, with the resulting panic situation in our confined quarters. However, there were the sounds of Japanese voices yelling and the engines cut back. We were docking. Now, with the boat being tied to the dock, the guard became nervous and insisted on half closing the one and only hatch cover that we had been allowed to have open. He stood with his bayonet facing the hatch and cursed anyone who dared to have a pee over the side.

In the morning we were off loaded to the dock and then marched and straggled with our sick a short distance to a road. Counted, re-counted and counted again they seemed to be satisfied that no one had escaped from our hell hole on the tiny boat. Much to our surprise no one had died on that short journey. Here, on the side of the road in a bomb devastated area that we were not familiar with, we had no idea how to tell the guard that water must be available near by. The streams on Haruku had been our friends. Now we were lost. The day wore on as we became dehydrated, having had only partial seawater to quench our thirst during the past twenty-four hours. And we were the lucky ones. Some of those who could not stomach the seawater had gone without. Diluted seawater stung the throats of men with ulcers in their mouth and/or lips. About noon a truck came to pick us up and drove around the bay to Wei Jami (why-ammee) almost directly opposite to the town of Ambon.

Wei Jami camp proved to be a recently abandoned native camp. The natives had been treated the same way we had. However, they did not have either a strong military or civilian organisation to back them up; consequently life was much more of an individual effort to survive. It is hard to imagine the utter hopelessness of their situation. They were dying like flies without the faintest chance of getting medical treatment, without even the rudimentary knowledge of collective sanitary living and nobody to turn to for advice. They were recruited directly into death camps to perform a few months or weeks of labour for their masters before making the supreme sacrifice. These were the workers of "the Greater East Asia Co-prosperity Sphere". In this case, as they were moving out of the camp, some of the men had died and no one had removed their bodies. We were moving into a camp not only with dead bodies in it but in a despicable condition. Graves were dug in great haste, the bodies disposed of and all men put to cleaning up the existing mess.

The first priority was to locate and dig latrines, then to clear the areas that had been used by the natives for this purpose, both inside and outside the wire and in the bushes surrounding the camp. Of course all our facilities had to be within the wired compound. Here again the problem was flies. We could clean the ground inside the camp perimeter but it was equally as bad on the other side of the wire. In true Japanese style of thinking the ground out side the wire, foul as it was, was not a problem connected with flies in the camp. The *bali-bali* (bamboo sleeping platforms) in the huts had been fouled in the same indiscriminate manner as the ground outside the huts and within the perimeter fence.

We could understand to a certain degree why the Nips were treating us as an expendable labour force. We were the enemy and they were acting the part of the uncivilised, barbaric conquerors. This could not, however, account for their attitude towards the Indonesians. To conscript, perhaps millions of men, throughout their newly conquered empire and then treat them with such utter contempt was unforgivable. One would have thought that a modicum of national prestige would have had them clean up the camp so we would not be aware of their method of treating the native population. "Asia for the Asiatics". Of course, as an expendable labour force it did not matter if we knew how they treated the Indonesians. This knowledge would soon go with us to our graves.

The water supply consisted of a single bamboo pipe that was stuck into a stream, somewhere in the jungle, above the camp. This trickled all day and was the only means for the two hundred or more men in camp to have any refreshment. This single supply covered all our needs - - hospital, cookhouse, drinking, cleaning and washing. As other prisoners arrived from various other camps (Liang, Rumah Tiga) our numbers swelled to approximately four hundred and fifty. We did not know it at the time but it appears that they were gathering us together in the face of American advances up the east coast of New Guinea. This cheap labour could be used on many other construction sites. At this time we did not know for sure that it was Japanese Government policy to murder all prisoners of war rather than have them released by an advancing enemy.

There were two other camps of our Haruku survivors on the island of Ambon. Liang and Rumah Tiga (translated from the Indonesian -House 3.) Rumah Tiga was in the same disgusting condition as Wei Jami. Liang was an established POW work camp and a complete hellhole with a comparable death rate to Haruku. It is hard to believe a camp could be worse than Haruku but the kitchen for Liang camp was located some distance from the camp and connected by a rough dirt track. This meant that a lot of food (soup) was lost in spillage between the two points. The staples of our diet were rice and soup. The rice arrived in good shape complete with small stones and weevils but the soup suffered. The cooks wanted to get around this waste by half filling the soup drums, but this was not allowed. The camp was established close to the runway that the men were constructing. This meant that frequent air raids and strafing missions by P38 fighters were an additional hazard that we had not experienced on Haruku. However the most mortifying condition for our men was the fact that the camp was run by British army officers and they had maintained rigid army discipline within the confines of the camp. It was an accepted fact that the Japanese controlled everybody outside the camp, but inside was run by the officers and non-commissioned officers resulting in some harsh punishments. As mentioned previously, on Haruku this had not been necessary.

As the Japanese had no compunction about the use of prisoners on military targets there was no lack of work in Ambon. At this time, July 1944, the Americans and Australians were on their way up the North East coast of New Guinea. At the closest point Ambon is little more than four hundred miles from New Guinea. This put us well within bomber and fighter range of the advancing American and Australian troops.

In early February 1942 the Australian contingent defending Laha on Ambon Island, consisted of approximately three hundred men. Another eight hundred Australians were located on the opposite side of the island. The Japanese invading force had totally overpowered this smaller unit with the result that the majority was captured alive. The Samurai Warrior Rear Admiral Hatakiyama then ordered his staff to murder all prisoners. Holes were dug in a nearby plantation and the unarmed prisoners were either bayoneted to death or beheaded with a sword. The total number murdered by Samurai command exceeded three hundred and thirty officers and men. Australian and Dutch defenders on Ambon. With this knowledge of the recent history of this island, what should we expect from this group?

On parade the following morning one hundred men and one officer, Flying Officer Haddow, were cut off from the main group and marched to an isolated area of Ambon Island. I was designated the medical orderly for this group as we were marched out of camp. If the Japanese would go for this situation it meant that I would simply have the job of applying pressure to any wounds that inevitably develop under these conditions, dressing existing wounds and ulcers with existing old and bloodied bandages and generally trying to be helpful to the sick and almost disabled in a situation where everyone is sick and almost disabled.

After about half an hour of marching we were stopped in an area where the road was only a few feet from the beach. This beach was located in a bay that seemed to be deep, for there was a freighter at anchor about two hundred yards off shore. A crude attempt had been made to camouflage the deck and winches with a liberal sprinkling of palm fronds cut from the surrounding shoreline. Much to our surprise we were told to sit and wait. This seemed to be the most unlikely place to have a group of prisoners working: a ship in the bay, a road close to shore, and jungle on the other side of the road. It was not long before a truck arrived with a lot of *parangs,* (native knives used for slashing jungle and bush—similar to a machete), *chunkel*s and other tools for jungle clearing.

There were no paths off the road but we soon discovered that our job would be to cut a path into the jungle and then make a clearing without destroying any of the high growth. This was obviously to be a storage area concealed from enemy air attack. With a boat at anchor in the bay there was only one part to the puzzle missing—how to get the war goods, for that is what they must be, from the boat to the shore. We worked all day slashing a long pathway and made a start on a clearing under the coconut palms. My job as medical orderly did not materialise as the Japanese wanted a full hundred-man working party, to work like there was no tomorrow. Our bowl of rice and *katella* soup arrived late in the afternoon, for this was the first day in a new camp. Nothing happened at what should have been suppertime. We were kept working. Then sunset and they still expected us to work on clearing the jungle, neither easy nor practical in the dark. Eventually we did get our evening meal - - more rice and *katella* soup. Then after dark, lights appeared on the freighter and the grinding of winches indicated to us that they were starting to unload. The Japanese started prodding us with their bayonets and motioning to the anchored boat. Without an interpreter it was difficult for us to get the message. It seemed to be that they wanted us to swim out to the boat to pick up the cargo. What a totally ridiculous situation! They had no idea if we could swim. While this mad pantomime was being carried out there was a terrific splash as if the cargo had been dropped in the water, with the result that we were now forced at bayonet point and determined screaming, into the water as far as the guards could reach with their bayonets. I doubt that any of them could swim or they would have chased us to the dropped cargo with a bayonet on us all the way.

There was a shout from the boat " *drumo drumo*." Someone on the boat was trying to get the message to us that the drums of gas were now our responsibility. We soon got the idea that we had to swim out to get them. So those of us who could swim went out to the side of the boat and grabbed a barrel. The non-swimmers stayed on shore to roll the barrels into the jungle. It quickly dawned on us that there was great danger in being under the unloading area with the Japanese operating the ship's derricks. The first load had fallen into the water. Each barrel was forty gallons, which roughly worked out to three hundred and fifty pounds (one hundred and sixty Kg). Not a nice way to go — crushed under a Japanese aviation gas drum being off-loaded to fight our own bomber and fighter pilots.

During the night we were fed once again with the usual rice and *katella* soup. Two skimpy meals with a bucket of hot tea for twenty-four hours work. We got organised at the start of the unloading procedure, as soon as we knew what was expected of us. Those who could swim went out to the boat, got hold of a gas barrel, swam ashore with it and passed it on to a non-swimmer who would roll it up the path we had cut that day into the cleared jungle area. Since most of us had clompers (wooden platforms with a strap across the toes) it was not easy to roll barrels into the jungle. Without clompers the trip was unbearable. There are all kinds of hidden sharp sticks, split bamboo, razor edged leaves and protective spines that grow with great profusion in the jungle. The swimmers could handle a barrel the two hundred yards from the boat to the shore much faster than a non-swimmer could roll the barrel into the jungle half the distance. The solution was obvious. We swimmers had to come right out of the water, bare footed, naked, and keep rolling the drums into the dispersal area. In this way there would not be a bottleneck. We were quickly covered with mosquitoes, our feet cut to shreds, with spines and brambles tearing at our bodies. We were once again in the monsoon season. The ship had to be unloaded fast so that it might sneak away to bring another load of war goodies to this advance supply base. It was only after the officers on the ship found that barrels were drifting free of the nebulous unloading zone that we were forced to stay in the sea and swim more barrels to shore. This was typical lack of communication between our two bosses. The gang on shore wanted the barrels dispersed while the crew on board wanted the barrels gathered before drifting too far out to sea. When dawn broke the unloading stopped as the fear of American bomber or fighter attack mounted.

As soon as the winches stopped grinding the Japanese quickly replaced the layer of palm fronds that we had seen the previous day, in an effort to camouflage the ship from the prying American eyes.

After we had been on this job for a month or more, and successfully gathered and eaten all the coconuts in the work area I had a lucky break. I was outside the hospital hut just before our parade time, at sun set, when I heard a " psst, psst," from the bushes out side the wire. Looking over, I saw an old man hiding in the under growth. As I walked towards the barbed wire, he glanced rapidly in the direction of the guards, and then he emerged from his hiding place with a large coconut in his hands. He offered it to me. I declined because I could not pay for it. He was quite shocked and made me understand that this was most definitely a gift. He wore a sarong from the waist down and looked to be in about the same state of hunger as I was. I refused the kind offer and pushed the coconut back to him. But he would have none of it and insisted that I take it. I gave in, knowing that it was easier for him to get another one. This was most welcome as we had stripped all the palms near our work site and had no way of getting any extra food on this job. The risk this fellow took to get near the camp and give a coconut to a prisoner is almost unbelievable. We had seen natives severely beaten for much less than this and heard of others being decapitated for just such an action. There is no doubt that he risked his life to bring some very welcome relief to a man he had never seen before and would never see again. It is obvious where their sympathies lay. The value of a coconut was enormous; quite apart from the food value the husk and the shell make excellent fuel. The husk will smoulder and maintain heat after the volatile shell has given off the required heat to cook some not so tasty morsel. The flesh itself doubled my rations for two days. A real prize. At this stage of our existence I was pretty well on my own as Taffy who had shared my 19th birthday Vienna sausages with me had died on Haruku. Jack had left Haruku on the first sick draft. Penny had died. Blackie had been moved with another group and I lost track of him. Humphrey, and Todd who had fallen out of the Canary nut tree, had left Haruku on the first sick draft. I had been moved from the workers' hut to the orderlies hut and was with a different group of fellows. During the next move I was to meet with Jock Bowman, the camp pharmacist. We both managed to survive the coming year and remained firm friends until his death in the mid nineteen fifties[2]. In fact Jock and I celebrated my 18th-19th -20th- 21st and 22nd birthdays together in 1946. Of all my pals in the Air Force he was the only one to survive those four gruesome years and celebrate with me.

This Laha work party of one hundred men and one officer lost one man, to dysentery, during the few weeks that it lasted. But the effects were to be disastrous for all of us. As it was a nighttime job we were constantly harassed by the guards during the day when we were supposed to be sleeping. We frequently had to take cover as the American bombers and fighters sorted out targets in Ambon just across the bay, and military dispersal areas in the neighbourhood of our camp. On many occasions shrapnel from the exploding bombs landed in the camp and the strafing by Lightnings was far too close for comfort. Many of the men contracted a new kind of fever that we called Ambon fever. It was not as bad as malaria and affected one differently to dengue fever. During the following few months the one hundred men of this party suffered an alarming death rate.

We were amalgamated with the main camp work force and taken to a variety of sites near the town of Ambon, always working on military targets and being harassed daily by P38 fighters. We worked amongst the trees dispersing bombs or petrol, sometimes making defence fox holes lined with coconut trees. It was on this job that I came near to being one of the POW casualties of allied air action. Liberators were over the work site in force, dropping a good load of bombs. We had constructed a six-foot long slit trench and roofed it so that there was enough room for only one man to enter at a time. The idea being that a direct hit would be the only way of killing the occupants, who would be Japanese.

When the bombs started exploding close to us, our guards found a nearby shelter and left us to this new creation. I was the last one to reach the shelter and had the advantage of being able to watch the Liberators with their P38 fighter escorts. I was standing in the foxhole. I had been there only a few moments when I felt as if a huge hand was pushing my head well down into the safety of the covered trench. I did not resist and was soon rewarded by hearing a piece of shrapnel lodge itself into the end of the trench just a few inches over my head. Everybody in the trench had been crouched down as the bombs were falling pretty close to us. Were the gods looking after me by pushing me into the trench at the crucial moment? Had I been standing watching the air display as I was just seconds before, I would surely have been cut in half. What was the force or helping hand that had pushed me into safety? The sliver of shrapnel was about two inches wide and fourteen inches long. Fascinated by this close call I grabbed the bomb sliver to show it to my friends only to find it burned my hand. I had not reckoned on the explosion and the resulting friction causing so much heat.

Unloading military supplies on the docks was one of the favourite jobs. The chances of getting some loot were far better here than on any other work party. The camp doctors had been asking the Japanese doctor - I do not know if we still had Major Shimada as the POW doctor for the area - for quinine and had been consistently turned down. Our doctors were always told that there were no supplies available. To have malaria without quinine under our circumstances was to start the journey to the Happy Hunting Ground. The Japanese doctor knew this, so his refusal was tantamount to giving the death sentence to anyone who had a recurrence of malaria. The work party on the docks came across huge quantities of quinine in storage. The docks were not so busy that this horde was unnoticed. Taking the quinine was not easy, as one had to wander from the work area on a trumped up excuse, or through evasive action, find a way into the godowns and then get one's fingers on the goodies. There were a lot of native workers in the general area, but by this time we did not worry about the attitude of the natives. The Japanese had been so cruel and behaved in such an uncivilised fashion that they were hated by each and every one of the Ambonese and no doubt by the entire population of Indonesia.

Once the quinine was stolen, the camp search had to be negotiated. The intensity of this often depended on the individual guards and the area of work that we had been in. A good tropical rainfall was a godsend. In time the outside work parties were able to supply the camp with enough quinine to treat all patients and have a small stock to boot. All this stolen from the "unavailable supplies". More evidence that they were determined to have an expendable work force!

My position depended on the qualifications of the medical orderlies in the particular group in camp. I was put on the work parties when men with more orderly training were available. On Ambon there were several camps and some movement of prisoners between them. I was working in the hospital when one of the Dutch doctors decided to operate on a man with advanced beriberi and an ulcer about two inches by four inches on his foot. One side effect of beri-beri is that it numbs the nerves in the limbs that are most affected. The main effect of beri-beri is the gross swelling that takes place, as the body is unable to get rid of its fluids. The feet on this unfortunate fellow were as big as a normal man's thighs. The ulcer had eaten deep into this insensitive mass, stank to high heaven and put the man out of action completely. Without anaesthetic, the doctor started to cut deep into the swollen flesh. My job in this operation was strictly that of holding the patient down — one of three men assigned for this duty. To our surprise there was no reaction on the part of the victim. The doctor cut away most of the top part of the foot to a depth of one inch. It was only when the knife got close to some wholesome flesh that the man showed any sign of pain. My job was made easy on this occasion.

On our way back to camp one evening the column was stopped by a Japanese army officer. The bowing guards were outdoing each other to get lower and lower and more frequent in their demonstrations of subservience. Something great was going on, as we were soon marched off the road and onto a jungle path. There was a great deal of shouting back and forth as the guards seemed to be arguing about what we were actually supposed to be doing or where we were headed. As darkness fell we found ourselves in the jungle miles from the road we had left about two hours earlier. Six guards with about thirty prisoners was a worry for them. They were lost and did not have the least idea what to do with us. Luckily we came across an abandoned hut. Built on stilts, the floor was about three feet off the ground and made of bamboo slats. The guards herded us here and told us to keep quiet and go to sleep. We had enough room to sit with our knees under our chins.

It was fairly obvious that the officer who had stopped us on the road had intended us to work somewhere. The guards, thinking they knew the instructions, had got lost in trying to carry them out. Now we were faced with another night in the jungle, but this time with only minimum movement. We spent most of the night killing hordes of mosquitoes and listening to noises of the jungle. This was interrupted frequently as the guards kept up their spirits by chattering. The occasional giant beetle, almost the size of a humming bird, with a tough horny shell, would drop from the *attap* roof with the resulting outburst of profanity as the surprise and fright hit the unsuspecting prisoner. The split bamboo floor had enough spaces in it for individuals to relieve themselves with out making an undue mess. There was absolutely no way the guards would allow anyone out of the hut into the limitless black jungle and freedom. By this time we were so demoralised, hungry and weak that escape was just a passing fancy.

When dawn broke we were herded onto the path again and kept going in the same direction. After a great deal of shouting between themselves we were about faced and headed back to the road. In camp we received our usual pap breakfast and were put to camp work for the day. We were so lucky that this little incident had happened, for later on we were to see a spectacle to brighten the heart of all prisoners. Ambon, right across the bay from camp, was visited by two hundred Flying Fortresses. Talk about over-kill! This was an excellent example. Maybe Ambon was just one town on a milk run and only a few bombers dropped their bombs. The Zeros were scrambled but they did not break up the formation or shoot down a single Fortress. Unfortunately, two of our men working in the town were killed and several wounded. I played with the idea that any day now I could throw away the three months time limit as the advancing Americans would over run the whole area. I considered shortening this period but was reluctant to do so as it had served me so well for so long

Rumours were rife that the Japanese would kill all prisoners before letting them be recaptured. We knew we could not trust them for an instant. Any suspicious actions on their part could at best be countered by making a break for it. Since we knew they did not want their treatment of prisoners to be known by the world at large it would be extremely difficult to escape their weapons. "Dead men tell no tales."

We continued dispersing their military hardware until the 8th October 1944. By this time the Americans must have been close [3]. We were put on a barge, this time in the open, and on the usual badly stowed stores that were being moved in the same direction as we were. Our stretcher cases were loaded first so that we could use the same stretchers to carry more men on board. There were never enough stretchers in spite of the fact that they were crudely made out of rice sacks and bamboo poles, both of which were readily available. Bamboo grew in great abundance locally and rice was brought to the islands in the very same sacks.

It was not long before all the "fit" men were moved off the barge and taken to Ambon. We were not allowed to take our sick with us. At the start of this move, early in the morning, it had been raining hard and we were all soaked and miserable. Now with the tropical sun on us the sick were left exposed to the vagaries of the weather and without the moral support of a few fellows to look after them.

In Ambon we were ordered to board a local wooden trading vessel, which soon cast off for another unknown destination. This time chances for survival were very much better. Just being on deck and unencumbered gave us a fair chance. Obviously we were to move in a westward direction as New Guinea and the Americans were only a short distance to the East. Most of the boats leaving Ambon had done so at night - why were we leaving in broad daylight?

It was now routine for the Nips to starve us even more on a ship journey, their reason being that there were more prisoners on board than crew and guards. This simplistic reasoning overlooked the machine guns that were trained on us. Possibly more graft was at hand as someone pocketed the rations or money that was supposed to feed us? For two days our rations consisted of a few biscuits for each man. We touched into Kendari on the east coast of the Celebes where the group collectively was allowed to buy some fresh fruit. This was shared between all the prisoners. Apart from the first wild day of daytime travel we had stopped each day in some isolated bay and moved only at night. This routine was followed again after we left Kendari for a new and unknown destination.

1   I have recently read *Pacific Sweep* by William N.Hess. He mentions that the aerodrome was operational and subject to visits by 35th and 80th squadrons of P 38s, USAAF.

2   In fact Jock Bowman survived to see the turn of the century. After the publication of "*My Life With the Samurai*" Jock heard of my book and contacted me from his home in Scotland.

3   Morotai Island is less than four hundred miles to the north. The Americans had landed there on the 15 September - unknown to us.

10

MUNA

THE DEATH CAMP

One thing is certain and the rest is lies;
The flower that once has blown forever dies.

EDWARD FITZGERALD (1809—1883)

Two days after leaving Kendari we arrived on the island of Muna just south of the Celebes, 11th October 1944. Nobody had the vaguest idea where this island is situated. It is fairly hilly and seemed to have a little cultivation. It is many times larger than Haruku and probably had several villages on it. We never did find out as the work parties were confined to the locale of the camp and cemetery area. However we soon got to know that there was a village upstream of the nearby river. The jetty we arrived at was of good construction and quite long. There was a gravel road that appeared to circumnavigate the island. The main method of travel was by ox cart. The Japanese controlled the only trucks we saw on the island.

The island trader docked smoothly about noon. We were hot, thirsty, hungry and keen to be away from this target - the jetty. The five days on the boat had taken its toll. We had all walked on to this trader in Ambon. Now, five days later, we had more than thirty people who could not walk at all. This had been the case since leaving Haruku where we were so close to death that the slightest reduction in rations saw more casualties. Inevitably we had men designated as "fit" by the guards but who were on the edge of total collapse. Men who were forced to work yesterday died today. Those who could not work unloading the boat were carried to one side and were abused by the guards for being sick. During the evening a few men were ushered down the road to our new camp to pick up bamboo poles and rice sacks. After midnight, when the unloading was finished, we put our sick on the rice sack stretchers and shambled off to our new camp. It made travel a lot easier for all of us. Even in our "fit" state it was not easy to support a sick man as we staggered and stumbled along the road.

It appeared we were to be housed in an existing transit camp. We found out that one or two of the previous drafts from Haruku and Ambon had called in here on their way to Java. It consisted of three or four dilapidated *attap* huts of standard design with bali-bali (bamboo) beds that were in great need of repair.

After arriving on Muna we had a very welcome addition to our diet - fish. Baskets full of tiny anchovy-like fish were brought into the camp every day. At last we felt that there might be some hope of getting fitter. Eating fish every day, even the small amount we received, was a great boost to our morale. Maybe our purple pellagra skin would metamorphose and ulcerated limbs heal. Sometimes there was enough fish to have a serving of two teaspoons full per man. On other occasions the fish would be thrown into the soup with the main enjoyment being the knowledge that there was some protein to help our emaciated bodies. The fish flavour was not enough to overcome the powerful, bitter taste of *katella* leaves but we were happy to know it was there. Our joy was short lived. After only a few weeks of this minuscule addition to our diet, it stopped abruptly.

The day after we arrived on Muna another draft of Haruku men caught up with us. The Japanese were trying to get their prisoners away from the advancing Americans. We had close to four hundred and twenty-five men on this camp located near the village of Raha. We were the last and fittest men of the two thousand and seventy one Haruku Island slave labour force.

There was a long jetty near the village with the only industry on the island, a sawmill, close by. It seemed that we were well clear of any military targets. The jetty was seldom used as the only Japanese on the island appeared to be our guards. No military garrison here. Just a nice normal native island that the war, for the most part, had passed by.

Our camp consisted of three *attap* huts running at right angles to the road and further back from the road a hut at right angles to this group. The guardhouse was on the south end of camp with our cook-house close by. For the first time since leaving Java we had properly constructed barbed wire fencing surrounding the camp. This was about ten feet high with the strands at six-inch intervals and all pulled taught. The poles for securing the barbed wire were placed about twelve feet apart and firmly dug into the ground. It turned out that this was a regular transit camp for returning prisoners. No doubt it was also used to house the locally recruited militia and the native forced labour battalions. It had all the trappings of a permanent camp in the Japanese scheme of things — no washing facilities. All the water for the camp had to be carried in. There was a river just south of the camp with a well-constructed bridge over it. A gently sloping hill made the backing for this nicely situated camp. This was a great convenience for the guards as they patrolled the hill and no doubt had a wonderful view of the straits between Muna and Butong Islands.

We had frequently heard Liberators flying along the coast at tree top height and on many occasions lengthy bursts of machine gun fire. It seemed that the

Americans were shooting anything that moved on the sea, including the local fish boats. Our joy at being away from military targets proved how old fashioned our thinking was. The conduct of the war had changed during the past three years. Virtually anything that floated, or moved by mechanical power on land, was a target. The main mode of transport on Muna was by bullock cart.

Christmas Day, 1944, was just another day with most of the camp sick, and the meagre rations as scanty as ever. One hundred and thirty six men had died since our arrival in October. We did not have a padre in camp so one of the officers thought it might be a good idea to cheer everyone with a Christmas Service. Strictly on a voluntary basis some of the men responded by gathering between the huts for an impromptu service. We attempted to sing a couple of hymns but it was not the way to go. After more than two years of starvation and the loss of hundreds of men there was not too much interest in the Great One Above. As we looked at each other it was evident that the kingdom of heaven is in the individual will to survive. There was no one looking after the collective group as the church service would lead us to believe. The attempt at singing was a dismal failure. Two verses of "Abide With Me" was the extent of our effort. Forlorn and discouraged we drifted back to the *bali bali*. If there really was a God directing operations could this kind of thing happen?

I was a medical orderly on Muna and on this particular morning had just come off night duty and collected my breakfast of watery rice and was sitting on the edge of the bamboo eating or drinking it when the silence of the camp was shattered by the four engines of a Liberator with all guns blazing at about two hundred feet above the camp. The terrifying suddenness of this roar made me react without thought of the consequences. I must have put into effect a long planned safety measure that I had subconsciously made soon after arriving on the camp. Frightened out of my wits I made a mad dash for the barbed wire and either went through it or over it, as I have no recollection of this. My idea was to get to the large trees just outside the wire. This was a rather unusual setting as several large trees grew in an open area that had practically no undergrowth in the immediate vicinity. I figured that the protection of the trees would offset the fact that this Liberator was using both his front and rear guns. As he flew directly over the camp I would be able to move around the tree and be protected by its large trunk from the front nose gunner, the belly gunner and the tail gunner. The thought passed through my mind that my brother, who was flying in Lancasters at the time I was taken POW, may have requested a transfer to this theatre of operations and actually be in this machine terrifying the very soul out of me. This whole scenario must have lasted just a few seconds and then we were back to the normal routine of camp life. Now I found myself outside the wire with three other fellows. The only course for us was to nip into camp as fast as our legs could take us. We all headed for the wire but one of the guards was a touch quicker than we were. He rounded us up and took the four of us into the compound behind the guardhouse. The four of us knew that the only punishment for escaping was beheading. Here we were in the Japanese compound, completely surrounded by their quarters waiting for the selection of an executioner. The guard halted us in the middle of their parade square and left us standing to attention. We must wait for the final details to be worked out. After two hours under the relentless tropical sun the Staff Sergeant appeared. Yellow Boots was a new entity to us. Blood and Slime had fortunately been moved with another draft so we had an unknown staff sergeant in charge of the camp. We had seen him around on the rare occasions when he performed some duty that entailed his talking to the men on guard but generally speaking he kept to himself and out of our sight. Now, dressed in his finery with the inevitable Samurai sword at his side he came to tell us the consequences of our actions. It seemed fairly obvious to us that he had dressed in this fashion to confirm our worst beliefs. It occurred to me that he might be merciful and order a straight forward execution as opposed to the course of action that Blood would take — merciless beatings followed by a public execution.

Surely with this staff sergeant dressed for the kill our fate was sealed. On this isolated island in the centre of Indonesia without a military garrison of any consequence the staff sergeant would not be dressed like this for his own comfort or to impress the men in the guard room. What could be more glorious for him than to dispose of four of the enemy in the traditional manner? Not only did he have the right to do this, it was his duty. Was the number four unlucky for prison escapees? The number of men left on Amahai was four beheaded escapees (so we thought at this time)[1]. The four of us were lined up with my own position being on the extreme left of the four as we faced him. He started his oration in quite a normal fashion but started to raise his voice at the same time as drawing his sword. This was a normal tactic for all the Japanese as they liked to work themselves into a lather before striking the first blow. The sun flashed on his sword as he raised it high above the first man's head. After a few harshly spoken words he brought the sword down flat on the top of the victim's head. I was feverishly thinking of his *modus operandi* and then in a flash it became obvious to me that he would need time to work himself into an effective killing machine. Starting with the first man in line he did not have enough room to swing his sword. We knew from long experience that they always took a few minutes to create the right conditions for a beating or an execution. I would be the first in line for decapitation. I must not go out like a lamb but there were few alternatives open to me. I decided the only thing I could do was to kick him in the crotch with all my sixty to seventy pounds and bare feet. What damage this would have done is open to speculation. However it would give me the satisfaction of a well-timed and last farewell to old Mother Earth. Timing was the crucial point of this whole exercise. If I kicked too soon there is no doubt the Kempetai would have had another victim to torture into a long and lingering death. If too late all would be lost. Hopefully I could kick just as the sword touched my neck. In this way we would both have our little victories, though bare feet were hardly a lethal weapon. Perchance my severed head would have a smile on it. He finished with the man next to me and then came smartly in front of me. He stood to attention and continued his treatise on the evils of escape or was it about the glory of the Empire and what it had done for "The Greater East Asia Co-prosperity Sphere?" I had no idea and was concentrating on my timing. Now I must be incredibly careful. Unnoticeably, I shifted my weight onto my left foot and watched like a hawk as he manoeuvred the sword over his head. It hung there for a long moment. Was he deciding which way to bring it down? I was tense as a spring. The timing had to be so exact. The puny little muscles in the back of my legs were like violin strings. Then the movement started. He brought the sword straight down with the flat hitting me a casual blow on the top of my head. I had detected in time the straight downward movement of the sword rather than the curved swipe necessary for decapitation. Both feet were well on the ground. Thank God!

He moved back to his original position about six feet in front of us, sheathed his sword, stopped talking, and indicated that we return to barracks. My God! What a morning - - having the living daylights scared out of us by both friend and enemy alike. But "Yellow Boots" proved to be a civilised Japanese. For the next few days the four of us met to discuss the chance of being called out to dig our own graves but it did not happen. Just how lucky can a fellow be?

We had a rather undefined feeling that with a man like Yellow Boots in charge of the camp, conditions might improve and we would get more rations and medicine. But it never happened.

The camp was situated about half a mile north of a river. This river was wide enough to boast a nice bridge that carried the road to the mill about a mile north of the camp. Our only means of washing was to be paraded down to the river. This parade took place most evenings an hour before sunset. It soon turned into the regular evening's entertainment for the local population. The guards would take up their vantage point on the bridge as we bathed ourselves, naked, on either side. By the end of the first week most of the locals had grandstand positions on the bridge and the riverbanks watching several hundred naked prisoners swab off - no soap involved with this operation. The population of the island of Muna had never in its history had so much open entertainment of such an unusual nature. There were animated discussions, with a great deal of pointing, as the

The stream on Muna Island where we were allowed an occasional bath, naked, much to the amusement, entertainment and delight of the local population who gathered on the bridge to watch our every move.

Photo by Jurgen Kaminski

Tony Cowling talking to the British Columbia Military History Society about his experiences in many different Japanese Death Camps. This address was given in the Beatty Street Armouries of the British Columbia Regiment during the spring of 2004.

men and women observed our rather crude ablutions. This camp was particularly dusty as the main gravel road on the island passed within a few yards of the camp. The motorised traffic was scarce but the oxen drawn carts and occasional horses created quite a dust.

A basic necessity for working under slave labour conditions in a tropical climate is salt. It was apparent after we had been on the island only a few days that Muna was totally lacking in this commodity, or so we were told. All requests for salt were denied on the grounds that there was not any available. Like the denial of quinine in Ambon, where we had found large stocks on the docks, we were most sceptical. Since it is an absolute necessity, a work party was organised to carry seawater from the beach to the cook-house where it was boiled dry leaving a residue of salt in the huge *wajangs* (woks).

The cemetery was about another half mile past the bridge. At one period there were so many sick men in camp that I was involved in all the stages of the burial process. Having been on duty when Johnny died, about 1:00 a.m., I carried him to the morgue and put him into a couple of rice sacks to wait for the morning burial party. As a worker on Haruku I carried dozens of men to the cemetery from the hospital. Now, as a senior orderly, I was taking men nightly from the hospital to the morgue. Johnny was another man sacrificed by Churchill and Wavell for a precious few days. After parade that morning there were only a few fit men for the burial party so I was ordered to grab a pick axe and accompany the men to the grave yard as a pall bearer. Here we began digging two fresh graves, for Johnny and another for a man that died earlier the previous evening.

We had dug to a depth of four feet when our friends the Americans were over again with two Liberators at tree top height. This time I was under complete control of myself and had a nice view of them as they flew within a few hundred yards of us. Waving like mad we had no idea if they were aware that we were prisoners. The situation was a complete reversal of the incident a few weeks before. Our guard was now in the grave seeking shelter from the enemy, while we watched these magnificent aircraft strafing the hell out of something quite distant from us. We realised at this stage that we really had no control over our reactions to the sound of aircraft. One day we would grovel in the dust and the next day we would be happy and cheerful at the sight and sound of our future liberators.

At the beginning of November 1944, there was a rumour that we were to be moved again. All very vague and secretive. It did not really bother us too much. The whole camp was resigned to accept the decision of the officers as to who would stay and who would be moved. The usual manoeuvring to get on or off a draft was passé. The stakes were life and death - - nobody wanted to stick his neck out to be sunk in transit or to stay and die a slow death by starvation. There were no alternatives. We were not alive, just existing from day to day. If fate said "go," we went. It was just impossible to know what was the smart thing to do. We had at long last been reduced to Zooid which flows so easily with the tide.

Major Gibson and Dr. Forbes made up the camp list for a move should it develop. In October when the two boats had arrived at Muna and this camp started we had very close to four hundred and twenty-five men. Now we were down to approximately three hundred, with one hundred of these destined to be moved again. On the 10th November we were told of the move and that it would be on the following day. There were seventy-five hospital patients with twenty-five "fit" men to carry and coax them to the jetty a mile down the road.

Since arriving on Muna I had been assigned to permanent medical orderly duties. The hospital consisted of about two-thirds of the hut running parallel to the road. The doctors and orderlies occupied the other one-third. Having once again lost all my friends to the Happy Hunting Ground I chummed with the chemist, Joch Bowman. There were no drugs to dispense but he was an operator, and somehow managed to keep himself out of the way of the Japanese and off any work parties. Dr. Forbes selected Jock and me to accompany him on this next move. Dr. Philps had been with our group at Semarang and on Haruku and had been separated from us as we left Ambon. His party of prisoners did not stop at Muna and took well over two months to reach Java. They had an extremely high death rate. Of the six hundred and fifty men who left Ambon only two hundred and seventy nine arrived in Java. A 57% death rate in little more than two months.

On the 11th November 1944, we paraded at dawn, with our scanty goods and even scantier bodies. It was now over a year ago that I had been weighed on Haruku Island at seventy-two pounds. With not a single meal of any substance since then I had no idea how much I weighed now. The march to the jetty was an agony in itself for all concerned. The sick were in most cases too sick to walk and the fit had their time cut out trying to get them there. The beri beri patients were the hardest to deal with because they weighed so much. With bodies so swollen and muscles so incapacitated they were both too heavy and too awkward to deal with. It took two men to carry a beri-beri patient, whereas the other sick could be looked after on a one-for-one basis. Beri-beri stops one urinating properly, with the result that the body swells from the feet up. The feet get to an enormous size, possibly as large as the skin will stretch. Now the fluid builds up to the Michelin man proportions. Allowed to go unchecked, the fluid gradually squeezes the heart to a standstill. There was no way for us to combat this. My own defence had been initiated that night on 'the hole' in Haruku. I only ate rice if there was 'something of a nutritious nature' to offset it - not scientific but effective. The 'something of a nutritious nature' had a broad interpretation and included everything from coconuts to leaves of any sort and all edible roots.

Tied to the dock was a boat of about a hundred tons with an overall length of one hundred feet - - a coastal trader with a large central hold, aft bridge, and a raised fore deck with a machine gun mounted. Constructed of oriental lumber with two masts, it made an ideal trader, not a troop carrier. After sitting on the jetty for hours we were herded onto the forward section of the boat. Before dark some native Javanese troops were embarked to the centre section of the boat. This now gave the Japanese a good definition of the mode of travel. Forward all the prisoners, centre the native troops and aft the Japanese guards, army and navy personnel. The only exception to this was the twenty-four hour watch, in pairs, on the machine gun mounted right over our heads.

Most of our sick were lying on the deck and forward hatch covers, with the officers and a few men, myself included, under the raised area of the machine gun. That night we cast off, but not under our own power. A vessel of similar size picked up a line that had been attached to our bow. We were neatly under tow. Every sea move that we had made to date involved us only as a last consideration in the movement of native troops and war supplies. Now we wondered what was in the hatches below us. More aviation fuel and bombs or hundreds of bamboo poles?

We had the usual wooden contraption hung over the side as a crapper. Conditions were extremely crowded. We could only walk from port to starboard and around the raised area of the hatch, picking our way between the prostrate sick. But we were on deck, which meant fresh air and a chance to determine our direction of travel. Just being in the open air is a luxury that can only be appreciated after being consigned to the cargo hold, usually half full of aviation fuel barrels. The night was typically tropical - calm, moon lit and peaceful. There being no engine in the boat we ghosted along northwards. Not much sleep to be had with so many sick around, with their groaning and moaning and the frequent call of 'plate'. We did not have bedpans so the alternative was the 'plate'. Just an ordinary enamelled plate placed beside the buttocks of a patient lying on his side. The motion did not help matters. It was never easy to get a man with diarrhoe or dysentery to soil on a plate without spills. The area of contact between the buttocks and the plate was about one inch for our scrawny bunch. Throw in a gentle movement to port or a dip of the bow and the equilibrium is upset. The resulting mess is unpleasant for all concerned.

Just after dawn we heard a four-engine job flying at twenty thousand feet and gave him a muffled cheer. That machine gun was too close for a display of exuberance. All was quiet as we headed slowly on our way to some unknown port to the north. The native troops were eating great quantities of fresh fruit, so we began scheming on how to make some of this change hands. The sick, some of whom would not see the end of the day, were groaning their way to oblivion while others knew only too well the value of silence. The weather was good, the sea calm, and we were summing up the possibilities of a take-over with this machine gun right over our heads. Was there another one mounted aft that we could not see? In spite of the unknown loyalty of the native troops on board, a machine gun gives the operator a great advantage. How to get control of the machine gun? The immediate target of a take over would have to be the bridge where the Japanese were gathered. Native troops would no doubt join us but we would still be a boat under tow. The idea was totally impractical.

Suddenly — "Look! Look!" was yelled in the most excited voice, followed immediately by the rattle of ten machine guns, two cannons and the roar of powerful engines. All hell was on us again. This was the most beautiful sight - two P38 Lockheed Lightnings, machineguns blazing, shooting the hell out of us and the towing boat. Many of the men were waving rice sacks at the strafing fighters but my back was turned to the attackers and my immediate reaction was to seek cover so I dived under the forward deck housing, a really foolish move as the machine gun was overhead, making this area a prime target. By the time the P38s had completed their first run I was on my feet and watching this wonderful sight. The machine gun was out of action and did not fire a single shot. The guard tried valiantly to make some adjustments to it but to no avail. After the first pass it was clear that the fighters were concentrating on the bridge of both boats and were firing incendiaries. With the second pass completed their job was done, and praise the Lord, they had recognised us. They left the devastation with wings wagging and a bunch of prisoners so happy that someone was meting out a little justice to these Shintoists. No time for sentiment now. The boats were on fire and all the troops and most of the crew were in the water. None of the prisoners had gone over the side. The Captain and a couple of his crew were surveying the damage.

Now was the chance to take over. An armourer leaped to the machine gun to see what could be done and the rest of us made our way aft to control the fire. But it was no good. A wooden vessel riddled with incendiary bullets burns like a firecracker. We made our way back to the bow of the boat. The flames were licking forward at such a terrifying speed that there was only one way to safety. The captain gave an order, which could only have meant abandon the ship. Everyone made for the gunwale and leapt over the sides. The sick were lying on the deck with the flames now amidships and being wafted towards them at an ever increasing rate. Dr. Forbes shouted to one of the fellows and we started to throw these huge beri-beri bodies overboard. Many of them could not swim and started protesting that they would drown. We convinced them there was no alternative. One could stay on the boat and burn to death for sure or go overboard and grab one of the hatch covers that Tom and some of the other fellows were tossing over. With the last body off the burning boat I looked around to see what the situation was. The heat of the flames reminded me there was no time to dally. Joch took a dignified step off the gunwale after warning us to look out for the bodies that were still close to the boat. Dr. Forbes followed him, having made sure that no one was left on the deck or in the shelter under the bow deck. The only other man on the boat was Major Gibson who told me he could not swim. I made some foolish remark like "good luck sir," stepped on to the gunwale and made a spectacular swan dive into the calm blue and bloody red tropical waters.

My first thought on surfacing was of sharks. There had been a great deal of bloodshed as the Americans hit mid ships and the aft sections pretty hard. No one saw the attack until it was upon us. Even then there was no protection from the onslaught. I swam like mad for the lifeboat, knowing that the law of the sea made friend and foe partners when a common enemy was facing them. Like the Geneva Convention, the law of the sea meant nothing to the Japanese. As I put my hand up to the gunwale and raised my head out of the water I saw a rifle butt about to be brought down with deadly accuracy. Moving like a fish, I was out of the way as the butt hit the gunwale with a resounding crack. This was definitely not hospitable territory. I swam off to find a hatch cover and some fellow prisoners. Tom was nowhere to be seen so I stuck with the crowd nearest to me. Jock and Dr. Forbes must be somewhere amongst that widely dispersed crowd of bobbing heads.

Now I had a chance to look around and assess the situation. Both boats were blazing like fury. The Japanese were in lifeboats, with the rest of us hanging on to whatever was at hand. The Javanese troops seemed to have been decimated as most of the floating lifeless bodies were in the green uniform that distinguished them from the Japanese in their brown/khaki uniforms. There was a good showing of prisoners so we had probably come out of this better than the other groups.

What were our chances? Where was the land? On the horizon to the west we could just make out the tops of some palm trees. This gave us a direction to work towards. At this time I remembered the plight of the crew of the H.M.S. *Jupiter* sunk in the Java Sea Battle. Many of them had been with us in *Jaar Markt* camp, Sourabaya. They had tried desperately to get ashore on the north coast of Java, only to find the tide was far too strong for their efforts. When they were washed into a position close enough to fight like mad to make the shore the tide would turn and they were washed out to sea again. This went on for three days until they were finally rescued. The Japanese would not be that concerned with our safety and they would have had no way of knowing how many to look for.

Being one of the fittest men on our hatch cover I organised a kicking party so that we were maximising our efforts to close in on the palm trees. After a couple of hours of kicking our way towards land the man just to my right said - "There is nothing left for me now." He let go of the hatch cover and sank. I tried to grab him but it was too late. He sank. I was surprised that some one could give up in this fashion. Even more surprising, to sink like a stone. I wondered why he sank as there were so many bodies floating all around us.

We kicked under a cloudless sky and nervously kept an eye out for sharks. This went on till mid afternoon when someone pointed to the native out-riggers coming from shore. We all looked eagerly ahead to see a whole fleet of white sails beautifully set against a backdrop of swaying palms. This meant we could relax for the moment knowing they would soon be upon us. Soon we started kicking again and pushing the hatch cover ever closer to land. There was no reason to take chances with so much blood and so many dead bodies in the water not too far from where we were. With the palm trees still many miles ahead of us one of the fellows stood up and announced that we could walk to shore. This rather shocked the more conscientious of us as the man was obviously slacking off while the rest of us were kicking like mad to make the shore. With only five feet depth we felt right at home only to lose this in another few paces. It was not long before we were standing on sand rather than coral. Now we looked for the fleet of white sails that were to rescue us. Nothing. Not a sail in sight. Were we all hallucinating? Was this a mirage? Apparently some native craft did venture out, with strict instructions to pick up Japanese only. Our rescue fleet had disappeared?

Escape was the prime thought in my mind. With this heaven-sent opportunity they would never know who was alive or dead. I swam and staggered onto shore for it would not be long before dusk was on us. I should have time to organise a hiding place for the night. I swam in only two feet of water to a mangrove swamp and stood up to find my way inland. I only got my head and shoulders out of the water when I was a black mass of insects. Every square inch of my body was covered with hungry biting black insects. I did not recognise any of them and did not want to hang around to try to identify them. This called for a rapid change of plans. I must swim away from this area, find a better landing spot, and warn the others.

Completely covered by water again my aim was to get as far away from the swamp as possible. Using my hands to propel me along the bottom I emerged from the swamp and headed in a northerly direction. Shouting a warning to the others that the swamp was a hive of insects I started swimming like fury to get around the point and over to a sandy beach. No sooner had I cleared the swamp than a boat came around the point with guards yelling and screaming. Looking up, I saw a large powered lifeboat with a Japanese at the helm and two rifles a few feet from my head. I was the first to be recaptured, having raced ahead of the others and not scouted the land properly. I was the first to become a guest of their God Emperor again. Soon the lifeboat was full. Both Joch and Tom were in this boat. After picking up all the men in the immediate vicinity we were put ashore with the two guards on a sandy knoll beside the island road.

Tom was safe with us again, but only by the grace of God. After he had abandoned the fiery boat he swam to the same lifeboat that I had. His greeting was worse than mine, as the Japanese had a bayonet at the ready and as soon as Tom touched the gunwale he was jabbed furiously by the terrified guard. He managed to move his head fast enough to avoid a direct blow into the skull. However the bayonet caught him over his right eye and into his cheek. He lost the sight of his eye from this attack. My friend Joch, always lucky, came through this without a great deal of trouble.

As the sun had set, the guard very decently allowed us to have a fire to try to warm up a little, but more importantly to keep the insects at bay. In our totally emaciated condition we felt the cold if the nighttime temperature fell more than a few degrees. Most of us had been in the water for close to eight hours. The chances of a nighttime strafing seemed pretty remote. In this group there were about forty men. We had started with one hundred. There must have been some deaths apart from the man beside me who gave up the ghost and sank. As the night wore on men came in under guard from every direction. In the morning the tally of recaptured survivors was seventy. One most amazing fact came to light as we saw men who were swollen with advanced beri-beri when we boarded the boat now as scrawny as the rest of us. Having exercised in the water they had peed themselves free of many pounds of fluid. Was this a new way to alleviate the horrors of beri-beri and take the pressure off the heart, the final killing stroke? We had to wonder if the doctors were aware of this remedy and if they would have tried it at an earlier stage of our prison life.

In the morning a truck arrived and all seventy of us were herded into the one vehicle for the drive back to camp. Now we knew why the boat had waited for darkness to move. The Americans were watching every move with their dawn patrol. It was a classic operation. We could visualise every move as the dawn patrol radioed base with our description and position. Two lucky devils dispatched for a milk run and a little target practice and the job was complete. What we wanted to know more than anything was their base of operation. Just how far had they advanced? Which direction were they heading? A hundred questions that had no answers.

Back in camp we had the wounded to take care of in addition to the normal complement of malaria, dysentery, and beri-beri patients. We had lost twenty-seven men in the twenty-four hours since leaving camp. My Christmas present of 1941 - the beautiful automatic watch that I had so carefully hidden from so many searches was now at the bottom of the sea. I had just kept it too long. It always had trading value and I had kept it as an insurance against the day when my need might be more desperate. It seems strange now that under those circumstances I did not pass it off to some native for something totally unbelievable - such as a cooked duck loaded with spices and so tender, or half a dozen eggs. Now with nothing but a downward slope ahead of us my little insurance had gone. But then, there were only three months to go!

Conditions in camp slowly got worse. One day, out of the blue, our rice ration ceased altogether and we were given corn {maize}. This was such an abrupt change that the serving utensils for rice were not practical for corn. Our first meal of corn consisted of eighteen individual kernels per person. How could we live on this? Eighteen kernels of corn and a cup-full of green *katella* soup! Our rice ration had been three hundred grams of rice per day per man. Breakfast consisted of eighty grams made into a type of porridge with a little of the local brown sugar in it. Lunch was one hundred and twenty grams of rice, dry cooked, with *katella* soup and "dinner" the same only with one hundred grams of rice. Eventually we were living on more maize than rice, a substitution rather than a supplement to our diet. The change over was hard on the fellows in hospital after so long on rice alone. Many patients with ulcerated mouths and throats found it impossible to swallow these comparatively larger kernels of corn.

With no military work to be done on the island the guards allowed us to cultivate gardens. This obvious solution to keeping us alive was only granted after a twenty-five percent death rate. As a by-product to this effort I managed to get hold of a sweet potato and plant it in a corner of the camp near one end of the hospital hut. Jock and I watched this like a couple of hawks. So did another two hundred pairs of eyes with the result that the first leaves to appear disappeared that night. This soon became routine, as I am sure the whole camp watched this one potato defiantly pushing up leaves that would never mature. Our rations were so restricted that a bowel movement once a week was quite satisfactory.

One day I was standing beside Dr. Forbes as he took the sick parade when one of the fellows who had reported sick with a badly cut leg mentioned, hesitatingly, that he had this gnawing pain in his stomach. Did Doc' have any ideas? I listened intently as I was suffering the same pains but was not about to admit it. Under no circumstances would you find me admitting to anything that might faintly resemble sickness. I was keenly aware that admittance to the hospital was, in most cases, a one-way ticket. Dr. Forbes was most reassuring as he told the chap that we all had this pain and it was basically a hunger pain. Much relieved he went on his way. We all knew that we were hungry, nay starving, so the pain was really of no consequence, just a signal that had to be ignored.

On one of our trips to the river for the evening bath I was happily dousing myself with water when I had an almost spiritual, though distant, contact with the healthiest, best fed man on Muna Island. There were many villages up stream of us so it was routine for us to be bathing in the toiletry of these villages. Slaves are not choosy. This particular evening I was astounded to see a two foot long turd about two inches in diameter float right past me on its way to the mighty ocean. Could we be more humbled or humiliated? Our every move watched by the island population and now this further degradation to ensure the prestige of the White man was ground to the lowest point.

Tammy was a Welsh miner with whom I had had many a good banter. He was as broad as he was tall and more powerful than I could ever hope to be. Now I looked after him as he lay dying of starvation, malaria and dysentery. He had always kidded me that when we were released he would make sure that I would have my first sexual encounter in some appropriate, macho fashion, getting drunk with the boys and stumbling into bed with some equally naive female. A man of some thirty years and married for some time, he thought that it was wrong to have someone as inexperienced as myself in the clutches of these heathens. The Japanese doctors always restricted quinine. Tammy had a fighting chance for recovery so he was given some of this precious medicine. Imagine my surprise, when we moved his dead body, to find some quinine tablets under the block of wood that he used for a pillow. Did he not take the medicine because he knew he would not make the grade and so left it for someone with a better chance? There were many noble souls in camp.

The chance of stealing drugs for the sick was an absolute zero here, for the only work parties outside the camp were on the gardens or digging graves. In fact quinine became so short that Dr. Forbes was forced to be selective as to who should receive it. A difficult position for him to be in. We could well sympathise with him as it was sometimes all too apparent that certain individuals would not recover. However some individuals looked to be beyond hope but had that spirit that never gives up.

Flight Lieutenant Allen was our dentist. He wore wings (under normal conditions) and had joined the air force to fly. Now he was to carry out his peace time task. One day while I was on duty there was a considerable commotion from the morgue. This was a small *attap* hut half way up the hill behind the camp and situated close to the hospital. A Dutch orderly and I were hurriedly sent for to help in holding down a patient who was having a tooth extracted. It evolved that this poor devil had a complicated root structure to the tooth being extracted. There were already three men holding him down when we were called to assist. We were all for ceasing the operation as the fellow was in terrible agony and the doctor not in a position to do anything about relieving the pain.

The struggle continued for some time as it seems that once the process has started there is no going back. I had thought my extraction to be painful, but it was a breeze compared to this torture. Eventually the doctor won and displayed the tooth to all helpers and the suffering patient. The whole process reminded me of the classical struggle between Capt. Ahab and Moby Dick.

We, the orderlies, made one terrible mistake with a fellow who was given up for dying and left to lie on the *bali- bali* unattended. After two or three days of neglect he was still breathing so I turned him over to give him a good clean up when to my surprise I found that he had hole at the base of his spine about two and a half inches in diameter full of rotten flesh and stinking. It was deep enough for us to see his spine through the puss and surrounding filth. We had a fair quantity of potash of permanganate on camp so the wound was cleaned post haste and the plucky individual revived. He was still alive when our party once again left camp some months later.

Sometimes a fellow would know when he was going to die and no encouraging words would stop him. I had already experienced this when the boat was sunk. One night I was talking quietly to Andy, who had been in hospital for a couple of weeks but was far from the most seriously sick, when he told me he would be dead before his birthday. Thinking his birthday was some weeks or months ahead I tried to encourage him and told him the Americans would be here in three months at the most. Then, just by way of getting his idea of what he was thinking about, I asked him when his birthday was. He replied in a good strong voice 'tomorrow'. Of course I tried even harder to talk him out of this depression when all his involuntary muscles relaxed and he died as I spoke.

American bombers were frequent visitors over this area. They even bombed the small saw mill just north of the jetty. I was fascinated by watching the bombs fall from the belly of the Fortress. Just watching them separate as they came out of the bomb bay and knowing that they were on their way to destroy some of the Japanese war effort was a perverse satisfaction. At night any sound of engines in the sky would be greeted by the guards with a shout of '*tutop api*'. Malay for 'stop smoking'. Since the only remaining pleasure in life for our dying patients was to smoke I did not enforce this cry from up on the hill. It was difficult to get a light again after putting out a cigarette so I let the patients continue to smoke. Occasionally some one would go out of the hospital to the urinal and take a long drag on his cigarette. This prompted the guard to call me, the duty orderly, up to his perch and demand that I report to the guardhouse in the morning. I was beaten several times for this but it was worth it. I am sure the Americans did not see our smokers and I know the satisfaction a smoke gave to the sick and dying. Some of the men were so addicted to smoking that given the chance they would trade their precious possessions for tobacco rather than food. The good tobacco at this stage was a black native tobacco shipped from island to island in hollowed out bamboo. The average tobacco was a mixture of this black stuff and dried jungle leaves wrapped, at best, in a page of the bible. Every evening we would see thousands of flying foxes (large fruit eating bats) pass over the camp, fairly low, on their way to their feeding grounds. This was grounds for many animated discussions on the best way to capture these tasty morsels. Eventually one of them turned up in camp, how it met its untimely death I do not know. It may have been traded for some treasure or found gasping its last breath beside the river. Whichever way it was, the end result was most unexpected. Having provided a meal for the hungry and proud possessor, all its bones were thoroughly examined to see what further use it could be put to. It was at this stage that it was noticed that the wing bone had a deep socket in it to accommodate the adjoining wing bone. On further careful inspection this socket proved to be just the right size to house a cigarette, added to which the bone was hollow and about three inches long. An ideal cigarette holder and oh! so sophisticated. Indeed a rare acquisition.

As the days wore on and our humdrum existence plodded from week to week we had a most believable and exciting rumour. A tall White man had been seen in a village on the south coast of the island. No doubt in our minds this would be an American naval officer sounding out the terrain for some future operation. The entire island was almost deserted of Japanese, and surely we were worth a rescue operation? We were really excited for a couple of weeks but nothing came of it.

The measure for serving rice that we had used on Haruku, and that we thought was so small, was large by comparison to the one now in use on Muna. One hundred grams of cooked rice does not fill a container much larger than a good-sized wine glass. This, plus the meagre cup of *katella* soup twice a day, was what we were now reduced to.

Joch had made arrangements with the cook, for some deal that he dreamed up. The cook should give us a bowl of cooked rice in return for whatever Joch had given the cook. Jock was always fussy that all food should be covered at all times, a wise precaution, since there was so much dysentery around. He asked me to pick up this extra ration that he had arranged. The cook was not there when I arrived but the rice was on his bunk covered with flies. In fact the billy can of rice looked black. It was so totally covered not a single grain of rice could be seen. I swished them off and returned to our quarters. The first question Joch asked me was 'was it covered?' 'Yes," I answered quite truthfully. We enjoyed the extra rice and did not suffer any ill effects.

Eventually a bamboo pipe was constructed from the tap down the road to the camp. This gave us a constant trickle of water for both the hospital and the cookhouse. However, the Japanese had a pipe with running water to their quarters right beside the camp. Just to keep their superiority to the forefront this tap was often left running and the water ran down the road to the river. Another reminder of our position.

Early April we heard that the abortive move of a few months previous, which resulted on our sinking, might be repeated. Jock and I immediately approached Dr. Forbes and said that, whichever way the kaleidoscope tumbled, we would like to stay together as a team. If he went on the trip, we would. If he stayed in camp, we wanted to stay with him. We had a feeling that our trio was lucky and to insure this luck we must stick together. He felt the same way and so, in the face of rotten odds we had cast our fate together.

Friday 13th April 1945 was not the best of days for the superstitious to depart this lovely and deadly island. Soon after our noon meal the selected group of about eighty prisoners was started on the "march" to the jetty close to a mile north of the camp. We had quite a few stretcher cases and walking sick, and the usual Japanese panic, hurrying and prodding us along. The fit assisted the walking sick and carried the stretchers. It was a long and desperate walk to a fate that was in the hands of some far off American air base, or perhaps an over-fed, submarine commander. We frequently fantasised that the air force would drop their dining room garbage cans in the camp. A once a week drop of this nature would have all of us back into a fairly healthy state.

There were never enough stretchers for all the men who needed them. Even the walking sick took a lot of looking after. If the situation had not been so desperate and painful the sound effects would have been well worth recording. The cries of agony mixed with the shouts of the guards to '*speedo, speedo, lakas, lakas*' (hurry, hurry). We arrived at the jetty before the sun went down to find that the hurry was pointless. The boat was not there, or in sight. We speculated that the boat might never turn up. The Americans had such complete command of the air that they must know every move these little fanatics were making.

Well after dark the muffled sounds of an approaching trader were heard. At last they were smartening up to the fact that night travel was the only successful way to get around. This time the vessel was smaller, about eighty tons and self-propelled. The guards did not waste any time, and loaded us and moved away from the dock in the shortest possible time. The skipper and the crew were urging the guards on to greater efforts and the guards in turn were yelling and prodding us with bayonets. As a result of this obscene panic our party of eighty was reduced to fifty. The stretcher cases with walking sick were left on the dock. Whoever was in charge of the move had wrongly estimated that eighty prisoners could be crammed into he hold of the tiny coastal trader.

Since our arrival on Muna[2] in October with approximately four hundred and twenty five prisoners we had buried, or lost to friendly fire, one hundred and seventy eight; our draft comprised fifty so we were leaving one hundred and ninety seven behind. It was a real gamble as to who would have the higher survival rate. A party of fifty is easily disposed of, but then the Japanese had starved and tortured more than the remnants of this camp on Haruku. We heard after the war that the Japanese moved the remaining men from Muna to the Macassar camp. This was carried out by moving small numbers of men in ever-smaller craft to the east coast of the Celebes (Sulawesi), in much the same fashion as our move. The last draft of forty men did not know about the cessation of hostilities and were moved as prisoners until the 4th September. Nearly three weeks after the end of the war.

No more deck travel. We were once again forced into a hold half full of rice sacks. It was tiny — about twelve by fifteen feet. There was no headroom to speak of as we hunched up with knees under chin, our hot sweaty bodies in constant contact with one another. Black as any black hole and hot, in spite of it being well past midnight. We cruised in this way until the dawn broke. Then the anchor chain disturbed the few little catnaps we had managed. Soon after the anchor was down a party was assembled on deck and we were told to go ashore and cut palm leaves. A skiff had already been lowered and a party was taken ashore. After many trips the skipper was certain that the Americans would not see us and the camouflage party returned to the hold.

There was a certain area on deck for cooking surrounded by the wood that had been stored for this purpose. Some of those who had not been on the camouflage party had been on deck to relieve themselves and discovered that, by a little fancy foot work, they could hide in this badly stacked pile of fire wood. This was a doubly good effort for all of us. Even a few bodies on deck made a world of difference down below. Because they had been to so much trouble to camouflage the boat they dare not cook on board, as the smoke would be a dead give-away. A few men were allowed to go ashore to do the chores connected with the cooking. The Japanese actually gave us some fried rice with nourishment in it. Normally on all boat trips the food was kept deliberately meagre, pap twice a day, to keep us in a weakened state. Now they fed us two nearly normal meals as far as taste went but the quantity was still sadly lacking. Was this a 'good' skipper or was the end of the war in sight?

This routine lasted for six days. There were no washing facilities. In spite of the hold being open during the day there was not much circulation of air as the boat was completely covered with palm fronds. At night the hatch was closed and the dinghy secured over it. After twenty-four hours in this rotten putrid hold, we stank. After six days our condition was beyond description. As usual with a boat trip, we ended up weaker than when we started. This time our destination was Macassar (Ujung pandang), the largest town in the Celebes. We had been moved over six hundred miles to the west and no doubt beyond the range of American fighters. Our morale boosters had been left behind but we knew that the Americans were on the move. Surely three months would see the end of this terrible existence.

It is interesting to note other opinions of Muna camp. Dr. Leslie J Audus who was with us on Hruku has recorded these comments, written at the time of our release, in his book "*Spice Island Slaves*". These men were patients I took care of on Muna.

A REPORT FROM A DUTCH OFFICER IN HOSPITAL ON MUNA: P234

Throughout the night there was the continuous sound of the singing and the loud talking from those whose minds were crazily trying to escape that miserable existence. Over it all one heard the monotonous and penetrating death rattle of the dying. Behind me for three long days a British officer had lain telephoning his wife; repeatedly he answered questions only he heard, alternating them with outbursts of anger when he screamed that the connections were bad. After three days he died.

The filth defied all description. The camp cookhouse got water from a bamboo conduit; it was usually just sufficient to prepare the food. Those who were in a condition do so were, now and again allowed to go and bathe in a rather dirty stream, but cleaning up the sick in hospital remained an almost insoluble problem. For me this was taken care of by a young man who, although a malarial victim, took upon himself all sorts of little jobs for me and now and then, in one or other canny way, tipped a little can of water over my head.

It goes without saying that under such cirumstances the extent of befouling was indescribable. Vermin tormented us and kept us from sleeping while scabies, widely spread, developed with many into a mass of sores, which covered particularly the lower part of the body.

THE COOPERATION BY BUDDIES CAN BE GATHERED BY THIS ACCOUNT OF A FELLOW RAF MAN. HE HAD UNTIL NOW BEEN AN ACTIVE WORKER BUT SUDDENLY COLLAPSED FROM MALARIA AND STARVATION. HIS FRIEND WOULD MAKE SOUP FOR HIM OF THE WEEDS GATHERED FROM THE ROADSIDE. (SATEH IS A MALAY MEAT DISH SERVED ON A STICK.) P 237

"In the morning before the working party left he carried me outside where, sitting on the ground, I kept myself busy catching grasshoppers which I threaded on a lidi (the mid-rib of a coconut frond) into a kind of sateh which Rob, when he came back, roasted for me over a little fire. In the afternoon he again took me back to the hospital. Through the loss of sensation over the greater part of my body I did not feel the lice, which reproduced unhindered because there was no way of getting rid of them.

In the camp we were also bothered with air-raid alarms but there was no bombing. An orderly saw to it that in a possible air attack the sick in hospital were laid flat on the ground, in that way we took cover.

P231

In the hospital hut lay a non commissioned officer, who for a long time had exhibited alarming symptoms of malnutrition, including mental aberrations. One of the most serious was an unconntrollable kleptomania. Whatever he saw unattended he pilfered. He could get around reasonably well and night raided all huts for booty. His aberration was known and in the course of the morning, when he sat or strolled outside, an orderly took away all the stolen articles from his bed-space. Who ever missed anything made his way to the orderly and, when he recovered his possessions, nothing more was said about the loss.

THE AFTERMATH OF OUR SINKING BY AMERICAN P38 FIGHTERS RESULTED IN THIS COMMENT BY DR. LESLIE J AUDUS. P226

"Many of the survivors were wounded and some needed operations. Dr. Engelen was ordered to operate first on 11 Japanese, then on 14 natives and finally on the prisoners. The seriousness of the wounds might not be considered in that priority, only the order of human importance in Japanese eyes".

1   In fact three men were beheaded on the Amahai camp. Four Dutch men had been involved and suspected by the camp guards but one man managed to convince them that he was too sick at the time. When they arrived on Haruku we were told the four men had suffered the beheading. It was not until Leslie Audus published his book "Spice Island Slaves" that I found the facts.

2   In December 1994 Tom and I returned to Muna on the Caledonia Star. Not only did we identify the old camp sight and the graveyard but we were received on the same dock by a bevy of beautiful girls singing a welcome and spreading flower petals at our feet. Both of us weighing more than twice our weight in camp, but not by any means overweight.

11

Clothes and Soap

FROM NEAR DEATH TO NEAR LIFE

*When two cultures collide is
the only time true suffering exists.*
HERMANN HESSE

Our party of fifty men was driven on the back of a three-ton truck to the Macassar POW camp. Having started the journey as the fifty fit men of a group of eighty, all in walking/working condition, we now had some men who could no longer walk. The stifling conditions of our airless, oven-like hold had claimed a few more casualties. Yet, though sick, weakened and demoralised by the journey, all the fifty had survived.

Macassar (Unjung Pandang) was a well-established camp consisting mainly of the survivors of the Java Sea Battle - British, American and Dutch[1]. The camp was run by the Japanese navy, relatively a more civilised bunch than the army. We were moved into a permanent building, not just an *attap* shack that we had experienced during our tour of the islands. The first meal we received was tasty — not too much of it, but a bit more than we had come to expect. The following day we received an issue of clothing. White vests, blue shorts, and then of all things, some soap and cigarettes! Man what a treat! We were developing into real city slickers. There was even electricity in our building. The order 'lights out' now meant something. Not only did we have electric lights but also we were far enough away from the advancing Americans to make use of them. A rather dubious, but possible life saving, privilege.

The Japanese kept us segregated from the main camp. We were strictly forbidden to talk to the permanent prisoners. But they could see that we had not fared well. Our average weight was well below theirs. There was even a library in this camp. We were not allowed there but arrangements were made for us to have some books. Imagine after two years of not seeing any paper, we could now actually have a book to read, rather than try to smoke it.

Food, books, soap, cigarettes, a hut without leaks, and electricity to boot. What a change in life style! We had arrived, but where? Macassar (Ujung

Pandang) was half way to our destination. With the Java Sea between us and 'home' our chances were less than fifty-fifty. We knew very well the Americans controlled the seas as well as the skies. But 'home' might never happen. We lived, or rather existed, for not even the day, but for the next 'meal' so why worry about this far off, maybe never-to-happen, event? We didn't. This camp was too good to miss. Enjoy it while it lasted.

On 30 April, after about ten days in this camp we were forced to work on the camp gardens. What a nice change to be working for our own good outside the camp wire. Being outside the wire always meant that an opportunity might present itself for some gain. Roots, leaves, snakes, iguanas. Who knows? Thirty of the original fifty men were fit to work. A sixty per cent capability after a six day sea voyage was probably better than the average working rate for the Java-bound moves from Haruku. We discovered much later that the group that left Ambon about the same time we did, the group that was fated to have Blood and Slime with them, started the journey with six hundred and fifty prisoners and ended the sixty eight day voyage with two hundred and seventy nine men. A fifty seven percent death rate in little more than two months.

The camp gardens were far more extensive than anything we had experienced since leaving Java. This was probably why the inmates of this camp looked healthier than we were. The inevitable cruelty of the Japanese was here. The first day we were breaking ground in a new area allotted to the camp for cultivation, some freshly buried bones were unearthed. Thrown to one side were two skulls and an assortment of human remains. Our guards were not the least bit concerned that these bones had no doubt been happy Celebes natives. A few days later, when we were put to work in an established garden, we found the body of an electrocuted man hanging on the barbed wire surrounding the gardens. Two prisoners were detailed to dig a grave just outside the wire and the man was buried on the spot. No thought was given to identifying the man and consequently no concern for next of kin.

Our small party of fifty men was confined to the hut after working hours, but there were strong attempts to communicate with the sailors of the permanent camp. The inevitable bashing followed but we assured them that the Americans were on the warpath and beating these martinets at their own game. It was about this time that the "Great Marinas Turkey Shoot" was under way, when the Americans were shooting Japanese out of the skies just for the hell of it. The tide having turned to such an extent that the Americans had all the experienced pilots and the Japanese had the untrained.

When we were clearing land for the garden extension we piled the bushes, dried grass etc. and left it for a few days to dry in the tropical sun. On one occasion I was lucky enough to come across a really nice six-foot snake. My immediate reaction was to grab it by the tail and give it a mighty flip, as one would crack a whip. I did not heed the fact that a guard was standing close to me. My action put the snake out of commission long enough for me to kill it. However, the guard who had watched the whole process was as white as a sheet and just standing behind me with his mouth open, lost in a deep daze. Too dumbfounded to say anything, he turned and walked off. Once again I was not in a position to tan the skin and could not find anyone who would make use of it. But the flesh was consumed with great enthusiasm.

A few days later, when the scrub clearing had dried and a match was put to it, we had the most exotic aroma we had sensed in many a year. Our nostrils were treated to the cooking of roast beef, or so we thought. This had to be investigated immediately. On some excuse the fellows persuaded the guard that the fire must be put out. Soon we discovered snails were being cooked by the hundreds. An added feature was the automatic opening of the shells so that we had ready access to these tiny tasty morsels.

We had been in camp a few days when the 6th May 1945 rolled around and I became twenty-one years old. It was quite by accident that I was made aware of the date as we had been so out of touch with days and dates and months. Luckily for me it was before we went to work in the morning so I was given the day off. What a luxury! The Japanese required a garden party of thirty men each day regardless of our physical condition. This finally worked to our advantage as the general fitness of our group improved. As more men became fit it meant that we could take turns in the garden work. The rotation in this manner was exceedingly slow as we seldom had more than thirty-one or thirty-two men capable of working outside. My buddies Jock, Jim and Steve, these last two being from Wales, arranged for me to have double rations for the evening meal and made a birthday card for me. How things had changed! Six months ago extra rations, let alone a card would have been out of the question — completely beyond the realm of possibility. Now my buddies were celebrating with me and even happy to get me some extra food. How good life could be! Before the end of the day rumours were circulating that another move was on the cards for us.

In spite of our improved conditions and the luxuries of a permanent camp we were still under the control of the Japanese army guards. It seems that in all nationalities there is rivalry between the services. Here we were on a navy camp with army guards. It was fortunate for us that the main impact of our guards was during the day and out on the working parties. The inevitable beatings continued with some nasty results. Our guards would not allow any communication with the regular camp hospital. Dr. Forbes somehow managed, in his own inimitable way, to circumvent this cruel little plan. He procured some medical supplies from the camp hospital. In spite of these improved conditions malaria, malnutrition and dysentery were still with us, but now there was some hope that we might be able to survive for a longer period than just the next few days.

In July we heard that there had been twenty-three deaths at the Muna camp since our departure. This news must have come from our army guards as there always appeared to be friction between the army and navy personnel. We received another issue of clothing — white vests, blue shorts, a shirt and a green tunic. Soap and cigarettes were a regular issue and we continued to get books sent to our compound from the camp library. It sure paid to be in a large camp even if we were segregated.

What had changed our captors to this new way of treating us? In the last three months we had more clothing and food given to us than during the last two years. Not much more, but more nevertheless. Was the attitude of the navy so different to that of the army?

On the 25th July we were ordered to parade at 5:30pm for the final move to Java. Taken to the docks by truck, we were dumped near a large tanker with a heavy list to port. The guards told us that we would be boarding that night in spite of the unstable condition of the tanker. We spent the night in a godown near the ship, praying that the Americans would not pay us a visit. We were fed fish and rice. Fish instead of *katella* leaves was a marked improvement.

At 7:10pm on the 26th July 1945 we boarded the tanker. The distance to Surabaya is approximately five hundred and fifty miles and should normally take less than two days for a tanker of this size. The ship was obviously not in proper sailing trim so one could only speculate as to how the machinery was maintained. The journey from Macassar to Surabaya, although not too distant, is across the widest part of the Java Sea, where the Japanese had trounced the American, British, Australian and Dutch navies in 1942. The sea must now be well patrolled by American submarines.

The deck of the tanker had a white line painted down the length of it and amidships. We were herded to the high side of the line and told that under no circumstances were we to cross the line. We were deck cargo and must only move from the allotted area to relieve ourselves in the usual overboard toilet. Our daily fare was rice and fish in small amounts for the evening meal, a nice change from the inevitable *katella* soup of the past two years, with a supplemental issue of sugar and biscuits twice a day. Water was very tightly rationed with little consideration given to the fact we were on the open windy deck of a steel tanker under the tropical sun. We had to hang on for dear life because of the list. The deck was burning hot under our feet and handholds were hard to find. We were now so far from the American air action and so completely surrounded by major islands of the Dutch East Indies (Indonesia) that any attempt to take over the ship was just a pipe dream. We were continuously under the muzzle of machine guns so there was little chance of our taking any effective action. Our main concern was still to get food into our emaciated bodies. As the tanker got closer to Java the water issue was cut back drastically. Under the tropical sun, on the hot steel deck without a glimmer of shade, we were being cooked. The constant breeze sucked sweat out of us until we were dehydrated skeletons. Water was absolutely essential. It was nice to have had a biscuit and a teaspoonful of sugar twice a day but we needed the saliva to get it down.

On 29th July we arrived in Surabaya at 4:30 pm. We had not seen an American aircraft during the entire trip and apparently evaded any lurking submarines. Our expectation was to return to Jaar Markt camp, that large, well-organised camp we had left more than two years earlier. If my friend Hengie was still there and working in the cook-house wonders would be performed. Jock, Jim, Steve and I would be well looked after.

This was not to be. As we stood on the dockside all eyes were peeled for any kind of tap or hosepipe. We had to get water into us fast. With crying empty bellies and parched throats we discovered a standpipe and made a dash for it. There was a mad scramble to get our faces, mouths wide open, under this sweet relief. Soon we were moved by truck to a small transit camp near a railway station. Had they closed Jaar Markt while we were away? If so, where were our buddies? We found the answer to this at the end of the war[2].

The work here was all of a defensive nature. We spent our time digging slit trenches for the Japanese garrison. What a change in attitude now! When we left here in 1943 the world was about to be dominated by the glorious Nippon forces. Now they were concentrating on their defence. The Americans must be a lot farther up the chain of islands than we knew about.

It turned out this was a native labour camp. The last one we had occupied was Wei Jami, Ambon. This one was bigger and cleaner and thankfully there were no dead bodies to move out before we settled in. The rice ration was again down to the minimum - two hundred and fifty to three hundred grams a day. We received a small serving of soup and some exceedingly salty fish. Our rations followed the normal pattern. The rice was the warehouse sweepings of spilled sacks complete with small stones and many maggots both dead and alive. The dried and salted fish was reject food that was not acceptable by the population at large.

On the 6th August our group of fifty left the camp, marched to the nearby railroad station, boarded the train, and headed for one of the largest camps in Java. The cattle trucks were the covered type so that we got some protection from the sun. For two days we rattled our way through this beautiful countryside to the capital city of Batavia (Djakarta). Arriving at 2:30pm we were directed to No1 POW camp where they had been warned that a draft was 'returning from the Islands'. Once again we were the pariahs of prison life - - accepted into this large and well-organised camp only to be excluded from all its activities. We were again separated by barbed wire from our fellow prisoners. It seemed that the Japanese did not want it known that we had witnessed the daily air activity over Ambon and as far back as Muna. The general health of the prisoners on the other side of the wire seemed to be good. They at least had some meat on their bones, not too much, but considerably more than we had. We heard that the spineless Kurishima, our camp commander on Haruku, was at this location but did not know if he was the CO. Where were Blood and Slime?

For the last many months we had been aware that as the Americans advanced the Japanese were not going to let us out of their clutches without a fight. A death march was the favoured method of mass killing. This method had the disadvantage of being a lengthy process compared to exterminating a whole camp by machine gun fire. In one case the disposal of bodies was not a problem, whereas it was a decided inconvenience in machine-gunning a whole camp. The Japanese were known for herding men and women into a confined area, such as one hut, and then setting fire to it. With machine guns placed around the hut it insured that no one survived and the disposal of bodies was practically a *fait accompli.*

Our very first impression of this camp was not good. Herded like sheep into a *kraal* we were the jetsam of a long-lost work party. Who would care about the fate of fifty men when the losses had been so heavy? But there was some light at the end of this tunnel. Like a wart on the main camp, we were attached for better or for worse. How could it be worse than the conditions of the last two years? Soon the advantages started to show. Our all-consuming concern was for food. One of the wonders of our diet before we left Java was *Katjang idjoe.* Today we know it as the Mong bean. This now miraculously appeared in our diet. Rice was of course the main staple but there were little additions that made existing worthwhile. The advantage of having barbed wire around us was that our own camp executive could see at a glance our condition. I am sure every effort was directed to giving us more than our fair share of the rations, not in quantity but quality.

On the 10th August 1945 two miracles occurred. We were given three Red Cross parcels to divide amongst the fifty of us and at 7:30pm I was given seventeen letters, all of them more than two years old, but this was not a worry. This was the most enjoyable half hour since I was taken prisoner on the 8th March 1942. I sat down and read and read and read. My Dad had made good his escape from Batavia. Mother was keeping the home fires burning and trying to organise a family get-together. My oldest brother Derek had been shot down, on a thousand bomber raid over Osnabrook and was now home and enjoying life as a Flight

Lieutenant. Colin my younger brother was in the 5th Airborne Division, and had volunteered in India to parachute into Malaya to rescue me. And little Geoffrey was still at school, thank goodness. What a life! Now I could afford the luxury of thinking of my parents and eating anything I could put my hands on. Such rashness was soon rewarded with an incredible dose of the killer dysentery. But at the same time we were allowed to organise a semblance of a hospital. For the first time since I had become a medical orderly our group was given some medical supplies, as opposed to stealing them out of some warehouse. Dr. Forbes, who had been with Jock, Steve, Tom and I on the fiery sinking boat, was once again in a position to bring his skills into play. Just about everything was looking up.

A day or two later we heard that the cook-house was issued with salt, pepper and curry. Something very strange was going on. Were the Japanese in some weird way trying to be nice to us prisoners? Was this just a fact of life in Java or were they actually changing their spots? No, that seemed impossible. I never did find out how the main camp knew who was in this last draft of men from the islands. The information did not come from our small group. The Japanese were interested in working bodies, not individuals, so the Cycle camp administration must have taken the initiative and found out who we were. It is most likely the camp authorities knew only that fifty men were arriving and then, after the usual hassle, found out our names.

Noah, Our Dutch interpreter, made a habit of squatting outside the guardhouse. He would listen to all the gossip the guards had, with the idea that at some time there would be a gem of information he could tell us. He was a patient man and must have listened to an awful lot of drivel before announcing to us that the guard commander had made a speech to all his men. The theme was that Java would not surrender. Java would fight to the finish. What kind of talk was this? Having just come from Muna and Macassar we knew that the Americans were not so close to Java that there would be any talk of fighting to the finish.

Now was the time for us to be doubly careful. If there was talk of fighting to the finish something very serious was happening. Were they scheming a final solution for us? Death march. All through our imprisonment they had searched our belongings. First it was to find weapons, then radios or radio parts, and finally, since moving from the islands, to destroy any written records of camp life. Every move had been accompanied by a thorough search. Any written record had been destroyed, with the inevitable beating being liberally administered. Spot searches had been carried out at any time of the day or night. In spite of this I was able to keep a small Union Jack in my possession until sunk by American fighters. A few men were able to smuggle some sort of written record past the searches having kept them buried most of the time[3]. It was too obvious to us that they were not about to admit publicly how they treated their prisoners. "Dead men tell no tales."

We were all scheming in our own ways the best action to take to evade this final killing ground. What was the best way to thwart what we knew from long experience the Japanese had in mind for us? Wasn't their ideal to have the last man die on the last day of the job at hand? The Samurai code - the Bushido conduct? We each had a score to settle with specific guards, but this was a luxury we would have to subordinate to our own survival. It seemed the time was getting close. My estimate of three months looked as if, finally, it was coming to fruition, and maybe with a vengeance as we heard news or saw signs of the guard's iniquitous intentions. It is interesting to speculate what would have happened if the guards had remained in camp after the surrender. I fear the officers would not have had either the ability or the desire to control some very angry men.

On the 15th August about noon the gate to our compound was left open - strange - no guards around. We curiously, cautiously, moved out of the gate to look around. A little braver we wandered into the main camp. Rumours were rife. There was a radio in this camp, but which of the circulating rumours was the real truth. An army officer, Lt. Foster, introduced himself to me. He had been taken prisoner in Java at the same time we had and knew my family. He was in touch with the radio news in camp and told us that the war was over. *The Japanese had surrendered. We were free.*

It was unbelievable. No last minute treachery. There had been no final solution, no mass murder, no machine guns trained on us for the final glory of their God Emperor, no death march, no mass immolation. What on earth could have made this happen? Dumbfounded, we just wandered around not knowing what to believe and not knowing if this was all some gigantic hoax. It was totally against the Japanese character to let us survive. Japanese who had considered us cowards were now surrendering. Impossible! They must all commit *hari kari* before surrendering. What would their beloved God Emperor think of an army that surrendered? All these men had left locks of hair and fingernail cuttings at home so that their loved ones might remember that they had died a honourable death for their God Emperor. Surely it would not be warrior-like for one to return home and collect their own hair and nail cuttings. This would defeat the whole purpose of the exercise. We could not believe this news as we wandered back to our compound and tried to think this thing through. First the open gate to the big camp — then my friend telling me that their radio actually confirmed that the war was over. Just what could have created this miracle? How could the leopard change his spots overnight? The divine intervention of the Atomic Bomb had saved us and thousands more like us.

Very soon a contingent of Indian guards appeared at the camp. The crafty

Japanese had taken their own men away and placed these former British Indian army men as our guards. We had been aware that many Indian army personnel had followed the call of Chandra Bose and defected to the enemy in the hopes of driving the British out of India. In fact Indian army men were carrying the Nipponese flag within a few weeks of Singapore falling.[4]

Just after this we were visited by a British army major who had parachuted onto the aerodrome to take the surrender of Java from the Japanese. A sight for sore eyes! His mode of dress was new to us. There was nothing about him that we could relate to the fighting man of 1942. We watched in awe as this man stood on a couple of boxes before us and told us of the Atomic Bomb. The whole conduct of this talk was totally different to the attitude of officers and men to each other when we went under the gun. This major was confidant, assertive, no nonsense. He knew his mission and would carry it out with a great deal of determination. I have no doubt this major was an outstanding officer to have been picked for this job — expendable and gutsy. He told us that he had brought with him a doctor and some telegraphists. These men would cater to our immediate needs. He also warned us not to expect miracles in being moved out of Java in a hurry. The end had come so quickly that transport to get men into Singapore and Malaya was a priority. Planning for the invasion and re-taking of Malaya was well advanced and might be carried out without the actual fighting taking place. To be free of our captors, who had deliberately killed so many of our friends, was satisfaction for now.

We were warned to stay close to the camp as the situation was not healthy outside. There were headless bodies to be seen in the canal every morning. Now was the time for uncontrolled revenge. The Japanese army had been defeated, the British had only token representation on the island, and the Indonesians were scrambling for independence and not knowing how to accomplish it at this early stage. In fact there was no real authority to maintain law and order. Hundreds of years of rule by the white man and then the unmitigated cruelty of the Japanese was not to be passed by the locals without retribution. Japanese and Indonesians were settling disputes that had accumulated during the past few years. Nighttime saw retaliation lurking for the unwary on every street corner.

One of the County class cruisers, H.M.S. *Cumberland*, steamed into the Tanjong Priok docks where I had stood next to the H.M.S. *Exeter* some years ago as the victorious Japanese had bombed the hell out of us. Nearly four years later, what had been won and lost in this terrible conflict, with millions of lives lost, hundreds of thousands by torture and inhumanity and starvation? Right now we were back to the *status quo* with the British and Americans rescuing and providing immediate relief for the oppressed. The native population under Sukarno was well on the way to independence from the Dutch, although this would take more fighting and loss of life until the objective was firmly established, for all they proclaimed independence on the fifteenth day of August 1945. This date did not mean that they controlled Java or any of the three thousand islands that comprise Indonesia.

Navy rations were delivered to camp. Food that we had only dreamt of for more almost four years was now available to us. Sad irony, we could not eat such delights as jam. It was sickeningly sweet and could not be kept down. Alas, we were back to the staple rice once again. We knew it was only a matter of time before we would be enjoying a great variety of food, but for now it was necessary to continue the rigid self-discipline we had naturally practised for the last three years. Our staple food was rice for the rest of our stay in Java.

The cruiser sent the ship's entertainment group to camp for our evening fun. What a laugh we had, now that we could enjoy ourselves without the fear of a lurking Blood or Slime. I remember so well the violin player who would ask a question of the audience and, hearing stunned silence, made his violin give us the unmistakable answer. This brought the house down. Just to think that ordinary human beings lived like this all the time, laughing and joking when it pleased them.

On the 2nd September two Swedish Red Cross representatives arrived on the camp and on this day the first of our comrades was moved to the hospital in Batavia. We learned that a hospital of this size had a mental ward. This was something that our harsh environment had not allowed us to even consider. It seemed that when the chips are at rock bottom death came before the mind collapsed for most patients. In the islands those who did lose their minds were so sick physically that they died within a few days. On both Haruku and Muna we had cases of men suffering from mental breakdown. They did not last more than a few days before they died. In one noticeable case on Muna a man suffered from kleptomania. He would wander around the hut during the evening and pick up anything that appealed to him. At first the men swore at him and would not let him get away with it. Gradually we realised that he did not mean any harm. The following morning the men would go to the hospital orderly and recover the "borrowed articles".

Two Japanese aircraft flew over the camp causing a lot of speculation and questioning on our part. Little did we know that the Indonesian independence leader, Sukarno, had already declared Indonesia an independent nation and thus caused a complication for the occupying forces.[5]

Jock, Jim, Steve, and I commandeered a staff car from the clutches of a Japanese officer who had the misfortune to be driving by the compound as we emerged. At this early stage of our relative freedom the Japanese were still responsible for the law and order aspects of the islands. In a grand style we told him and his driver to get out and walk. We did not have any thoughts of revenge as we did not know the individuals. We just wanted to assert our rights! We drove to the nearest women's camp, Tjideng I believe, to see how they had managed to survive these inhumane times. Their condition was terrible and seemed to be without any immediate relief. There was no civilian organisation to take care of them. Like us, food and medicine were the most important requirements for them. We inquired of the camp administration if there was anything we could do to assist. But, of course, the problem was far greater than we anticipated. At this time there were two women's camps in Batavia (Djakarta) with many hundreds of occupants. Soon after the surrender in 1942, the Japanese had been gathering women and children into central areas and housing them in deplorable conditions.

I was keen to return to Canada as this had been my home for the two years immediately prior to arriving in Singapore. But the authorities would not hear of it. I was an RAF member and I must return to the UK for rehabilitation regardless of my own wishes.

Naturally we were now part of the main camp. In fact we stayed in our barbed wire compound but we were included in all the camp activities. These encompassed a fairly wide variety of lectures, readings etc. Much to our surprise an Aussie pilot who had been shot down just five months previously brought us up to date on the progress of the war. He told us of the defeat of Germany and how the Americans had fought their way along a string of islands in the western Pacific. We lapped up such incredible news like thirsting peasants. An air gunner who had completed many sorties over Germany gave us an account of his experiences. There was just so much news to catch up with.

The next day I considered myself most privileged as my new friend Lt. Foster invited me to listen to a BBC broadcast, the first time I had heard a radio in nearly four years! It was very exciting. My notes show that there was an item number sixty-one which was apparently a direct order to the Japanese to carry out some direction. It was so good to know that democratic people were in charge of the world again. My stomach was still recovering from dysentery and my appetite not what it should have been. This was not a worry when there were so many good things to look forward to.

On the 7th September Dr. Forbes took over the sick parade for an extended group. In this big camp the doctors had to be responsible for more than fifty men each. At last we were integrated with a larger group giving us some safety in numbers. Two more of our fifty, Tierney and Connolly, went to the Batavia (Djakarta) Hospital. This pretty well insured their survival. Two Liberators flew over the camp at about two hundred and fifty feet wagging their wings which was greeted with a great uproar. A lot of fellows took in the town and enjoyed our newfound freedom. This resulted in discipline being tightened with strict after dark curfew. An American broke the curfew one evening and spent the night in town. He spent the next few days in jail, probably for his own protection as much as a lesson for the rest of us. Our food was kept at a pretty mean level but slowly showed some improvement. There was some form of entertainment every night and we got regular news bulletins. The officers continuously reminded us to be patient and reassured us that everything was being done to arrange transport for our move from these rotten surroundings.

I heard that a Mrs. Fernando, a friend from Singapore, was in one of the women's camps so I hopped on a truck going the rounds of the other camps and tried to locate her. No luck at either Tjideng or Adack camps. Camp conditions at Adack had improved greatly and we were offered a cup of coffee by their office staff. They had removed a sign that the Japanese had put up, "Loose Women Quarters", meaning that any woman who wanted to supplement her rations or get other privileges could report to the Officers quarters. I believe something like ninety nine point nine percent of the women would rather suffer the terrible indignities of prison life than cohabitate with their captors. What was really surprising to all of us was the number of children that had suffered the ire of the past four years.

On the 13th September we received word that the most seriously sick cases would be sent to Singapore. Slowly aircraft and boatloads of men were leaving camp. Priority was given to the sick and wounded. A few days later Joch, Steve, Jim, and I were drafted for departure. Dave Harries and Tom Coles were to follow sometime later. As we packed our precious belongings Dave looked over to me and said 'Smile Tony —I always liked your smile'. A little embarrassed, I looked at him and said 'Dave, you know we are going to be real people again'.

Soon we were on our way to Singapore as very small cogs in a huge piece of machinery that had passed us by. Time had overtaken all of us. Little did we realise as we joined the world of civilised people again that our very basis of thinking was way out of line. Having hoarded everything we could lay our hands on that might have some conceivable use - pieces of stick, a twig here, a shell there, a coconut husk for the fire that evening, we were now in the world of the expendable. Our little treasures were trash. We must think on a big scale. More clothes, more food and those lovely apparitions. — Beautiful women in uniform, nurses, Wacs, Wrens, Waafs. A new world awaited us.

We were in Singapore for a few days before boarding our homeward bound transport. During this time the first test of freedom proved to be too much for some of our comrades. Bound for the old fashioned 'good time' they roamed the streets of the city in search of booze and women. Lavender Street was the whorehouse capital of the Far East. Everything was available there. It was a one-stop shoppers' delight for the man in uniform. Unfortunately the booze was mainly wood alcohol and had disastrous results for those who really tied one on. Some fellows were returning to camp escorted by their buddies because they were blind. Others were in various stages of severe hangover recovery, wondering what on earth had hit them. Blindness, numb extremities, partial paralysis. They were worried out of their minds as to what to expect next.

It was not easy for me to get around the city and make inquiries as to who of my friends had survived. In fact I really did not know who had been captured and who had managed to escape in those last desperate and tragic days of a destroyed and dying city. Information was scarce. I did make contact with Robert Kinloch, the man who had tried to stop the Chinese labourers from leaving Tengah aerodrome at the onset of an air raid. We chatted by phone but it was not feasible to meet before our ship left for the UK. He had survived and had many stories to tell. On arrival in the city I was compelled to visit the hospital because most prisoners harboured a variety of worms and I was no exception. Thank God we did not know about this any earlier as we were contending with enough overt diseases, to say nothing of the great variety of ulcers, cuts and bruises. We had already been deloused and treated for scabies before leaving Java.

After we had been on board the M.V.*Celicia* for a few days, on our way home, the crew told us that they had been warned to humour us as we were not yet normal. In Singapore as we hung over the rail, talking to the local population peddling their goods from sampans surrounding the ship, our jargon was half English and half Malay, with Japanese and Dutch swear words thrown in for emphasis. It must have been a strange sight for the crew who had been braving the hazards of the deep while we were devoting our total energies to finding more food.

As we progressed through the period of prison life, my friends died off one by one. It was essential to work on a buddy buddy system, so as time went by I picked up new buddies to share the food gathering and cooking chores. As mentioned in this chapter Jock, Steve and Jim were my companions at the end of the war. Jock and I celebrated my 18th, 19th, 20th, 21st, and 22nd birthday together in London. Jock took up his old job as a pharmacist with Boots. I lost track of him in 1956 and thought he had died. In 1994 he surfaced in Scotland and we corresponded. He had retired from Boots, the chemist shop, and returned to the house he was born in. Into his nineties, he is doing very well for an ex POW. Steve and I met in Singapore in 1947. I had been on night duty as a member of the Harbour Board Police, grabbed a couple of hours sleep and then walked out of the barracks towards the centre of the town. It was just by chance that Steve was walking in the opposite direction when we came face to face. We both dropped our plans and headed for the nearest bar to have an old fashioned

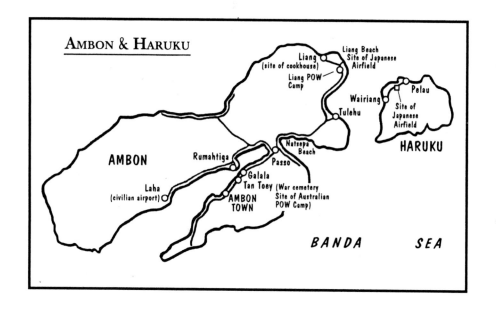

Tel. No.—HOLBORN 3434,
Ext....1257...

Correspondence on the subject
of this letter should be
addressed to
THE UNDER-SECRETARY
OF STATE,
AIR MINISTRY,................
and should quote the reference
A.966808/46.............

Your Ref........................

AIR MINISTRY,

LONDON, W.C.2.

30 September, 1946.

Sir,

    I am directed to inform you that the King has been graciously pleased to approve the award of a mention in despatches to you, in recognition of your services whilst a prisoner of war in Japanese hands.

    The award will be announced in the London Gazette issued on 1st October, 1946, and the certificate will be forwarded to you in due course.

I am, Sir,
Your obedient Servant,

A.C.2. A.H. Cowling,
Grantleigh,
Wray Lane,
Reigate,
Surrey.

Letter from the Air Ministry, London, informing author that he has been awarded a mention in despatches.

We check out the Haruku camp well. Fifty years later and still in use.

Tom Coles, Fred Ryall and the author inspect the roller we pulled on the coral airstrip for the Japanese. The airstrip is now overgrown and useless.

On the author's return to Haruku in 1994 with a group of ex-POWs. Happy Kiriu children provide a welcome by the Haruku camp river. The camp site was on the right behind the trees that look so beautiful today.

POWs return. Tom Coles, second from the left, and Leslie Audus who performed his magic by making yeast to save the fellows from going blind, at Tom's left.

The Kiriu village girls choir greets us near the former Haruku camp entrance. Many children followed us around and we located the well—still in existence, and the cookhouse—where only one stone and mortar fireplace stands in ruins. The dam on the river has gone and the graveyards are overgrown. All the bodies have been removed to Ambon Island.

The ladies of Muna greet us fifty years later. Tom Coles and I left here twice. First to be sunk by American P38 fighters, later as 60-70 pound slave labourers.

pow wow. Steve had stayed in the RAF. and was now stationed in Singapore. This was the last time we met. He retired from Air force and died in the UK some years later. Jim, the powerful Welsh miner, I did not hear about until 1986 when Tom Coles and Dave Harries, both of Muna and Macassar camps, told me that he had moved to California. Jim died in 1990 having proved himself a most resourceful and enterprising individual. Blackie Blackmore corresponded with me for a couple of years. He moved to Rhodesia, now Zimbabwe, and joined the police force. I sent him a Christmas card in 1990 with no response for two years. We renewed our friendship in August 1994 when he visited Canada and spent a few weeks with my wife and me. We planned to meet in Singapore in December 1994 and cruise the islands with a group of survivors. Unfortunately he was not able to accompany us. Hengie of Semarang camp I never heard from again.

1   The Java Sea Battle (February 1942) was the major engagement fought by the combined forces of the ABDA Command. Rear-Admiral Doorman, RNN, in command of American, British, Dutch and Australian Naval units. A decisive Japanese victory.

2   After the war was over we discovered that many of our Haruku men had been moved on to other areas for a variety of work programs

3   This record has been compiled from notes taken immediately after the surrender.

4   Chandra Bose the Indian nationalist, left wing extremist established the Indian National Army to fight for the Japanese against the British. The INA fought in Burma with the Japanese.

5   Of course the Dutch were keen as punch to take over the reigns as the Colonial Masters again. The original post war plan called for American jurisdiction over Java, however they soon realized that for all practical purposes the British should be given control of the area. The subsequent war of independence was complicated by the fact that the British did not have enough troops to effectively occupy the area. Therefore Japanese troops, under British direction, were used as policemen to maintain a modicum of peace and discipline to ensure the establishment of a government. Eventually Dutch troops were introduced into this complicated triangle, which led to the complete independence of Indonesia and the nation as we know it today.

12

HOME

LIBERTY IS ALWAYS DANGEROUS

True friendship is like sound health,
the value of it is seldom known until it is lost.
CHARLES COLTON 1780—1832

Civilisation - the victory of persuasion over force
PARMER WRIGHT

I soon learned more details of my Dad's successful escape from Singapore, having been sunk three times in the endeavour. After arriving in Perth he put the story of his escape into letter form for me. I read this exciting account some four years later in the comfort of his London office. My older brother Derek, who I thought might be strafing the hell out of me on Muna Island was, in fact, in Stalag Luff 3, POW camp in Germany. He was shot down on a night raid over Osnabruck. One of my younger brothers, Colin, had volunteered for the Royal Air Force only to be turned down as they had too many pilot applications. He joined the Paratroops after cutting short a stint at Edinburgh University. While serving in India in 1945 he volunteered for the Malayan invasion forces, telling the authorities that he was fluent in the Malay language. His idea was to release me from captivity. My youngest brother, Geoffrey was still at school and luckily avoided all this terrible business. My mother kept the home fires burning for all of us. She tried very hard to arrange things so that we would all meet at home for a grand reunion but the forces of the world were too much for this to ever take place. We all survived but were never again to all meet at the same place at the same time. Now Western Australia, Canada, England and Tasmania have each laid claim to one of us.

After a year of being in and out of hospital and losing a kidney to the Haruku beating, I returned to Singapore to help my Dad try to regain some of his contracting equipment. Blue Valley Tea Estate had grown into a forest of tea trees and the factory had been burned to the ground when someone had tried to run the diesel engine on preheated coconut oil. At first this unusual and experimental system worked but it took a lot of careful manipulation to make it successful. Eventually the preheated oil ignited with disastrous results. The factory on this isolated estate was levelled to the ground, resulting in the whole place becoming useless. The staff and labourers were content to eke out a living until my Dad returned to get the show on the road again.

In Singapore we were successful in recovering a certain amount of equipment simply from casual observation by friends and employees of the company. The Bucyrus Erie tractor I had seen on Haruku was no longer there. The Japs must have moved it to some other construction job in the area. As the Americans advanced on the east coast of New Guinea landing strips throughout this area became an essential defence measure.

Before returning to Canada I joined the Singapore Harbour Board Police (S.H.B.P.) on a one year contract. Our purpose was to stop the wholesale looting of shipments arriving on the docks. The only qualification required for this job was to have seen front line action during the war years. It was a hastily contrived force in which the authorities did not have the time or money for training. We were most successful. Our first night of duty saw the arrest of dozens of dock workers drunk on the job. Men were lying around the godowns sandwiched between broken crates of fine Scotch whiskey. Bottles, unopened, were secreted in convenient corners for later consumption. It did not take long for our impact to be felt, but with this simple form of looting being stopped the challenge for the more sophisticated criminals came into play. Forged papers and large consignments of goods were regularly being spirited out of the harbour area. At the end of my contract year the S.H.B.P. had complete control of the situation, so I looked farther afield for my next job in spite of being offered an extension to my contract.

In his efforts to regain his lost equipment, my Dad had a business associate in Sumatra. I wrote to Mr. Van Dongeran to see what the prospects of a employment were like in Sumatra. Much to my surprise the whole island was in desperate need of European supervisors for the rubber estates that were coming into production after years of neglect. I joined Harrison Crossfield, Sumatra branch. As a budding young rubber planter I enjoyed the life a great deal. There were many advantages to living in a remote and beautifully simple area where the culture and people were so sensual. Hand in hand with the advantages were some dangers in this field work, as the Indonesians were struggling for independence and the white men were the targets.

On my rounds of the labour force one morning I came across the freshly killed and still warm carcass of a wild pig. It had its belly ripped open by one great swipe of a tiger's paw. Because of the political situation and the ever present threat of the Indonesian freedom fighters I went to work armed with a .303 rifle everyday, so I did not fear a confrontation with the beast that I had frightened away from its kill. The Indonesian farmers experienced a great deal of trouble with the wild pig population. I was requested on many occasions, when the crops were sprouting, to sit in their little 'watch towers' and wait for the arrival of wild pigs. This always happened at night. I don't think I ever hit a pig but soon after dark the noise of a .303 frightened them away and I was able to get a partial nights sleep. The farmers would stay up all night or share the watch with family members.

Under pressure from my family I returned to Singapore and tried to find a tea planting job in Ceylon (Sri Lanka). This did not materialise so I returned to a safer and more stable part of the world - Canada.

My first job after returning to Vancouver in 1949 was to sort Christmas mail at the main Post Office. Since the Cold War was in full swing I applied to the Reserve Air Force with the idea of taking flying training. They would not consider me as I had only one kidney so I joined the army Ordnance Corps (RCOC) in the early 50s. Eventually this was to lead to a most satisfactory outcome. In 1952 I was invited, as a blind date, to a Valentine's Day party sponsored by a group of graduates of Montreal's Royal Victoria Hospital and the Montreal Neurological Institute who had moved to our beautiful city. In 1953 I married my blind date – Norma and issued forth four wonderful boys; Christopher, Geoffrey, David and Michael.

In 1961 I was unemployed and had made arrangements to move my lovely wife and four boys to Montreal, where my brother-in-law would assist me in finding a job. We had purchased a house in Richmond and, because of my lack of funds, I was desperate to sell and find some gainful employment. All arrangements for the movers to come in and load the furniture had been made for a Monday morning. On the Sunday immediately prior to moving, my Commanding Officer, Major Bill Maxwell, phoned me to say that the Federal Government was starting a Special Militia Training Program (S.M.T.P.) to alleviate the large number of unemployed. The program was to train young people, for a period of six weeks, in the rescue of citizens from demolished buildings, as part of the cold war preparedness in case of the outbreak of hostilities. To carry out this program they would employ regular Militia soldiers to do the training. At this time I held the rank of Captain and immediately applied for a spot in the S.M.T.P. I was most fortunate in being accepted right away and cancelled all plans to move to Montreal. Luck was with me as the Brigadier at Headquarters BC Area wanted a staff officer for "G" branch. Out of all the officers in the training program I was picked to work at HQ— a job that lasted for three years and allowed me to save enough money to attend UBC. A rather strange situation arose when I applied for a university loan. There had been a program of loans for veterans. However by this time, 1964, the program had ceased and the awards were made to the children of veterans. I was not considered eligible for these loans. I was really dismayed. With all the educated people in charge of programs of this nature no one was in a position to authorise a loan for a veteran. I did manage to find a job as a night watchman and completed my Baccalaureate in four years.

At the end of the first year, just before the exams were to be written, I did not have a penny in the bank. With a wife and four hungry boys at home and at least a two months' wait before I would be paid for a summer job I was in a real pickle. I appealed to the Legion for a loan. They told me the only course of action open to them was to ask their branches to put a can on the bar counter and request donations. After two months this brought in $50.00 which helped with our current bills. I worked during the summer at the Vernon Cadet Camp training young recruits.

After becoming a teacher and settling down to a regular job I accomplished, to a lesser degree, one of my ambitions, to fly. I could not afford instructions in powered flight so I took up gliding with the Vancouver Soaring Association. Every weekend during the summer I would drive, a hundred miles, with my boys, to Hope in the Fraser Valley. We usually slept, on Saturday nights, under the wing of our club Schweizer 2-22 trainer. During the weekend we shared the glider with the other club members. Hope is a town at the east end of the Fraser Valley surrounded on three sides by mountains. Occasionally we could get some favourable lift and stay aloft for a fair amount of time. There was always the consideration of sharing the time with other members on the ground and knowing just how they felt if you overstayed your flight. The other hobby I took up immediately was the art of bee keeping, a really pleasant and rewarding past time. I still maintain two or three hives in the back yard but the art gets progressively more difficult as new diseases such as the varoa mite infest the industry and the hobbyist.

I retired from the teaching profession with a Masters Degree in Education and a great desire to sail the beautiful coast of British Columbia. This is one of the most attractive sailing areas of the world. With a multitude of islands that protect the coast from the storms of the Pacific Ocean and with balmy summer weather it is the sailors' paradise. I was fortunate enough to sail from the frozen reaches of Glacier Bay, Alaska, to the exotic and historical shores of the Society Islands. Tahiti welcomed us after three months at sea from the Florida coast through the Panama Canal, Galapagos Islands and many other adventures in the south Pacific.

After the Atomic Bombs were dropped and the lives of thousands of war prisoners and internees saved by that action, it became apparent that the treatment of people under the auspices of the Japanese was far from satisfactory. From the Mukden Incident in 1931 to the end of the Pacific war in 1945, the Japanese had behaved in a most unbelievable manner. In all theatres of the Pacific war the senior officers had not only turned a blind eye to the actions of their troops but also had actively encouraged, and in many cases participated in, behaviour that the western world abhors. Their ability to deny the truth and put their own interpretation on facts that the rest of the world sees in a different light is most disturbing. No doubt this is based on the belief of *Hakko Ichiu* espoused by God Emperor Jimmu in 660AD, a belief that Japan must rule the eight corners of the world, or in simple terms, become the master race accountable to no one. The Japanese armed forces has several names for their disciplinary actions; the army calls the routine striking and bashing of soldiers *bentatsu,* the navy goes for *tekken seisai* or the iron fist, civilians refer to the whip of love or *ai-na-muchi.* The unfortunate recipients of this discipline are told that this violence is done in the name of love. Love for family, village, city and to the ultimate father figure their God Emperor.

Military War Crimes tribunals were held in Tokyo, Manila, Hong Kong and Singapore, to bring the perpetrators of these sadistic crimes to justice. In the clash of cultures and by the very nature of *Hakko Ichiu* the Japanese do not admit to any wrongdoing.

The Singapore Tribunal was the centre for all crimes committed in South East Asia and Burma (Miramar?). Both Squadron Leader Pitts, our Commanding Officer in Haruku and Doctor Alaistair Forbes, who was with me on all our camps after Haruku, testified at these trials. Whiskers (Col Anami) was hung for his part of the atrocities. Gunso Mori (Blood) was hung. His story, the early part of it, prior to leaving Java, is told by Laurens Van de Post in the book *The Seed and the Sower*, later made into the movie *"Merry Christmas Mr. Lawrence"*. This was the Mori before he went to Haruku. A mad man even with an officer to control him, and in the more controlled atmosphere of Java. It is interesting to note that the Japanese made the Van de Post movie and naturally turned it into a propaganda piece. The immorality of it is lost in the 'clash of cultures' theme and Mori's crimes are justified. Kasiyama (Slime) was sentenced to life in prison, but because of the lack of English/Japanese interpreters he only served a short sentence. I have no official confirmation of this but it is widely believed by many ex POWs. The man who bayoneted Tom and lunged at me after we were sunk by the American P38 fighters was dealt with in a Dutch military court in Java. Tom and I did not hear of the results. I was assured by a major of the War Crimes Tribunal in Singapore that the Dutch authorities would be harder on him than the British.

Either in Java or Singapore, in 1945, we were asked to give details of any atrocities that we had suffered. I did not look on the beating that I had suffered on Haruku as an atrocity. It was an excessive reaction to a broken rule. However the bayoneting of a survivor from a sunken ship was to my mind against all international law. This to me constituted a real atrocity. I listed the incident without knowing the date or the individual concerned and submitted it to the authorities. There were literally hundreds of other submissions made at this time. It must have been one piece of paper amongst thousands so I forgot about it, thinking this was really a psychological exercise to placate abused troops. This was in September 1945. In 1947, after my return to Singapore, I was working in the office one day when the phone rang and a voice on the other end identified himself as a major of the War Crimes Commission. He stated that he had my report of a bayoneting off the island of Muna and that the individual concerned was in a prisoner of war camp in Java. Needless to say I was absolutely staggered. I had not given this incident a thought for many months and was once again enjoying the life of a free man. We discussed the situation for a while during which time he told me that the Dutch had other atrocities attributed to this individual and that their punishments were harsher than anything the War Crimes Tribunal in Singapore would pass out. I believed him and left the Dutch to deal with the situation.

In 1986 Dave Harries, as mentioned, organised a return trip to Haruku. Seven of us managed to fly there and see that the village of Kariu now surrounds the camp. The only two recognisable features are the well, constructed at such cost in human life, and the river that provided water for the camp. In true native style all the villagers use the well, but for convenience they have erected a screen just next to the well and made it into a urinal. They have not considered the fact that the urine drains neatly into the well. With several acres of untended land next to the well it did not occur to them that this practice may not be beneficial. The campsite is now overgrown with palm trees and scrub land. The airstrip is covered with three feet of undergrowth. After I became a medical orderly the fellows constructed anti-aircraft gun pits for the defence of the strip against American fighters. These were now neatly planted with chilly bushes that were flourishing. There is a new dock at the village of Pelau. There are hundreds of happy children playing in the water and in the dugout canoes that abound there. The fishing is good and life is prolific and normal with many more villages on the island. Only one man that we met remembered the Japanese days of terror. I believe the life expectancy on Haruku is approximately fifty years. He had been employed by the Japanese to finish the *attap* roofing on the buildings we occupied. He looked old and frail and had difficulty walking. I took him by the arm while he showed me the area where we had the cemetery. He walked with a single stick in much the same manner as we had provided for Marcel many years previously. With an injured leg one can take a lot of weight onto the stick by holding it across the chest and placing it on the ground on the side of the injury. The natives do not use a stick in the fashion of a western walking cane. My Indonesian was too rusty to get the story of what had caused the injury to his leg.

The seven of us felt that by contributing one hundred dollars a year to a fund that would buy supplies for the school we could turn what had been a hellhole for us into a really worthwhile project for the inhabitants of this tiny village. We would obliterate the torture, disease, and starvation of bygone years and make this one village a place where the children would grow up to be proud of themselves and their home turf. They would have a school that was well equipped, and possibly a dispensary at some future date.

Mrs. Leleh, the school teacher who organised a sing song for us, with one of her boys proudly playing his guitar and singing "White Christmas", had admired my little solar calculator when I produced it to calculate payment for the bananas and coconuts that they had given to us during our visit. I told her that as soon as I got home I would send her two of them for the school. We left there with really great plans.

I wrote to Mrs. Leleh soon after returning to Canada to confirm her address and advise her that the calculators and other miscellaneous school supplies would be sent as soon as I could establish that the mail was getting through. Bas Trevethick, one of the members of our party whom I had not met in prison camp, contacted the Indonesian Embassy in London and arranged for two boxes of books to be sent by courier to the school. We felt really good about this as the official at the Embassy was from Ambon and would have an interest in seeing the delivery of the books to the right place. It was not to be. The books never arrived and my letter was not answered. Two years later Geoff Lee, anther member of our group, sent a parcel of ballpoint pens to the school and many months later received a letter saying that the supplies had arrived and that Mrs. Leleh had heard from Tony Cowling. On the strength of this second hand information I wrote to Mrs. Leleh and enclosed a solar calculator. I told her that I was keen to send some more calculators and other miscellaneous supplies. More than a year has passed now without an acknowledgement. We are well aware of the translation and writing difficulties but hope eventually to cultivate our little school on far off Haruku. I feel sure that all the men who suffered on Haruku would be most pleased to know that a little school on the island is now enjoying a better than average education as a result of our having been there.

Now (2001) with a second printing contemplated no word has been received from Haruku. The graft and mismanagement in Indonesia is, I am sorry to say, the cause of so much suffering. The little project I initiated to create happiness and education on a small island would have been unique and so beneficial to the village of Kariu. It was destined never to come to fruition. The happy children we saw playing in Peleau village in 1986 have since been the targets of religious fights on Haruku. The Indonesian government policy of resettling families from Java to the Moluccas Islands has not worked favourably for the majority Christians of Haruku.

APPENDIX   1

XMAS DAY 25TH DECEMBER 1942. (NB. We were given a sheet of paper with these sentences and instructed to select three numbered sentences. We were allowed to add twenty words to this. My parents did not receive this letter for approximately two years.)

1   We prisoners are permitted to write home by the generous Government of Nippon.
2   I am now in a Japanese Prisoner of War Camp in Java.
3   My Health is excellent (not excellent).
4   I am now in hospital on account of sickness. I was in the hospital but now I have recovered my health
5   I hope you are all healthy and living well. Are the children well. Have you enough money for food to keep yourselves.
6   My daily work is easy and we are being paid for the number of days we work. We have plenty of food and much recreation.
7   We officers are being paid the same salary as that of the Japanese officers according to the ranks per month
8   I am always wishing that this miserable war would be over, and that I should return home.
9   At present I am now working.
10   I am constantly thinking of you. It will be wonderful when we meet again.
11   Our camp is well equipped, and the accommodation is comfortable. Our daily life is very pleasant.
12   The Japanese treat us well, so don't worry about me and never feel uneasy.
13   Would you kindly look after so and so (Mr or Mrs).
14   Good bye. God bless you. I am waiting for your reply earnestly.

APPENDIX 2

In 1946 when I was released from RAF Hospital Cosford, I visited my Dad in his office in Caxton Street, London. He gave me a sealed letter date stamped March 1942, Perth, Western Australia. He had addressed it to me in Java but it had been returned to him. He kept it for me. This was the enclosure:

Escape from the Japs

Aldelphi Hotel
St. Georges Terrace
Perth. W.A.

SINGAPORE

On the afternoon of 10th February 1942, I said Goodbye and Good Luck to my friend, Lieut. Gordon R. of the Malayan Royal Naval Volunteer Reserve, who had been ordered to take his ship to Batavia. He and I shared rooms in the same block of buildings at the Hotel, and, when he was in port, he invariably called at my room to warn me when the alert was signalled. Imagine my surprise when he walked into my room at 10:30 that night with the news that he required me to take a watch on his ship (HMS Panglisma) or an Admiralty Tug, because the Malays had refused duty. As I had not anticipated being able to leave Singapore because there were still women and children remaining, there was much to do before I could get away. I had no sleep that night attending to my affairs as far as I could and packing up. But I made it, and reported for duty at 5.30 a.m. after seeing General Wavell land at a nearby aerodrome, just as it was getting light.

In an endeavour to save certain vessels under repair, the Naval Commander in Singapore ordered a tug (*Trebova*) to tow several ships to the Dutch East Indies, and I was ordered aboard one of these. On going aboard, I found that there was very little food, and already there were quite a few white people asking if they could be taken away. Four ladies were refused on the grounds that there was bound to be trouble, and they were told to go to the docks where they would probably find another ship. There were several air raids around us up to 9 a.m., and very large shrapnel bursts were taking place over the aerodrome adjacent to the shipyard where we were getting ready for the tug. I dashed off to town to obtain some food from a small store I had made for myself, getting back to the ship just as my Lieut friend was moving off. Incidentally, there was much action in the suburbs of Singapore, and I heard machine guns chattering as I loaded the car. I could see that if we did not move soon, the Japs would land bombs and shells right on us in the shipyard. Half an hour later, a patrol vessel confirmed that the place where we had been parked had been bombed soon after we left. We cruised about the harbour outside the breakwater, and got bombed for our pains. At 3 p.m. we were off, and as a parting present, an island called Blakang Mati - where we had heavy guns firing on the Japs - was badly bombed continuously just as we were passing it. As we were closer inshore we got some of the trouble.

By this time Singapore was a burning island; and so were the surrounding islands, which mostly contained oil tanks. The smoke pall was so thick that the air observation in the afternoon was quite impossible. The result was that the Jap Air Force paid attention to escaping shipping. In particular one episode stands out in my mind. A crowd of soldiers were trying to get away in sampans to some junks lying just outside the breakwater. Down came the bombs from 27 Jap planes and we had to rush to the rescue - but there was not much left to rescue.

Fortunately we were small fry, and beyond a couple of inquisitive Jap planes, we were left alone for the rest of the evening, and so had a grandstand view of the bombing of other ships until darkness fell. After doing spell of duty till 8 p.m. trying to keep the ship on a course (the steering had gone wrong due to the bombing) that would cause the hull the least strain, I retired for the night completely exhausted in a bunk I found below. I took the precaution of preparing an 'abandon ship' bag - in fact my office bag, before I lay down, and it was just as well that I did. At 2 a.m. I heard a yell of " all hands on deck". I cursed the fool that shouted and asked "what for?" and was told the ship was sinking. I lost no time in jumping into about 2 ft of water swishing about in the cabin, grasping my office bag, and making for the companion way, down which I fell and hurt my back badly. The prospect of a watery grave, and the stillness of it all drove me to Herculean efforts, and after five minutes I joined my shipmates on the fo'castle. There were only two of them left, the others having already been rescued by a patrol vessel, which in the light of a watery moon, I could see approaching us. The sea was rough, and it meant a jump at the right time, otherwise ..! As the other vessel approached, I threw my office bag over (by the way we had no life belts) and while I was arguing the toss as to who should jump first, I was pushed and fell luckily into the arms of a bunch of chaps on the rescue boat. My back was most painful, and I was carefully lowered into a space below where I literally passed out. What woke me at 7 a.m. (12th) was a salvo of bombs bursting around us, and I dragged myself to the deck just in time to see another bunch of planes bomb us once more. I must have been one of the oldest men on board, and as such I considered I was privileged to offer advice, which was to get out of the track of shipping (Banka Straits), as we were inviting bombs and destruction to about half a million dollars of naval ships. The advice was at once acted upon, and we turned West. Once again we had a grandstand view of bombing by Japs of our ships escaping Singapore. When we got to the coast of Sumatra, the officers decided to scuttle all towed ships and get aboard the Tug which was standing by.

It was a fortunate decision as will be seen.

We were now party of about 120 on the tug, including one lady we had rescued from the water, and a party of PWD (Public Works Dept.) officers who were stranded at fishing villages which we passed. On my advice we stuck to the coast along the 2 fathom mark, eventually reaching the mouth of the river of Palembang in S. Sumatra. Here we saw several ships sunk at the mouth, but I was able to tell our skipper just where he could get a pilot, because I had been to this place before. He proved to be a Dutch Malay, and informed us that there were only two left, but he would take us up, It was too late to go up that night, so at dawn we started on our 60 mile trip up river. About 6 miles from Palembang, we picked up a pilot from a crashed Hurricane, who had been trying to stop some paratroops who had just floated down alongside us on a Refinery area. There were about 500 of these paratroops - Japs of course - and the town of Palembang was in a state of great alarm when we arrived there an hour or so later. We could get no Dutch people to attend to us, and we could only wait until the 'alarm' was over. This did not take place till 2.30 p.m., when we went alongside the wharves to report, and ask for stores and coal. I should have mentioned that I was of no use in the engine room or the stokehold, I was given the job of 'writer', which took me ashore with the skipper, and the Malay pilot.

I was in luck, for the Dutch Harbour Master was a friend of mine whom I had known in Singapore. At my request he telephoned the No 1 (head) of the refinery which we had passed, and after considerable delay, due to the disturbance caused by the Jap paratroops, gave me a message that Mr Elliot, the chief man, sent word that I was to use his house and car, and that he would be over as soon as possible. I got leave from the skipper and had a grand swim in the cool pool of this rich man's air conditioned house. I was inches thick in dirt and grime, plus blood from cuts and bruises, and I never enjoyed a whisky and soda as I did that afternoon. After resting on the beautiful patio in a long cane chair , I donned the car driver's clothes (Mr Elliot's were too big for me as he is 6' 8" tall), and went for a joy ride in the town area to see what was happening. The place was in an uproar, as paratroops were being rounded up, so I made for the wharves again to seek out my friends of the Tug (*Trebova*). I was feeling pretty good as the temporary owner of a Packard limousine.

It was at the wharves that I first met our (British) Naval Control Officer, to whom I shall refer to as the BNCO in future. He informed me that I had better take the first train to Batavia, as I was now surplus and had a bad back. But he permitted me to remain with the tug, sending, however, all surplus people down by train. When he heard that I had a car, he made me sort of transport officer - driver, and I was glad to be of use. I invited him around to Mr Elliot's house for a drink and some food, and he accepted. Owing to 'phone calls he did not arrive till 10 p.m. (14th) and informed us that he was standing by because the Japs had been reported off the mouth of the river we had just come up. At 1030 p.m. he had a radio phone call from Batavia saying that some 30 Jap transports were outside the river mouth and were unloading barges of troops, and that our Blenheims had been sent to attack them. Half an hour later, another call came through that another 60 transports had been sighted by our Blenheims, and we were told to destroy Palembang - and good luck.

So there we were, the four of us. My friend, Lieut. Gordon R., the Skipper, the B.N.C.O. and myself. The problem was to destroy the town and the refineries. For a start, I got the B.N.C.O. to speak to my friend, Mr Elliot, at 1030 p.m. When I saw Mr. Elliot some weeks later at Perth, W. Australia, he told that my information enabled him and eleven others to escape after taking action in blowing up the refinery and letting the petrol down the river; that he went straight to the oil-fields and evacuated some 250 Americans at 2.30 a.m. that morning. I was very gratified to hear that I had been of use.

Reverting to the nightmare of Palembang, our little party had no sleep that night (14/15th February) what with the arrangements that had to be made to destroy Palembang, and particularly the two refineries, and to meet and attend to casualties coming up river in a couple of bombed mine-sweepers. At dawn, we set off for the docks to board our tug to take it up river, and on the way we noted the native population running around in a frenzy of fear. So they too, must have had the news of the Japs' approach. Demolition explosions were too numerous to mention, except one at the docks, which brought down nearby buildings, causing us to abandon the car, and run as fast as we could to the tug and cast off into the river, up which we were soon steaming under a pall of smoke so thick that the orders to the helmsman had to be given from the lower deck of the Tug! We arrived shortly at the coaling yards, just in time to see huge cranes and bits of RSJs toppling over or hurtling through the air. The Naval partly took about half an hour to get their baggage off the Tug and mine-sweepers, which were scuttled after being set on fire, and then we set about the long journey of 450 kilometres to Oosthaven in the southern top of Sumatra. We had no means of transport, and viewed with envy the RAF and other Military lorries passing us on their way South. At the Railway Goods yards of Palembang, which was clear of smoke, Jap planes frequently came over to have a look at us, and we expected bombing at any time. I suggested to my friend, Lieut. Gordon R. that as there were some engines and wagons in sight, I could see no reason why we could not use them instead of foot slogging. What exactly happened after that I do not know, a train a mile long with two engines with steam up was ready to move at 9.15 a.m. It was crammed with escaping women and children, civilians and soldiers, and our party, of course. Bren guns were mounted in front to protect the engine drivers; in the centre, and in the rear of the train, and off we went full speed ahead, every man being warned to keep his gun or rifle ready for instant action. It was well that this precaution was taken, for in a few minutes we came under fire from the paratroops who had landed the day before, and who lay hidden in the jungle on either side of the railway track. Our fire, however, was so hot (and probably unexpected by the Japs) that we got through with only a few casualties, after about 15 minutes, we were in good country. We had a miserable journey to Oosthaven, with no food and very little water, in the burning sun by day, and with the rain and cold at night. All the time, we had the foul smoke of the engines in our faces, as we were all in open trucks. I should estimate that we were about 2,000 people in all who got to Oosthaven on that train at 1.30 a.m., all miserable wet and filthy. There was not an ounce of food to be had, but the Dutch had given us some coffee at a stop a few miles back from the port. My Lieut. friend, although absolutely worn out, refused to rest, and in a couple of hours had persuaded some Artillery cooks to serve a most welcome meal of hot tea, biscuits and hot sardines in tomato sauce; this at 4 a.m. on the morning of the 16th Feb. 1942. The dawn was bleak and misty with an incessant drizzle. It brought a staff officer enquiring for the Naval party, who were given the job of taking two tugs and five speedboats to Batavia. It was decided that Lieut. Gordon R. and I should proceed ahead, and after reporting to the British Naval HQ at Batavia, we were to make arrangements for the reception of the members of the party. This was done by travelling on the "Roseboom", one of the ferry boats plying between Sumatra and Java (since sunk trying to escape from Padang in Sumatra) to Java, whence a train took us to the Capital, where we reported at 11 p.m. on the 16th Feb. 1942.

The next day I was thanked by Naval HQ for my services, and given a free ticket to the U.K. via Colombo. I decided, however, it would be quicker to travel by paying my own way via Australia, and either S. Africa or America. I duly landed in Fremantle where I was 'marooned' for some three months waiting for a ship to take me home, and when it did turn up (it was delayed by a strike by the Chinese crew) it was so slow that I left it at Durban, and got a ship - a fast Cunarder - at Capetown a fortnight later. I arrived Home in mid-July 1942, very glad to be back after a sea voyage full of anxious moments - after leaving Fremantle; then nearing Durban; and again at Freetown and off the Azores; to say nothing of the Irish Channel approaches.

(Since there had been no greeting at the start of the letter and no sign off I gathered that this was primarily a record of Dad's exciting escape from a doomed city. A truly harrowing experience for a man in his fifties).

APPENDIX 3

Certified true copy of an appendix to:-

Medical report of certain Prisoner of War camps in
Java and the Ambon group, with special reference to
the diseases encountered and the treatments thereof.
April 1942 – August 1945

-110-

MEDICAL APPENDIX No 4.

List of Outstanding British Medical Orderlies.

The undermentioned airmen did particularly good work during the dysentery
epidemic and at all times and maintained the traditions of the Service.

A.C. Flant   )

A.C.Pouden   )   Royal Air Force Medical Orderlies.
                      They left Haroekoe* either in November, 1943,
                      or May,1944.
A.C. Graham   )

A.C. Turbutt   )

A.C. Barnes   )
                      R.A.F. personnel acting as R.A.F.
                      Medical Orderlies in Hospital.
A.C. Cowling)

A.C.Cowling did particularly fine work although his trade was not medical
orderly. He remained with me all the time and returned to Java in July 1945.

*The difference in spelling is the British and Dutch version.

APPENDIX 4
THE CODE OF BUSHIDO

Some examples of the behaviour of the Japanese in other areas of the Asia Pacific war are listed below. For confirmation of these unbelievable stories I suggest to the reader that he or she refer to the following books on Japanese War Crimes titled *"The Knights of Bushido"* by Lord Russell of Liverpool CBE, M.C., *"Betrayal in High Places"* James McKay, is based on the papers of James Goodwin, an investigative officer with the Australian War Crimes Tribunal, Tokyo, and *Hidden Horrors, Japanese War Crimes in World War 11*. Yuki Tanaka. Many other books, noted below, are personal accounts of Japanese behaviour.

In Singapore and Malaysia:

Saburo Ienaga in his book the *Pacific War 1931 - 1945* states that over seventy thousand Chinese were arrested in Singapore for subversive activities. Of these an unknown number were murdered. He quotes a Japanese account **"The executions were carried out in a heinous way. A large number of Chinese were tied together, loaded on a boat, taken out to sea, and pushed overboard."** Others were taken to the beach and machine-gunned after being tied, in groups, with their hands behind their backs. Other murders were so gross in the defiling of the human body that they are best left unprinted. British investigations after the war based on eye witness accounts estimate the figure at between forty thousand and one hundred thousand disposed of by torture, beheading, drowning, machine gunning and other methods. In contrast to this we have the Japanese admission at war crimes trials of a figure *"not less than five thousand"*.

Robert Hammond in his book *"A Fearful Freedom"* tells the story of a British soldier cut off from his unit in the Battle for Malaya who tries to survive, successfully, behind enemy lines. This particular incident takes place soon after his separation from his unit. The Jim & Fred of this story are in the Malayan jungle when they come across a remote village far from the fighting front.

"With Fred covering him, Jim inched forward intending to search the houses for food. The smell became nauseating as he got closer, and then he saw the cause of it. The Japanese had been there. Stuck on poles and hanging from trees were the heads of those they had executed, and even worse - tied to the trees were the bodies of pregnant women who had been disemboweled so their unborn children hung out between their legs. Many also had their breasts cut off".

Off the coast of Sumatra.

Nurses Massacred on Banka Island

On the 12th February1942 the senior Australian medical officer in Singapore decided to evacuate all Australian nursing personnel. Many of them departed on the *Empire Star* and arrived safely in Batavia (Jakarta). On the 14th February the remaining sixty-five nurses boarded the *Vyner Brooke*, a small vessel of 1669 tons. On board were about three hundred other evacuees escaping from Singapore. The ship was bombed and sunk near the island of Banka off the coast of Sumatra. Only two lifeboats remained functional after the destruction of the *Vyner Brooke*. Consequently most of the passengers had to fend for themselves in the best way they could. The Australian nurses and about thirty passengers were lucky enough to be in one of the lifeboats. They landed on Radjik beach on Banka Island. Some time later a group of twenty soldiers from the *Vyner Brooke* joined them on the beach. Their immediate reaction was to find a way off the island and continue the fight against the invaders. However they soon realised that the native population was frightened of the Japanese already on the island and they were reluctant to co-operate. With this in mind and the fact that they had a considerable number of wounded in the group one of the soldiers, with the consent of the group, walked towards Muntok, the main town of the island, with the idea of surrendering to the Japanese and getting aid for the wounded.

About 10AM on the 16th February the soldier returned with a Japanese officer and 15 Japanese soldiers. The surviving British soldiers and the nurses were separated with the result that the British soldiers were taken away, out of sight, and bayoneted. A few of the soldiers who tried to escape were shot. The Japanese then returned to the twenty-two Australian nurses and thirty civilians still on Radjik beach. The civilians were sent down the road to be interned.

Nurse Bullwinkel the only survivor of this massacre describes what happened next.

"They came back and we knew what had happened... they came back wiping their bayonets. We realised what was going to happen. I can remember one of the girls saying, 'two things I hate most the sea and the Japs, and I have got both of them'. We were all sitting down and we were ordered up, and then told to march into the sea. Which we did. As we got about waist level they started machine-gunning from behind. I was hit at the side of the back. The bullet came through, but I wasn't aware of it at the time. I thought that once you were shot you'd had it. What with the force of the bullet and the waves I was knocked over into the water. And in doing so, I swallowed a lot of water. I became violently ill, and as I stood I realised very much alive. Next thing I thought, they will see me heaving. So I tried to stop and I just lay there. I wouldn't know how long. When I ventured to

sit up, there was nothing. All my colleagues had been swept away and there were no Japs on the beach. There was nothing. Just me. I got up, crossed the beach, and went into the jungle."

Eventually Nurse Bullwinkel met with a surviving soldier hiding in the jungle. Since the Japanese had captured the island they had no alternative but to surrender. It is not known if the soldier survived the years as a prisoner. I had the pleasure of meeting with nurse Bullwinkel, in Brisbane, Australia, during an ex - POW meeting, in 1986.

In Borneo

CRUCIFICTION

Wong Hiong, a Chinese cook for the Japanese guards at Sandakan POW camp, North Borneo, witnessed the following incident in August 1945. During the time of this observation Wong Hiong was hiding in a nearby building.

"The prisoner was made to stand with his back to the cross and was supported in this position by Hinata. I then heard the Jap officer give a shout, whereupon a Jap soldier by name Nishikawa emerged from the administration office carrying a stool and a knife with a blade about 8 inches long. Nishikawa took the stool and the knife to the Jap officer who was standing near the cross with the prisoner. Nishikawa then returned to the office. The Jap officer then stood on the stool with the hammer in his right hand. He then raised the prisoner's left arm and driving a nail through the palm of the left hand fixed it to the left arm of the cross which was the height of the prisoner's shoulders. When the officer commenced to pierce the palm of the prisoner's left hand with a nail the prisoner tried to wriggle and scream, whereupon Hinata held the body of the prisoner up against the upright post of the cross and put a piece of cloth into the prisoner's mouth. The Jap officer then placed the stool towards the prisoner's right hand and nailed the prisoner's right hand to the cross in the same manner by standing on the stool. He then put the stool aside and nailed both the feet of the prisoner with two nails to the horizontal board on which the prisoner was standing. Thereafter the Jap officer then stood on the stool and fixed the prisoner's head to the cross by driving a large size nail through the prisoner's forehead. The Jap officer then took the knife and first cut a piece of flesh from the left side of the prisoner's stomach and placed the flesh on a wooden board nearby. He then cut another piece of flesh from the right side of the prisoner's stomach and also placed it on the board. He then put a rubber glove on his right hand and pulled out the intestines of the prisoner which were also placed on the board. Taking the knife again, the officer then proceeded to cut bits of flesh from the prisoner's left and right thighs, both arms and neck, all of which were placed on the same wooden board".

Two other prisoners were forced to take the wooden board to the parade ground where the human flesh was displayed to the other prisoners and a lecture given by the Japanese officer. Wong Hiong was too far away to hear the words.

The Crucified prisoner was left to rot on the cross until the evacuation of Sandakan. Eventually the cross and the human remains were burnt.

In 1947 The Australian War Graves commission investigated the spot where Hiong said the cross had been located. Their findings: **"human remains, some wire, four nails 15 centimetres long, and four 7.5 centimetres long".** This confirmed, beyond doubt, Hiong's story. The human remains were too decomposed for identification. But Hiong's description of the prisoner leads the investigators to believe he was a British Marine Officer.

In New Guinea and the nearby islands

The *Akikaze* Massacre

The following are eyewitness accounts of Japanese behaviour in the New Guinea area:

On Friday 17 March 1944 Japanese naval officials rounded up the German missionaries in the Wewak area of Northern New Guinea and the surrounding islands. These missionaries, including nuns and their Chinese servants with children, were ordered to board the destroyer *Akikaze* for transport to Rabaul. After being under way for some time Lieutenant Commander Sabe assembled the crew and told them he had received an order from 8th Fleet Headquarters to dispose of all the allied civilians on board. Elaborate measures were then taken to assemble a gallows on the aft deck where each civilian would be taken for final disposal. The Captain ordered the engines to run at full speed so that the noise of the engines would drown out the machine gun fire and the screams of tortured individuals. First the male missionaries were removed from their quarters and taken one at a time to the aft deck where the gallows had been assembled. Each man, and later the nuns, were strung up on the gallows and then machine gunned to death - cut down and their bodies thrown overboard. The reason given for the aft gallows was to facilitate clean up after all sixty civilians had been disposed of. Two children were thrown overboard alive in order "not to waste ammunition". When it was decided to kill the civilians with machine guns and rifle fire why was it necessary to hang them first?

The Kavieng Massacre

It was decided in March 1944 that twenty-three plantation owners and their employees must be killed. The reason given for this decision was the expected invasion by the Americans. The invasion never happened. Samurai Warrior, Rear Admiral Tamura Ryukichi decided the men, including a fifteen year old boy, should be killed in Kavieng and their bodies weighted down in the deep sea area off Nago Island.

Sublieutenant Mochizuki Shichitaro was given the job of actually disposing of the men. The following is quoted from "*Hidden Horrors*" Yuki Tanaka. The method of killing:

"**The executions began at six o'clock. The detainees were told that they would be taken one by one to a barge that in turn would take them to a boat off Kavieng port. A few soldiers were responsible for taking each person to the middle of the wharf, and another would follow carrying the person's suitcase. In the middle of the wharf, the detainee was blind-folded and handed to Horiguchi, who instructed the detainee to carry his own suitcase. Horiguchi then took him by the hand and led him to Muraoka. Muraoka told each detainee that the barge was waiting under the wharf and that for safety sake he should sit on the edge of the wharf with his legs dangling over the side and his suitcase next to him. As soon as each victim sat on the edge of the wharf, Muraoka gently put two nooses over the victim's head — one from each side — and his men, who were holding the end of each rope, would pull violently. Muraoka would then make sure the detainee was dead by listening for a heart beat, remove the ropes, and throw the body onto the barge two meters below the wharf. Some of Muraoka's men were on the deck of the barge and tied each body to a concrete block with the wire cable. The detainee's suitcase was taken to the opposite side of the wharf and thrown into a pile. Suzuki, as supervisor, moved among Muraoka, Horiguchi, and Takada and ensured that the whole operation went smoothly**".

Blood Carnival

New Guinea, October 1943. Under the heading **Blood Carnival**, in the diary of a captured Japanese soldier dated March 1943, after a young Australian pilot of a Dauntless dive bomber had been captured, the diary states:

"**Unit commander Komai, when he came to the observation-station today, told us personally that, in accordance with the compassionate sentiments of Japanese Bushido, he was going to kill the prisoner himself with his favourite sword. So we gathered to see this happen....**

It will not be long now. As I picture the scene we are about to witness, my heart beats faster. I glance at the prisoner: he has probably resigned himself to his fate.... The truck runs along the sea shore....In a little over twenty minutes we arrive at our destination and all get off. Unit Commander Koumiss stands up and says to the prisoner, "*We are going to kill you*" ....Now the time has come, and the prisoner, is made to kneel on the bank of a bomb crater filled with water. He is apparently resigned . The precaution is taken surrounding him with guards with fixed bayonets, but he remains calm. He even stretches his neck out and is very brave.

The unit commander has drawn his favourite sword....It glitters in the light, and sends a cold shiver down my spine. He touched the prisoner's neck lightly with the back of the blade, then raises it above his head with both hands and brings it down with a sweep....I had been standing with my muscles tensed but in that moment I closed my eyes.

SSh... It must be the sound of blood spurting from the arteries. With a sound as though something had been cut, the body falls forward. It is amazing he has been killed with one stroke. The onlookers crowd forward. The head, detached from the trunk, rolls in front of it. SSh...SSh...The dark blood gushes out.

All is over. The head is dead white like a doll's. The savageness which I felt a little while ago is gone, and now I feel nothing but the true compassion of Japanese Bushido....This will be something to remember all my life. If I ever get back alive it will make a good story to tell, so I have written it down".

Salamaua Observation Post, March 30, 1943, 0110hrs.

CANNIBALISM

From page 236 of Lord Russell's account of Japanese War Crimes:

ORDER REGARDING EATING FLESH OF AMERICAN FLIERS

1.   The battalion wants to eat the flesh of the American aviator, Lieutenant [junior grade] Hall.
11.   First Lieutenant Kanamuri will see to the rationing of this flesh.
111. Cadet Sakae [Medical Corps] will attend the execution and have the liver and gall bladder removed.

Battalion Commander: **Major Matura**
Date: **9th March 1945**
Time: **9 a.m**
Place: **Miyazaki Hill Headquarters**

Method of issuing orders: Called to my presence First Lieutenant Kanamuri and Cadet Sakae and gave verbal order.

Place to report after completion of the order: Brigade Commander: Major - General Tachibana
Also informed: Divisional HQ Detachment, Major Horie, 308 Independent Infantry Battalion.

Another target of cannibalism was the Asian Prisoners of War. Hatam Ali was captured in Singapore in 1942. He refused to join the Indian National Army being formed by Chandra Bose to fight for the liberation of India and against the British in Burma. As a result of this he was transported to New Guinea as part of a slave labour force. After witnessing the Japanese select a man a day for their rations he managed to escape. In fact they did not kill their victims at all. Hatam Ali told the War Crimes Commission; **"At this place the Japanese again started selecting prisoners to eat. Those selected were taken to a hut where flesh was taken from their bodies while they were alive and they were then thrown into a ditch alive where they later died. When flesh was being cut from those selected terrible cries and shrieks came from them and also from the ditch where they were later thrown. These cries would gradually dim down when the unfortunate individuals were dying".** Hatam Ali as quoted from *Hidden Horrors*, Yuki Tanaka.

In The Philippine Islands

A PRISONER OF WAR EXAMPLE

Gunnery Sergeant Douglas William Bogue of the United States Marine Corps was one of five survivors in a camp of one hundred and fifty prisoners. The Japanese sounded an air raid alarm and hustled all the prisoners into the crude air raid shelters dug within the camp confines. Gunnery Sergeant William Bugue of Puerto Princesa POW Camp, Palawan Island, Philippine Islands, related this experience to the International Military Tribunal for the Far East [Knights of Bushido Lord Russell of Liverpool]:

"No sooner had we got under cover than I heard a dull explosion and incessant screaming, laughing and the shooting of machine-gun and rifles. As I was near the entrance of my shelter I stuck my head out to see what was taking place. The first thing I saw was a black pillar of smoke coming from the entrance to A Company shelter. It appeared to me that about fifty to sixty Jap soldiers, armed with rifles and grenades, light machines and carrying torches and buckets containing gasoline, were attacking A Company shelter which was next to mine. The buckets of gasoline were thrown into the entrance of the shelter and a lighted torch was then thrown in to ignite the gasoline: and as the men were forced to come out on fire, they were bayoneted, shot, clubbed, or stabbed. I saw several men staggering about still in flames, and saw them fall down shot. Some of the Japanese attacking force then branched off and attacked the north-east entrance of C Company's shelter and the north entrance of B Company's shelter.

Due to the confined space the whole attack was visible at a glance. I saw several Japanese shooting and stabbing with their bayonets directly above where Stidham was lying helpless on a stretcher. I saw one man whom I presumed to be Dr. Mango with his clothes smouldering, staggering towards the Japs with his arms outstretched, when he was mowed down by a Japanese soldier with a light machine-gun. Other American prisoners of war, who were coming out of these narrow entrances were shot as they emerged, mown down as they made for the fence above the cliff.

The Japanese soldiers participating were yelling, and in such manner that it seemed to me as if they were enjoying their task. Lieutenant Sato was running about with his sword drawn, giving orders, urging his men on. Before I withdrew my head the Japanese guards outside the fence had commenced a covering fire over the entrances that the Japanese attacking force had not yet attacked, in an endeavour to keep the men down [the shelters] until the attacking force could get to them and mop them up. I told Sever and Kozuch, who were in the same shelter as I, what was taking place and that our only escape was to get out of the entrance one at a time, and try to get through the fence above the bluff and get down to the beach.

I then quickly emerged from the entrance of my shelter, and somehow scrambled through the double barbed wire fence. Hanging onto the bluff I yelled back to Sever and Kozuch that they could make it now. In the few seconds that I was exposed I was hit by a bullet in the right leg. Kozuch was next to try, and Sever was directly behind him. Both of these men were shot down hanging partly through the fence and lying across the shelter. I could see the bullet holes in Kozuch's back as he was hanging on the wire.

A number of other men were now scrambling down this cliff from C Company's shelter where they had previously arranged an escape hatch. This escape hatch was made due to indications that we had received through conversations with the Japanese that just such a thing might take place.

At the southern entrance of B Company's shelter I saw one man crawl under the barbed wire fence and tumble down the bluff. I then let go of the bluff and scrambled down the cliff to the water's edge. Upon arriving there I noticed the bodies of two American prisoners of war lying face downwards, half in the water. They had been shot in the back. The Japanese taking part in the attack were standing along the barbed wire fence above the bluff, and shooting at the men who had managed to get over it, either through the fence or the escape hatch.

It was then that I was joined by two other prisoners named Ayers and Hale. I told them that I was going to follow up close to the rocks on the beach around to the south west by the dock area, and try to get into the underbrush, circling from there into the jungle. Neither Ayers nor Hale agreed with my plan and attempted to swim the bay, but both lost their lives. Hale, after swimming approximately thirty yards from the shore, was brought under fire from the Japanese on the bluff and, after a few shots struck the water alongside of him, he was hit. Rolling over on his back he said, 'They've got me," and drowned.

After seeing Ayres and Hale killed I proceeded around the rocks towards the dock area I previously had in mind. After going about thirty yards the rocks ended and I stumbled on three Japanese sailors attempting to set up a Lewis gun to cover the path I had just come over. I had no alternative but to jump on these three sailors in an attempt to get the machine gun away from them. We finally fought our way into the water where, due to their weight, I fell under the water and remained holding them under with me, forcing them finally to release their hold on the gun and on me. They then tried to get back to the beach.

Coming out of the water myself, I pulled the actuator [cocking handle] back on the Lewis gun and managed to kill all three sailors. But seeing another machine-gun being set up a little further down the beach I was forced to return the way I had come, in an effort to find a hiding place amongst the rocks.

In order to crawl into a small crevice to hide, I was forced to get rid of the machine-gun which I threw into the water. While in this crevice I could easily discern the difference between the Japanese hollering and laughing, and the Americans' screams being killed. I could also distinguish the smell of burning flesh and the odour of dynamite.

Very soon afterwards a Japanese landing barge patrolled within a few feet of the rocks where I was hiding. They were looking for prisoners who had managed to get away. Any who were found were shot from the barge. Patrols continued to comb the rocks and beaches for the rest of the day and about 9p.m., along with the other four survivors, I swam the bay and managed, after a few days in the jungle, to join up with the Filipino guerrillas.''

Many of the badly burned and wounded men who had jumped off the bluff on to the beach below were later buried *alive* by the Japanese patrolmen.

UNDER THE DIRECT AUTHORITY OF THE JAPANESE GOVERNMENT

The following is a copy of an order issued by the Commander of the Japanese First Submarine Fleet on the 20th March 1943:

"All submarines will act together in order to concentrate their attacks against enemy convoys and totally destroy them. Do not stop at the sinking of enemy ships and cargoes. At the time carry out the complete destruction of the crews of the enemy ships; if possible seize part of the crew and endeavour to secure information about the enemy".

When the British requested the Japanese Government to look into this barbarity they denied that Japanese submarines had anything to do with the "facts alleged in the protest". Some of the facts:

The Master of the *Daisy Moller* described how his ship was hit by a torpedo between number 1 and 2 holds, and immediately began to list and sink by the head. All boats were lowered, but the starboard forward boat was smashed during the process. " **The Captain took the compliments of both boats with him in the port forward boat. All on board got safely away and within three minutes of abandoning her the *Daisy Moller* sank.. As the vessel sank the submarine appeared about one hundred yards to the north of where she had just gone down and approached my boat after firing a tracer bullet at us. No words were passed and the sub turned away, but three minutes later came straight at us and rammed us at an approximate speed of sixteen knots, opening fire with machine-guns directly after. I swam to a raft about one and a half miles away. The submarine then rammed the other two boats and machine-gunned the water over a large area. The total number on board the *Daisy Moller,* when she was hit by the torpedo, was sixty-nine. Only sixteen survived".**

The detailed story of the *Jean Nicolet* and how the survivors were taken on board the submarine and made to run a gauntlet of Japanese sailors armed with bayonets, swords and a variety of blunt instruments for the sole purpose of beating the individual survivors and casting them into the sea at the end of their run. This story is told by two survivors who were rescued a few days later by *HMS Hoxa*.

The sinking of the British *MV Behar* by the Japanese Cruiser *Tone* where seventy two survivors were murdered on the direct orders of Samurai warrior Vice Admiral Sakonju.

Unit 731 the Japanese human experimental facility under the command of General Shirr Ishii, located in Manchuria conducted the most heinous crimes against humanity on record, during the occupation of China. Recent evidence has confirmed that the Commander-in-Chief Emperor Hirohito directly authorised the operation of the facility and it is a fact that his younger brother Prince Yasuhiko Asaka, the *"Butcher of Nanking"*, visited the unit and did NOT take steps to have the operation stopped. One word from the Emperor and the whole inhuman conduct of this experimental station would have stopped immediately. It was common practice to operate on live humans to find out what the results of certain injections were on specific organs of the live body. Deliberately injecting Chinese and other captives with deadly viruses was part of the normal routine. The patient would then be observed as he died without any attempt to counteract the known disease. In many cases the patient was operated on without anesthetic in order that the conditions of the body may be realistically observed

On Sado Island in the Japanese archipelago, 387 men were buried alive in the mine they were operating. Work was being carried out at the four hundred foot level. Lt. Tsuda reported this incident after carrying out the instructions of his commanding officer Maj.Sadakitchi. There is evidence this order originated with Field Marshal Terauchi, the commanding officer of S.E.Asia. During the night 1st/2nd August 1945 Maj. Sadakitchi gave orders for demolition charges to be placed in the mineshaft at the one hundred, two hundred and three hundred foot levels. The 387 prisoners were working the four hundred foot level on a daily basis. Between 8:45 and 9:00 on the morning of the 2nd August all the guards were ordered out of the mine. When the mine was clear of all the Japanese **"a number of wheeled ore bins were pushed to the mine's downward entrance and allowed to gather speed into its depths. At 9:10 am with no further bins to dispose of, the signal was given to blow up the mine."**

Of course there were no survivors. The mine entrance was filled in and the whole area covered over to blend in with the surrounding countryside. All the officers and men were dispersed with instructions not to reveal what had happened to the mineworkers.

General Douglas MacArthur ordered a stop to all war crimes investigations in 1951. The war criminals in prison at that time were released and the investigations into many mass murderers ceased. Col Tsuji who organized the killings of many thousands of Chinese in Singapore was never apprehended and later elected the Japanese Diet.

APPENDIX 5

INTERESTING FACTS OF THE PACIFIC WAR

Prime Minister Churchill's association with Singapore goes back to 1921 when, as a member of parliament, he voted to establish a naval base on Singapore Island. Throughout the twenties and thirties he was instrumental in curtailing expenses for military spending. This attitude on his part directly affected the construction of the 'Impregnable Fortress of Singapore'. At no time did he foresee a threat to Singapore from the Japanese. His attitude is typified by such official statements as "measuring our naval strength against this fancied (Japanese) danger" and "unduly stressing the Japanese danger". At this time the Japanese Navy possessed the three biggest and most powerful Battleships (Yamato, Musashi and Shinano) ever built.

This great leader in the European Theatre of the war was at a complete loss when it came to the affairs of the Far East. He was incapable of seeing his own weakness in this respect. On memorable occasions he did not take the advice of his Chiefs of Staff. In July 1941 it was decided at one of these meetings that Singapore should not be reinforced if it was attacked. Shortly before the city fell to the Japanese onslaught he directed that the 18 Division, trained in desert warfare, should be sent to Singapore and the surrounding jungle terrain. They arrived, for the most part, just in time to take part in street fighting as the city of Singapore fell to the Japanese. Their fighting equipment was sunk by the Japanese a few miles from the city that they came to save. The men arrived without equipment to fight an enemy with outstanding equipment! His instructions to Wavell were to the effect that these men should fight to the last man. There must be no thought of surrender. If they had been sent to Burma as Field Marshal Sir Alan Brooke suggested, their jungle training could have been initiated and their contribution to the war effort would have had some impact on the hostilities. Instead, they provided a slave labour force for the Japanese, paid for by the British Government. Approximately twenty seven percent of these men were to die an agonising death in prison camp. *All of them suffered at the hands of the Japanese.*

THE AUTOMEDAN INCIDENT

In August 1940 the Chiefs of the Imperial General Staff (CIGS) in discussion with Prime Minister Churchill decided that in the event of a Japanese attack in the Far East, Singapore could **not** be held. This **top-secret** decision was to be conveyed to the Commander in Chief, Singapore, Air Vice Marshal Sir Robert Brooke - Popham. The document was put in a weighted bag and given to Captain M.L.F. Evans, (Merchant Navy) an Admiralty Courier, with strict instructions that it must be thrown overboard from the Automedan, a merchant navy vessel, in the event of any danger.

On November 11th 1940 the German raider Atlantis ordered the Automedan to 'heave to' somewhere in the Indian Ocean. The Captain immediately sent out a distress signal, which provoked the German Raider into immediate action. The Germans pumped 28 shells into the Automedan some of which hit the bridge and killed the Captain and all crewmembers on it. The German boarding party on the Automedan made an incredible discovery. *Not only was this top secret document in their hands, but also the merchant navy code books and some seven million dollars in Malayan currency.* The Atlantis sailed directly to Tokyo, wired the information to the German High Command who after deliberation ordered the information be given to the Japanese. From this time, to the date of the attack on Malaya, all planning was based on the fact that the *British had no intention of reinforcing the defence of Singapore.* In fact this news strengthened Yamamoto's resolve to attack Pearl Harbour. Until this time he had repeatedly stated that he was not willing to divide his fleet in half - half to look after the British Pacific fleet in Singapore and the other half to take care of the Americans in Hawaii. Admiral Wenneker of the German Embassy in Tokyo stated in his diary that Admiral Kondo mentioned to him many times that weakness of the British position in Singapore and their unwillingness to strengthen it would not have been so apparent by the normal methods of espionage and code breaking. The Automedan Incident was a major coup for the Japanese. As far as we know the captain of the Atlantis was the only white man to be decorated by the Japanese Government.

The British journalist and brilliant naval strategist Hector C. Bywater developed the plan that Admiral Yamamoto followed in his invasion of the Philippine Islands and the attack on Pearl Harbour. In his book *The Great Pacific War* he details how Japan must attack Pearl Harbour in order to have an advantage over the United States. The Japanese were so enthralled with this book that two versions were printed for Japanese reading after the Kokumin newspaper had run the book in installments. In one version the ending was changed to show a Japanese victory, as the nationalistic nature of the Japanese could not bear to read of their defeat. *Taiheiyo kaiken ron* the Japanese translation of Bywater's previous book *Sea Power in the Pacific* became required reading at both the Japanese Imperial Naval Academy and the Naval War College. The civilian version *"Taiheiyo no Soha-sen 1931-1933 (The Great Pacific War, 1931-1933)* was widely read in Japan. Bywater was heard to comment that he never received, or was offered, royalties on the Japanese versions of his books.

Major General Woodburn Kirby in his excellent book *"Singapore the Chain of Disaster"* tells us that Colonel Haley Bell investigated Japanese espionage activities in Malaya in 1936 and was so successful in discovering an extensive network of activity that the Governor asked for his recall to the U.K. Not only was the information unwanted but also the efficient organisation built by Colonel Haley Bell was disbanded. This head in the sand attitude towards the Impregnable Fortress of Singapore made it into an almost defenceless city ready for easy picking.

Another prime example of the British head in the sand attitude towards Singapore and Malaya is the case of John Becker, arguably one of the most successful spies the British ever employed. The amazing story of this man's accomplishments is detailed by Peter Elphick in his latest book *Singapore the Pregnable Fortress*. John Becker, like Haley Bell before him, advised the Governor of Singapore and the military commanders that the Japanese planned to attack Singapore. This news was given to the British authorities in August 1941 after John Becker had spent a considerable amount of time in Thailand. He had determined that the Thais were secretly encouraging the Japanese to establish bases in their country while making the British believe they were in fact pro British. Sir Josiah Crosby, the British Ambassador to Thailand, was considered a very doubtful asset to his country by the foreign office in the UK. The American Minister in Bangkok, Hugh Grant, was convinced that Pibul, the Thai Prime Minister, was working hand in glove with the Japanese. A fact that Sir Josiah Crosby denied until the day of the Japanese attack.

Authorities in Singapore and Malaya knew of many covert Japanese operations in progress during the prewar years. Some examples of this: Submarines supplying the Japanese owned mines and estates on the east coast of Malaya. These submarines were actually berthed at the companies' wharf at Endau. They had evaded detection by the Royal Navy who were patrolling the east coast at that time. Surely this would cause major suspicions and no doubt it did. However the policy of the government at this time was *laissez faire,* so the inevitable blind eye was turned.

Captain Bob Collinge of the Straits Settlement Volunteer Force was mobilized some months before the attack on north Malaya. During one of his military exercises with a company of armed cars at Endau he was resting during a lunch break when to his surprise a car drew up in front of him and disgorged a Japanese military officer in full uniform. The Japanese officer walked down the wharf, boarded a powered sampan and was taken out to sea. The detailed report made by Captain Collinge to HQ in Singapore was never acted on. The reason given to Captain Collinge was appeasement. Any incidents concerning the Japanese must be avoided at all costs. Captain Collinge was later advised that HQ was aware that Japanese officers were frequently landed on the coast of Johore in uniform, changed to civilian clothes while conducting their espionage activities and then changed into uniform to return to their pickup submarines.

In total contravention of all International Standards for the conduct of war, the Japanese planned to equip their army with Thai army uniforms for their attack through this country. It was only after their landing had not met with the anticipated opposition that they did not proceed with the planned deception. However they did not hesitate to put their soldiers in civilian sarongs and use native women and children as a screen to infiltrate British lines during their attack down the Malaya peninsula.

All the lights of Singapore were on when the Japanese bombers attacked the city on the night of the 7/8th December 1941. My father's good friend Bobbie Coles who was living over the Aux Chat Noir ladies shop in the heart of Singapore phoned the Civil Defence Head Quarters to complain of the bombing taking place while the city was lit up. Civil Defence HQ told her that a practice raid was under way. She then told them in no uncertain terms that live bombs had landed near her apartment. This little episode is typical of the authorities' attitude to events that were actually happening. It is indicative of the lack of information being given to the public when one considers that the Military authorities had been tracking the approach of the Japanese attacking forces for at least the previous three days and the fact that Kota Bharu had been under attack for approximately three hours before Singapore was bombed.

The Military plan for the defence of Malaya included Operation Matador. This involved the army taking some high ground near Singora and Patani in Thailand where the Japanese were expected to land. This plan could not be put into effect because of a catch 22 situation. The military authorities required thirty-six hours to put the plan into action. The political branch of the government would not allow the violation of Thai territory prior to a Japanese attack. If the Japanese attacked Thailand in order to have a base of operations against Malaya then it was too late for Matador. This fuzzy thinking was typical of the whole Malayan campaign. Malaya was lost because of inept leadership and not because of the fighting qualities of the men on the spot as Churchill led the world to believe after the fall of Singapore. In this same tone of complete disregard for even a modicum of preparedness was the fact that the CIGS in London, in mid and late December, were discussing a *policy plan* for the destruction of airfields in the event of their possible loss to the enemy. This in a campaign that lasted only ten weeks and after five airfields had already been captured by the enemy. Now fifty-six years after the end of the Second World War only a partial release of Churchill's papers has been made. We are told now that more of Churchill's papers will be released after another fifty years. One can only guess that there is nothing to be proud of in these papers!

It is interesting to note that British Officers, in the front line, facing the Japanese in Malaya did **not** have detailed maps of the areas they were fighting in. This after well over one hundred years of occupation. The Japanese officers were equipped with the most detailed maps of every mile of the territory they were attacking. This was the result of an extremely efficient espionage system. Lt. Chippington (Leicestershire Regt) in his excellent book *"Singapore The Inexcusable Betrayal"* relates his fundamental lack of basic equipment and how, when actually confronting the enemy, he received an order to send his Bren guns to the rear area. This action would leave his unit facing an enemy equipped with heavy machine guns, light machine guns, anti tank guns and rifles when his sole means of defence would be the antiquated Lee Enfield .303 rifle. What courageous men he led that they should put up with such crass stupidity!

My good friend Van Vandergaast, a Lieutenant in the Malay Regiment, told me that they were equipped with the Northover Projector, an antiquated piece of artillery that more often than not back-fired with a wicked flame immediately after the trigger was activated. The trick to firing this gun was to move away from the flame of the backfire as soon as firing had taken place. Not a practical proposition in close combat and highly dangerous at the best of times. Van also mentioned to me that he had received a message from Army HQ when facing the Japanese, in the front line on the West coast of Singapore Island and just a few days before the surrender, stating that his routine practice at the rifle range was scheduled for the routine time this week. What were the Staff Officers at army HQ doing when the Japanese army was on the verge of capturing the city?

Sir Shenton Thomas was an ideal **peacetime** Governor for the colony. A man whose primary concern was for the welfare of the population was totally lost in a war environment. His policies, ironically, were to lead to the loss of many hundreds of lives of the people he so strongly wanted to protect: 1) Air raid shelters must not be built because it would be bad for morale. 2) The Chinese population, long time enemies of the Japanese, were not to be armed for the same reason. 3) Storage of rice and other basic products for emergency situations was out of the question as it would lead to poor morale in the civilian population. 4) Planning for water conservation or storage was not to be seriously considered. The planning and distribution system for water supply in Singapore, the fortress, had been neglected from the outset. The British Government had by 1941 convinced the world that Singapore was an Impregnable Fortress when in fact its major artillery was pointing out to sea and its air defence was primarily redundant and equipped with out of date aircraft.

Air Vice Marshal Sir Robert Brooke- Popham, The Commander in Chief of the Far East Forces, declared that the Brewster Buffalo was a match for anything the Japanese could come up with. Apparently he had not read the report on the capabilities of the Japanese Navy Zero fighter, readily available to him, and on file at his HQ. . This report was based on the findings of a group of Allied aviation experts who inspected a Zero that had been shot down in the Chinese theatre of the hostilities. It stated that the Zero would no doubt outperform any allied aeroplanes in operation at that time. The Brewster Buffalo had a top speed of 275 MPH and the Zero over 330 MPH. The Brewster Buffalo was over a ton heavier than the Zero and is the only operational fighter to be written up by James Gilbert in *"The Worlds Worst Aircraft"*. Australian pilots of the Buffalo were continually told, by senior officers, that the Japanese flew biplane fighters with fabric covered wings that were no match for the Buffalo.

Gregory Board, Buffalo pilot, RAAF, is quoted by James Gilbert in *"The World's Worst Aircraft"*:

Intelligence briefings almost daily by the most learned of men, who came in from the other side of the Japanese bamboo curtain, and told us the best of the Japanese fighters were old fabric-covered biplanes which wouldn't stand a chance against the Buffalos. With this ringing promise of slaughtering the Japanese in the air should they get too big for their britches, we concentrated on flying and learning different methods of drinking gin and tonic.

The entire squadron was wiped out to a man. Suddenly we realized what we had in the Buffalo — a barrel which the zero could out fly, out climb, out gun, out manoeuvre and out do in almost anything else that was in the book for a fighting aircraft.

The RAF and the Americans in the Philippines lost approximately fifty percent of their aircraft to the Japanese during the first 24/48 hours of hostilities.

Sir Robert Brooke-Popham was relieved of his command on the 27th December 1941. This was only twenty days after the outbreak of hostilities and a good indication of the turmoil that the leadership of the Far East campaign was experiencing. He had been appointed Commander in Chief on the 17th October 1940 having retired from a distinguished career in the RAF in 1936. He was out of date with current developments in the RAF and had no interest in the Command and Co-ordinating position to which he was appointed. This one gathers from the fact that he was known to fall asleep at any time of the day and particularly during conferences (Gen. Woodburn Kirby, Singapore Chain of Disaster). Who was responsible for appointing this man to the position of C in C of an area that was vital to the interests of Great Britain?

Lt. General A.E. Percival, the Commander of ground forces in Malaya and Singapore had written a defence paper for Staff College during his promotional exams in the thirties. Of all the Officers in the British Army he was probably the most qualified (not suitable) to protect Malaya from aggression. What happened? He was a brave and courageous leader in World War 1 and totally out of his depth in action against the Japanese. He had no concept of the situation in which he found himself. Like Brooke-Popham he should have been replaced immediately after hostilities broke out, preferably long before this. He was not the aggressive determined leader that was required to face General Yamashita on the field of battle. His predecessor Major General Bond had not carried out the defence recommendations made by Maj. General Dobbie in 1938. Dobbie had carried out manoeuvres on the east coast of Malaya during the north east monsoon (October-March) in order to prove to the General Staff in London that an attack on Singapore would probably come during this period, with the obvious result that Singapore would be attacked from the north and not the south as the prevailing command structure believed. It appears that General Dobbie was the only GOC, Malaya, who actually understood the defence requirements to make Singapore safe from a northern land attack.

Admiral Sir Thomas Phillips, Commander in Chief, Eastern Fleet, known to those who served under him as Tom Thumb because of his small stature, was a traditionalist who believed that the Navy was capable of defending its own battleships without the aid of air cover. This attitude after his enemy had learned two exceedingly powerful lessons that Phillips apparently ignored. On November 11th 1940 the Royal Navy sank three Battleships and damaged many other lesser craft at Toranto, Italy. This was carried out with the obsolete Swordfish torpedo bombers. These same aircraft damaged the German Battleship Bismarck to such an extent that it was sunk shortly after by British surface craft. Two days before he so boldly lead his ships to disaster the Japanese had reinforced the lesson of air superiority over battleships at Pearl Harbour. These vital lessons, ignored, were to cost the navy dearly in both manpower and capital ships. The Admiral had recently been given command of Z force by Prime Minister Churchill. This active duty command followed several years as a desk bound Staff Officer in London. The HMS *Prince of Wales* and the battle cruiser HMS *Repulse*, were both sunk after two hours of heavy air attack by determined Japanese flyers. In the finest tradition of the Navy, Admiral Tom Phillips went to the depths with his battleship. The air attack must have caused a primary distraction as both ships were hit by five torpedoes and sank within an hour of each other.

Duff Cooper was appointed by Churchill to co-ordinate the efforts of the military and civilian organisations in Singapore. From the time he arrived on the scene with over one hundred pieces of luggage (much frowned upon in war time) he was a thorn in the side of both the military and the civilian authorities. Churchill gave him a Ministerial rank; this lent a great deal of weight to his efforts to advise both parties. He was most unpopular and contributed nothing to the co-ordination he was attempting to carry out. He left Singapore, in early January, well before the city fell to the Japanese (it is not recorded if he left with the same amount of baggage). He arrived in Singapore in September ostensibly to co-ordinate the civilian / military aspects of the fortress. Between his arrival and the outbreak of hostilities, some three months, he managed to visit Australia, New Zealand, Java, Bali, India, and Burma, which must have left him with little time for his official duties. All this traveling at the public expense.

Col G.T.Wards, British Military Attaché in Tokyo visited Malaya and Singapore in April 1941. He lectured the senior military officers in Singapore on the efficiency and determination of the Japanese fighting man. He warned them that Japanese intelligence was second to none and that they were familiar with the current developments in Malaya, particularly troops strengths and deployments. At the conclusion of the lecture General Bond, the General Officer Commanding Malaya, advised the officers that what they had just heard was the personal opinion of the lecturer. He, Bond, knew exactly what the Japanese capabilities were and that 'I do not think much of them and you can take it from me that you have nothing to fear from them'. Unbelievable! (*The Chain of Disaster* Maj. Gen. S.Woodburn Kirby) It should be noted here that the Japanese had an extensive propaganda campaign aimed at the Indian troops stationed in Malaya. The gist of it was to question why the Indians would want to fight for the very people that were subjugating them. During the fighting for the defence of Singapore Island, Lt.Col. Phillip Parker CO of the Baluch regiment reported that three companies deserted to the Japanese forces while facing them on the front line. This of course left a considerable area undefended, a disastrous situation which demanded immediate remedial action. After the fall of Singapore many Indian troops joined the Indian National Army and fought with the Japanese army against the British in Burma. Those who chose not to join the INA were treated in the most abominable way. (See appendix 4 cannibalism.) Singapore is renowned in British military history as the campaign that suffered more desertions than all previous military undertakings.

Lieutenant Peter Kemmis-Betty of the 2nd Gurkha Rifles notes that they were training for Desert warfare in India prior to their departure for Singapore. This type of training requires the participating platoons to be located several hundred yards apart. In jungle warfare the platoons are frequently located a few yards apart. To totally confuse and demoralise first class fighting troops that were either in Malaya or sent there too late to be effective is tantamount to a criminal act. Major General Woodburn Kirby in his book *"Singapore the Chain of Disaster"* on page 184 states "In effect these reinforcements would be best summed up as the equivalent of a physically unfit British Division, two almost untrained Indian brigades, a number of partially trained Indian and Australian reinforcements and aircraft which could but be a wasting asset." Who ordered these troops to be sent to Singapore and Malaya after many weeks of retreating British forces and the obvious outcome to the defense of the Impregnable Fortress?

This roll call of Military and Civilian leadership was no doubt ideal for the 1920s but entirely inadequate, inappropriate, and ineffective for the defence of Malaya and Singapore against an aggressive enemy with fanatical determination. The mistake for putting these men in this position at this time is not theirs but rests with the seat of power in Great Britain.

Civil/Military Administration in Singapore from 1931 (Japan attacks China/Manchuria) until the day Singapore surrendered is a study in theory over practice. General Woodburn Kirby covers this in detail in his *"Singapore the Chain of Disaster"*. The petty squabbling between military commanders and then between these commanders and the Governor and his civilian advisers is almost beyond belief. One certainly gets the impression that they are far more concerned with their own authority than with the fate of the British Empire. This situation is exacerbated by both the military and civilian authorities in London who were incapable of identifying the problem and appointing individuals capable of rectifying the situation. If this part of the Empire deserved to be lost to incompetent administration the end result was well justified. The really sad part of it is that the impotent, ineffective government of the day blamed the fighting man. The Foreign Office gave top priority to the production of rubber and tin for sale to America and Canada to strengthen the British dollar position. This policy was carried to such ridiculous lengths that the military could not cut down a single rubber tree for sighting defensive positions without permission of the civilian Government. The Japanese of course had no restrictions. Finally, when it was too late, the government in London made no bones of the fact that the defence of Malaya was not on their priority list.

The blame for the sacrifice of the 18th Division in Singapore in January 1942 must be borne by the Prime Minister who was trying to mix politics and military strategy and failing miserably at both. Many thousands of men landed in a situation where retreat had been the most frequent order of the day. These thousands of men were sacrificed for a whim that the Chief of the Imperial General Staff called "a half baked idea." Having decided in August 1940 that Singapore could not be held it seems to be a criminal act to send these men, untrained in jungle warfare, into a situation that would involve either jungle warfare or street fighting. After giving over 700 combat aircraft to Russia, at the expense of arming Singapore, the Prime Minister was now giving thousands of men to Japan as a labour force. This was of course in addition to the men already in Singapore. Many accounts of the fall of Singapore state that seventy thousand troops surrendered to thirty thousand of the attacking force. On the surface these figures are correct and take into account all the troops in Singapore — navy, army and air force. Many of these men were administrative personnel and not trained for front line fighting. The Japanese equivalent - navy, army and air force attacking Singapore amounted to over *one hundred and thirty thousand troops*. These are figures only and do not take into account the quality of the equipment employed by either side or the quality of leadership. In virtually all the battles on the Malaya peninsula the Japanese out numbered the British fighting troops. Once again, poor planning and organisation was the primary reason for this disaster (*Singapore the Inexcusable Betrayal*). There were over seven hundred combat-ready aircraft in Indochina and three hundred tanks (In Yamashita's attacking force) as opposed to approximately sixty obsolete aircraft after the first twenty-four hours and no tanks in the British forces in Malaya. On the 9th December there were ten serviceable obsolete aircraft in North Malaya (at Butterworth) opposed by one hundred and fifty, first line, modern aircraft just across the Thailand border (*The war against Japan, Kirby*). Why was the Prime Minister trying to save the great naval base when there was no navy to make use of it? Why was he trying to save a *paper tiger fortress* that was in reality a magnificent dry dock with a few misplaced big guns to one side of it?

In London, during April 1941, The Vice Chief of Air Staff turned down a suggestion by the Royal Navy that Hurricanes be sent to Singapore as a precautionary protective measure on the grounds that the Brewster Buffalo Fighter "would be more than a match for the Japanese aircraft". Once again it is obvious that the assessment, so painstakingly acquired, of the Japanese Navy Zero fighter, was completely ignored by the most senior staff.

Many of the Australians sent to Singapore for the defence of that city were raw recruits who had virtually no military training. Some of these men had been in the army only two weeks before embarkation.

Colonel Tsuji, the outstanding officer who wrote up the battle plan for the attack on Malaya, advised General Yamashita, "Tiger of Malaya", that sixty percent of the troops defending the peninsula were Indian. The Japanese considering themselves *the master race* saw this as heralding an easy victory. This, added to their knowledge that the whole area was already sacrificed to them, must have been a great morale booster. Col. Tsuji prepared his battle plan after flying reconnaissance missions over Malay in an unmarked aircraft during peacetime. He also toured Singapore and Malaya prior to writing up his battle plans. Our intelligence officers knew of this and eventually had him discretely followed with strict instructions that he must not suffer any embarrassment as the result of being followed. He had the advantage of an extensive and efficient espionage network that had mapped every creek and jungle path in the country. In actual fact the Japanese invading forces had more detailed maps than the defending forces. It is ironic that in 1936 at the official opening of the Naval Base a Japanese company was awarded the contract to record on film the opening procedures and the details of the pride and joy of the British empire. Once again we must ask ourselves who was responsible for this invitation to conduct a little espionage at our public expense?

After the unconditional surrender of the Japanese, the Occupying Forces in Japan were told that the Japanese did not have an atomic weapons program. Many years later the scientists studying in Japanese Universities found not only a well advanced atomic program but also advanced studies for the development of bacteriological and germ warfare weapons (Unit 731 Testimony, Hal Gold) and experiments with a death ray. All these advanced methods of destroying human life were denied by General Douglas MacArthur when he decided to close the war crimes tribunals then in progress. This was done in an attempt to curry favour with the God Emperor in order to make his control of Japan an easier proposition.

It is common knowledge on the west coast of North America that the Japanese were drifting balloons over the Pacific Ocean with the idea of setting the forests of British Columbia, Washington, and Oregon on fire. On May 6th 1945 Elsie Mitchell and five children were killed by a bomb that they were investigating in the forests of Oregon whilst on a fishing trip. The remoteness of the bombsite and future investigations indicate that it was a Japanese balloon bomb that they were attempting to play with or identify. Two weeks after this incident the US Government ceased its censorship of Japanese bomb threats and warned the public not to tamper with strange objects found in the Pacific North West. This is just the first part of Japan's scheme to introduce a variety of killer diseases, anthrax, cholera, plague and other pathogens to the USA.

On 7th Dec 1941 at 6:45 am, the USS Ward, Destroyer, sank a midget submarine in the "Self defence area" around the entrance to Pearl Harbour. The USS Condor had already tracked and missed a midget sub that entered Pearl Harbour earlier that night. The attack on Pearl Harbour came some two hours *after* the attack on Kota Bharu in North Malaya.

Emperor Hirohito in his speech of surrender to the Japanese people, spoken in high Japanese, which was unintelligible to the commoner, did not allude once to the word surrender. He stated that the situation was *"not to the advantage of the Japanese people"*. In fact as a nation they have never admitted to surrender.

The Americans have always considered that dropping the atomic bomb offset the unprovoked attack on Pearl Harbour. The Japanese do not look on this situation quite so simply. They have always attacked an enemy without warning. It is their *modus operandi*. The Japanese are still trying to justify their concept of the Master Race and will stop at nothing to bring this about. The real reason for the Japanese surrender was the rapid advance of the Russian army. If the Russians had occupied Japan the outcome of the occupation would have been very different to the American occupation. The atomic bombs were a timely excuse for the Japanese and lent themselves to endless post war propaganda.

In December 1944 the Naval General Staff in Hibiya, Tokyo, were completing plans for their largest submarine, carrying three floatplanes in a watertight hangar, to surface off the west coast of the USA. Their mission would be to drop bacteriological and germ warfare agents over the highly populated areas of the coast and the submarine crew would spread their deadly cargo ashore. (Unit 731 Testimony Hal Gold) This naval operation was stopped by General Umezo Yoshijiro, Chief of the General Staff.

One of the last submarines to leave Germany before the surrender was a large supply vessel. Hitler ordered this submarine to take the most valuable cargo in Germany at that time, heavy water, plutonium and other materials for the manufacture of atomic bombs to Japan so that the effort to conquer the Allies could continue. Luckily the surrender came when this vessel was still in the Atlantic and the skipper reported to an American port to surrender.

The American torpedo disaster lengthened the war far longer than a few days' fighting to the last man in Singapore and Java would have done. American submarines and torpedo bombers were equipped with malfunctioning torpedoes for the first two years of the Pacific campaign. This was due primarily to US Ordinance refusing to believe the reports of their submarine commanders that the torpedoes were running lower than the actual setting and that the detonators were defective. In spite of the incredible tonnage of shipping sunk by the submarine service there was only a thirty three per cent hit rate which resulted in one ship in eleven, fired at, being sunk.

The Japanese built the largest battleships in the world; the *Yamato* launched in August 1940, the *Musashi* in November 1940 and the *Shinano* in December1941. (See the specifications below versus the fixed defences of Singapore)

The largest battleship in the world was the *Yamato*. Sunk by American dive-bombers and torpedo planes it had an effective fighting life of just 40 minutes. This one battleship had 33 large calibre anti aircraft guns, many specially designed for this purpose. Fortress Singapore had a total of thirty-six large calibre guns. The paper tiger fortress, some twenty years in design and building can be compared and contrasted with one Japanese battleship;

Fortress Singapore	HIJMS.Battleship *Yamato*
5 * 15 inch guns	9 * 18.1inch guns
6 * 9.2 inch guns	12 * 6.1inch guns
16 * 6 inch guns	12 * 5inch guns
Number not known	146 * 25mm anti aircraft guns.

The *Yamato* carried 6 aircraft.

Fortress Singapore was out gunned by a single Japanese battleship.

The converted sister ship to the *Yamato,* the *Shinano*, was completed on the 19th November, 1944, sailed from Yokosuka on the 29th November and was sunk by the USS *Archerfish* just a few miles offshore. The worlds biggest supply ship had an effective life of about twelve hours and never accomplished a single mission.

In 1936 a Japanese naval officer wrote a book he published in both Japanese and English called "*Japan Must Fight Britain*". There were so many indications of the Japanese intentions to create an Asiatic Co-prosperity Sphere that it is a wonder that the British relied on a propaganda fortress rather than a real fortress. Even the maps given to Japanese children in 1938 showed that Asia was to be a sphere of Japanese influence, a part of their Empire.

In 1923 General Smuts warned the British "tensions in the pacific would probably arise only when troubles in Europe would make it well-nigh impossible for the whole or even part of the British fleet to be moved to Singapore" Maj. Gen. S.Woodburn Kirby, *Singapore the Chain of Disaster*.

APPENDIX 6

EGOD.   SECRET.   AX. 705
         CYPHER   TELEGRAM.

To:- BRITAIR, JAVA.
FROM:- AIR MINISTRY WHITEHALL.
         DESPATCHED A.M.C.S. 1329 HRS. 26.2.42.

__IMMEDIATE. NOT W/T.__

AX. 705 26/2. __PERSONAL__ FOR MALTBY FROM C.A.S.
THE PRIME MINISTER HAS ASKED ME TO SEND YOU THE
FOLLOWING PERSONAL MESSAGE FROM HIM. BEGINS.
    I SEND YOU AND ALL RANKS OF THE BRITISH
FORCES WHO HAVE STAYED BEHIND IN JAVA
MY BEST WISHES FOR SUCCESS AND HONOUR IN THE GREAT
FIGHT THAT CONFRONTS YOU. EVERY DAY GAINED IS
PRECIOUS, AND I KNOW THAT YOU WILL DO EVERYTHING
HUMANLY POSSIBLE TO PROLONG THE BATTLE. ENDS.

TIME OF ORIGIN:- 1125 G.M.T.

COPIES TO:-

MINISTER OF DEFENCE (10)

King.

Copy to the King.

PRIME MINISTER'S
PERSONAL TELEGRAM
SERIAL No. T day/2.

Cr

APPENDIX 7

"Man's inhumanity to man is often beyond our imagination except through our experience". Daniel Mckeown.

Quotations from "Spice Island Slaves", Leslie Audus, fellow POW with me on Haruku. Leslie was a F/Lt, RAF, and initiated the yeast making program on Haruku. This worked wonders for many men that were loosing their sight.

I was asked to be a medical orderly long after the worst of the conditions in the hospital had ameliorated. The dysentery epidemic had improved. Beri-beri, avitaminosis, huge tropical ulcers, general debility and starvation were all increasing at an alarming rate. I was not aware of the conditions at the height of the dysentery epidemic. Following are a selection of comments made by doctors, officers and medical orderlies who were lucky enough to have paper and pencil to record their views.

Page 87. On the 12th May 1943 only a few days after our arrival on Haruku a doctor noted:
"The plague of flies is horrifying. In the hospital huts one hears the buzzing of millions of flies accompanied by the groans and hiccups of the mortally sick men. Maggots crawl over befouled sleeping places and over the exhausted men. The little that orderlies can do is gratefully accepted but is inadequate for effective help".

Page 89. F/Lt Audus records;
Deficiency symptoms continued to increase. More and more men develop sores on the mouth and in the throat, indicating pellagra. Some could scarcely swallow because of the swelling; bleeding from the nose and gums pointed to scurvy; stomach pains were universal. Without proper medication the doctors tried to arrest diarrhea with gambir, a tannic acid extract from the leaves of a native plant of the same name.

P93.
Mid June 1943, Audus writes;
In the sick huts there was heated wrangling over the belongings of those who had died, some clothes, a mosquito net, a blanket, a bed covering of some sort, sometimes only a few rags. Tragically many could not wait until the men had died before they took possession. Some were completely blind when they died.
Excreta everywhere is mixed with slime, sometimes just pure blood. Minds become more and more deranged. Many acquire a sense of euphoria. They feel they are getting better;

they have too few bowel motions to be ill; they become disoriented and feel they have eaten well and so on; after this they are no longer capable of communicating and go into a quiet delirium after which the end comes quickly.

P 96.
On the 14th June 1943, a Japanese morbid anatomist visited the camp with the idea of carrying out post-mortems. Our doctors had requested permission to carry out this procedure on many occasions but had been denied. Dr Forbes report:

Nowhere in the bodies was there a trace of fatty tissue to be found. The intestines exhibited necroses and perforations, the lungs were inflamed, the heart enlarged.
He and another Japanese doctor accompany him but fought shy of the huts for the seriously ill. They could have seen for themselves the unstoppable befouling and stink of urine and fecal discharge, could have seen patients who, from constantly lying on the hard, sometimes sharp-edged baleh-baleh (bamboo), in which fly maggots crawled, could have heard the hiccoughs of the dying.

P98.
A Canadian officer (Squadron Leader), boasted to one of the orderlies that he had made a century. He had been to the latrines more than one hundred times that day. There is no mention of his survival.
Towards the end of June 1943 (only 6-7 weeks after our arrival on Haruku;
Since proper medication was lacking the doctors certainly improvised. There were no more bandages so wounds were covered with strips of mosquito netting, or failing that, large washed leaves. For those who had eye troubles and could no longer tolerate bright sunlight, bamboo half-cylinder shades were made with a horizontal slit cut in them so that most of the light could be screened from the eyes.

Page 99.
Dr Philps comment at this time gives us some indication of the general attitude of the sick and dying in the hospital. "What impressed me most…the chaps managed to stay cheerful…one was made to feel very humble, seeing the quality of the human spirit – with certain death only a few days away"

Page 100 / 101.
For the whole month of July the camp remained one of filth, disease, emaciation and death.

July 31st. Of the 2071 men who had arrived 3 months earlier only 200 were considered fit, by Japanese standards, to work on the airfield. The attitude of the guards is summed up neatly when they declared "when the sick men die there will be more food for the workers". Dr Morioka declared the solution to the epidemic was to blow up the hospital, presumably with the sick men in it. The Japanese efforts must be directed to "victory not on curing the sick".

A Dutch doctor's diary comment at this time.
Painful neuritis, scurvy with intense itching, great infected bed sores, all prevent sleep when men can hope to escape from the reality. We have nothing here with which to fight these conditions; the 'gifts' from the Japanese are only sporadic and meager".

Page 103.
There are men with varied symptoms of kleptomania, disturbances of sensory perception and wide spread paralysis, accumulation of fluid in the legs and abdomen, sometimes amounting to litres, swollen scrotums sometimes to the size of small balloons. By stretching of the skin many splits occur therein from which the superfluous fluid drips. Everything remains hopeless. Still very many more are destined soon to die in the Haruku hell hole.

Dr Bruning finding "Blood" in a good mood managed to convince him that eggs would be beneficial for the hundreds of patients in hospital. Blood generously allowed him to have one egg for ten patients.

Page 105.
August 9th 1943. A Dutch doctor enters the following in his diary:
"Extreme emaciation down to skin and bone, numerous infected wounds, skin parasites, pellagra, mental disturbances, gross filthiness, chronic diarrhea, impaired movement even to the extent of complete paralysis, swollen stomachs and legs due to the enormous accumulation of water, that is the human suffering here, the like of which beggars description. Many now with pain and abject misery under those hopeless conditions. The fact there is still a young British soldier who begs me shortly before his death to tell his mother that he "died like a soldier" testifies to the strength of spirit which exceeds all comprehension".
Tropical ulcers have become so extensive that we have to admit men to hospital for treatment. Then for a few days they can be tended with bandages soaked in a solution of rivanol, chloramine or potassium permanganate. The only salves, which we sometimes receive in the form of boric and ichthyol ointments are presumably made up of unpurified lard so that when we use them eczema is often the result.

Dr Phips notes at the end of August 1943:
The most firm loyalties develop among groups of men, each group carrying their mates when they fell sick. Such was their fierce devotion to each other that few would have hesitated to give their lives for their friends, and in a subtle way, many did. Often they shared their rations to the extent that they themselves fell ill.

Page 106 / 107.
A comment from a fellow POW on Haruku.
We are completely cut of from the outside world. From one point in the camp we can see a little church and the Moluccans trudging to it up the sloping path on Sunday mornings,

the men in black and the women in colourful costumes. That is all. What else is happening in the world remains unknown.

Page 109. 6th September 1943.
Men are starving to death... but the plague of flies is distinctly reduced, a positive improvement.

Page 110;
Unknown to some of us workers on the airstrip an occasional gift from the unknown (heaven forbid) happened to the ever conscious and astute workers in the camp area, a couple of examples;
F/Lt Roy Fitch knowing full well the starvation plaguing the camp noticed an airman keeping a close eye on a friendly goat. The gang was selecting rocks from the stream near the camp to build a well for the Japanese, if the flow is beyond expectations the POW camp may participate if Blood condescends. F/Lt Fitch noticed the goat wonderingly near to the working party in the stream and diverted the attention of the Japanese guard. The result was rapid action by one of the airmen dragging the goat into the stream and drowning it. Who had that meat for supper?

Once again Fitch, the cook house officer was involved in a little deception, he took eight men to the village of Pelauw to collect a crocodile that the villages had caught and offered to the prison camp for the princely sum of CDN $8.00. "They brought the animal back to camp, decapitated and minus legs, to the guard room where the Japanese commandant came to inspect it. A surreptitious kick in the animal's ribs administered by the officer (Fitch) caused a violent reflex action in the tail which, switching around, knocked the Japanese officer off his feet. It 'really hurt trying not to laugh' Fitch commented.

Page 114.
19th October 1943.
The Amahai group, originally one thousand Dutch army men, arrived on Haruku to help with the completion of our airstrip. They had been located further from Ambon, the supply depot for the Moluccas Islands, and had suffered only 34 deaths. They had completed the construction of an airstrip on Ceram Island just to the east of Haruku in only six months.
An officer commented;
"When we came into the camp through the dank steaming jungle a clammy fear gripped us. There was something indefinably cruel in all the trees and climbing plants which grew over them and parasitized each other threatening to engulf the damp palm-frond huts to form a green hell. It was forbidden for the healthy to go into the dysentery huts, a sort of parody of a rule of hygiene, but one day a sailor came and asked me "will you go to visit our big marine sergeant for a while? He would be so happy to see you for while before he goes". I slipped into the hut of the "Serious dysentery cases" and there naked on the baleh-baleh was a man I once knew as a strong robust chap. Only the eyes were still alive. Maggots crawled over the immeasurably befouled baleh-baleh and over his dying

body. It was impossible for the two orderlies to clean up those Augean stables, and it was no use contemplating more orderlies. Everybody had to go to the airfield, Mori (Blood) took good care of that".

Page 124.

In November 1943 the Japanese administration, presumably on orders from higher authorities decided that the worst of the dysentery, beriberi, starving and blind POWs should be returned to Java and made fit for the Sumatra railroad project. Originally 776 men were to be transported back to Java. However this number changed rapidly as wounded Japanese soldiers from New Guinea arrived on Ambon at about the same time as the POWs and of course they had priority of movement. Our POW number then shrank to just 548 transported with the remainder staying at the Liang camp on Ambon. The Suez Maru with all these men on board was sunk by the USS Bonefish in the Java Sea.

NO POWs SURVIVED. Those in the holds at the time the torpedo struck were sealed in and those on deck who were lucky enough to get overboard were machine gunned in the water by the escorting destroyer which was picking up the Japanese survivors. (Due to the panic situations that accompanied all moves the figures kept by the Dutch and British officers varied considerably. In this incident the original number of POWs leaving Ambon on the Suez Maru was thought to be, according to British records, 650 with the Dutch claim 620. The British figure for the loss of prisoners on the transport is 548 while the Dutch records state 539. The difference in the actual number of men on this transport was established later when those men diverted to Liang camp confirmed (?) that only 548 or 539 had actually boarded the Suez Maru).

As POWs were being loaded on to the transport a Dutch doctor notes in his diary; In this twentieth century it is extremely saddening to see that men can behave so badly to others that they become skeletons riddled with skin diseases, blind, no longer able to walk by themselves, sunk so low spiritually that they are utterly unresponsive – mere vegetables.

P126. A Dutch orderly writes on the transport between Haruku and Ambon;
I keep watch over the dying, just watch since it is too late for any nursing. A few die each day and then the corpses, in sacks, are overboard within half an hour. Funeral solemnities there are none. I sit by Martin, a British service man who is weakened by dysentery and is now dieing of beri-beri. "Orderly what will happen to me? My father died of dysentery in the First World War in Mesopotamia. But what about me?" I hold his hand tightly and try to turn his attention away from the subject, he looks at me with warmth, and then before I know it, he dies, his hand still in mine. Just after that Martin is committed to the waters of the Bay Ambon in two rice sacks.

Page 131. After an American air raid F/Lt Audus writes;
After 3 days of delay our camp doctors were allowed to administer to the people of
Pelauw village that had been hit by the bombing raid of the 10 December.
As soon as air raid of the 10th December was over and our own wounded had been
attended to our doctors volunteered to administer to the wounded of Pelauw village. The
village we marched through every day on our way to the air strip. Japanese permission
was denied for 3 days. Eventually Dr Forbes and his colleagues were allowed to see the
villagers. Dr Forbes comments:
Horrible wounds, all without exception, are inadequately treated or not at all. I suspect
that no real medical attention has been given to any of them. Massive wounds are simply
covered with leaves, tied with strips of plant stems, with dirty rags on top. Proper care of
these wounds should have been taken three days ago. A local anaesthetic (novacaine) is
also put at our disposal but nothing much can be done with it because all wounds are
infected. Under the circumstances we can do little more than clean up the wound. The
majority of those hit are bound to die since we have no permission to continue treatment
afterwards. It seems extremely clear that the inhabitants of the island exist under
conditions that are not much better than ours. Many mothers come to us with small
children that are undernourished and with diarrhea and infected skin conditions. But
because we have nowhere near enough medicines we can not offer much help. The sights
there appalled even us who had become accustomed to the Japanese methods of
treatment. There we saw wounds with pieces of shrapnel still sticking out of them, three
days after the receipt of the injury. Compound fractures of arms with no splintage. One
case of a severe brachial artery had her gangrenous arm merely in a sling. The arm was
amputated and the girl was put in a temporary Japanese hospital. The three of us worked
for four hours on the patients. The next day permission was asked to see these same
patients. This was refused. After a few days we learned that the amputation case "doing
splendidly: she had turned yellow".

The total disregard by the Japanese for their grand sounding pronouncements of 'Asia for
the Asiatics" and "The Greater East Asia prosperity Sphere" could not have been more
abused. The total needless civilian deaths after the Japanese conquest of S.E. Asia
exceeded by far the total deaths of military and civilian personnel in camps.

BALDWIN, HANSON W. *Crucial Years 1939— 1941*. Harper Row NY 1976

BARBER, NOEL. *Sinister Twilight: The fall and rise again of Singapore*. London: Collins,'68

BARKER, A.J. *Yamashita*. New York: Ballantine, 1973

CHANG, IRIS, *The Rape of Nanking*. Basic Books 1997.

CHARMLEY, JOHN, *Duff Cooper*, Weidenfeld and Nicholson. London 1986

COLLIER, BASIL, *The War in the Far East 1941-1945: A Military history*. London Wm. Morrow,1968.

DAY, DAVID, *The Great Betrayal*. Angus & Robertson Pub'. London, 1988

DUNN, WM J. *Pacific Microphone*, Radio reporters last days in Java.

ELPHICK, PETER, *Singapore the Pregnable Fortress*, Coronet Books, London, 1995.

GOLD, HAL, *Unit 731 Testimony*, Yenbooks, Tokyo, 1996.

GOUGH, RICHARD, *Escape from Singapore*, London 1987.

HATUSHO, NAITO, *Thunder Gods*. The Kamikaze Pilots story.

HOLMES, RICHARD, and KEMP, ANTHONY. *The Bitter End*, The fall of Singapore. Anthony Bird Pub. 1982.

HONAN, WM H. *Visions of Infamy*. St. Martins Press NY. 1991.

HOYT, EDWIN P. *Japan's War The Great Pacific Conflict*. McGraw Hill Book Company,1986.

IENAGA, SABURO, *The Pacific War 1931-1945*. Pantheon Books NY .1978

INOUYE, *The Emperor's Responsibilities*.

JAMES, R,R. *Churchill a Study in Failure. 1900-1939*. World Publishing Co NY 1970.

KIMBER, WM, *S O E Singapore 1941/42* London; 1985

KIRBY, S WOODBURN, *History of The Second World War: The War against Japan*, Vol 6.

KIRBY, S WOODBURN, *Singapore the chain of disaster*. London: Cassell & Company Ltd 1971.

KNIGHTLEY, PHILLIP, *The Second Oldest Profession*. Pan Books. 1986.

LEASOR, JAMES, *Singapore the Battle that Changed the World*. Doubleday & Co., GardenCity N.Y. 1968.

LORD, JOHN & LE VIEN, JACK, *Winston Churchill the Valiant Years*.

MACKAY, JAMES, *Betrayal in High Places*, Tasman Archives (NZ), 1996.

MORAN, LORD, *Churchill from the Diaries of*. Houghton Mifflin, London, 1966.

LORD RUSSELL OF LIVERPOOL, *Knights of Bushido*. A short History of Japanese warcrimes. Cassell & Co London: 1958.

RUSBRIDGER, JAMES & NAVE, ERIC. *Betrayal at Pearl Harbor*. Summit Books NY.

SAPPOZHNIKOV, BORIS, *China theatre in WW2 1939—1945*. Progress Pub. Moscow. 1985.

SEAGRAVE, STIRLING & PEGGY. *Gold Warriors*, Bowstrung Books © 2002 Highly recommended. Japanese plunder of the Far East, China, Korea. American coverup of their share of the plunder.

SIMSON, IVAN, Singapore—*Too little, Too late:* Cooper, London, 1970

SMYTHE, JOHN, *Percival and the Tragedy of Singapore*. London: Macdonald, 1971.

STANSKY, PETER, *Churchill A Profile*. Hill & Wang, English Historical Review, Longman. 1972

TANAKA, YUKI, *Hidden Horrors*, Westview press, Colorado, USA, 1996.

TOLAND, JOHN, *The Rising Sun. The decline and fall of the Japanese Empire 1936-1945*.N Y: Random House, 1970.

VAN DER VAT, DAN, *Pacific Campaign, WW2*. The U.S.-Japanese naval war 1941-1945. NY. Simon & Schuster. 1991

WALDO HENDRICHS, *Threshold of War*

WEINTRAUB, STANLEY, *Long day's journey into War.*

WIGMORE, LIONEL, *The Japanese Thrust*, Canberra, Australian War Memorial. 1957

WILLMOTT, .H.P. *Empire in the Balance Japanese and Allied Pacific Strategies to April 1942* Annapolis: Naval Institute Press. Maryland. 1982.

INDEX

Adack 191
Akikaze Massacre 212
Allen 173
Amagi Maru 87
Amahai 91
Amani, Lt. Col. 84, 93, 96, 98, 198
Ambon & Ambonese 89, 90, 92, 93, 95, 112, 113, 117, 120, 149-153, 156-159
America and Americans 19, 35, 51, 80, 86, 106, 110, 111, 118, 120, 121, 122, 127, 129, 134, 135, 136, 137, 145, 146, 147, 149, 150, 152, 155, 156, 158, 159, 161, 162, 165, 169, 171, 174, 175, 176, 177, 178, 179, 180, 181, 183, 184, 185, 186, 188, 190, 191, 193, 195, 198
Andy (school friend) 13
Argyll & Sutherland Highlanders 27
Asia for the Asiatics 49, 63, 117, 119, 133, 147, 151, 231
Atomic bombs 78, 103, 141
Auckland 26
Audus, Fl. Lieut. 117
Australia & Australians 27, 34, 36, 38, 41, 53, 58, 80, 81, 86, 152, 153, 183, 193, 203, 206, 207
Automedan Incident 220, 221

Babs (aunt) 12
Bali 89
Bandung 50
Banka Island 36, 210
Barnes, George 134
Batavia (Jakarta) 31, 32, 34, 35, 36, 37, 57, 81, 127, 184, 185, 189, 190, 203, 205, 206, 207
BBC 190
Becker, John 222
bed bugs 82, 129

Behar, MV 218
Bell, Lt. Col. F.H. 221, 222
beri-beri 107, 146, 166, 168, 171
black market 63, 64
Blackmore (Blackie), Sgt. 44, 147, 148, 193
Blenheim Bomber 27, 44, 206
blindness 68, 117, 192
'Blood', Japanese Sgt. See Mori, Gunso
Blood Carnival 213
Blue Valley Tea Estate 12, 45, 81, 194
Bofors 30
Bogue, sgt D.W. 215
Bond, Maj. Gen. L. 225
Borneo 25, 211
Bose, Chandra 188, 193
Bowman, Jock 155, 166, 169, 172, 175, 176, 182, 184, 186, 189, 191, 192
Bren gun 32, 206
Brewster Buffalo 19, 27, 35, 225, 229
Britain & British Empire 13, 19, 24, 27, 33, 34, 35, 37, 80, 81, 86
British Columbia 12, 229
Brooke-Popham, Sir Robert 225
BSA motorcycle 16
'Bull' (camp officer) 75
Bullwinkel, Nurse 36
Burma (Myanmar) 81, 170, 173
Burma railway 72, 81, 86
Bushido Code 35, 36, 51, 86, 92, 187, 209-219

Cameron Highlands, Malaya 11, 45, 81
Canada 12, 23, 190, 193, 196
cannibalism 105, 123, 214
Cantonese 14
Carlile, Squadron Leader 63
Celebes (Sulawesi) 159, 160, 177, 181
Ceram 90, 106, 129, 138, 139

Ceylon 196
Changi (POW camp) 36
China 24
Chota (estate foreman) 15, 16, 17, 18, 21, 22
Churchill, Winston 19, 37, 57, 76, 80, 165, 220, 223, 226
clompers' camp footwear 103
clothing 58, 81, 102, 103, 128
Coles, Bobbie 223
Coles, Tom 137, 169, 171, 179, 186, 191, 198
Collinge 222
Cooper, Duff 226
Coral Sea 67, 80, 86
COTC (Canadian Officers' Training Corps) 23
Cowling, Colin 194
Cowling, Derek 194
Cowling, Geoffrey 194
crabs 82
crucifixion 211

Daisy Moller 218
Darwin 46, 80
dengue fever 107, 139, 156
Des Indes 34, 36, 57
dive bombers and bombing 30, 71
Dobbie, Jack 25, 44, 126, 155
Dobbie, Maj. General 225
Double Cross (camp newspaper) 80
Dutch 34, 38, 40, 41, 43, 46, 50, 54, 57, 58, 59, 60, 61, 64, 67, 68, 71, 72, 75, 76, 79, 80, 81, 82, 85, 86, 92, 98, 104, 109, 118, 145, 146, 147, 149, 153, 157, 173, 178, 179, 186, 188, 192, 193, 198, 199
dysentery 75, 85, 87, 89, 94, 95, 97, 100-105, 107, 110, 113, 115, 116, 124, 126, 137, 142, 146, 149, 150, 156, 167, 171, 173, 175, 183

'Emperor' (guard) 107, 123
Emperor (Japanese) 45, 61, 128, 132, 140, 187, 198
Empire Star 32
escape 45, 46, 51, 52, 54, 58, 60, 67, 68, 70, 74, 81, 82, 83, 84, 88, 92, 94, 108, 116, 137, 138, 163, 164, 178, 206
Exeter 36, 188

Fernando, Mrs. 191
Flores 89
Flying Fortress 118, 158
Forbes, Dr. 147, 166, 168, 169, 172, 173, 176, 182, 190, 198

Gammon Malaya Ltd. 14
Geneva Convention 51, 60, 63, 67, 139
Gibson, Major 166
'Goldie' (camp guard) 63, 74
Grant, Hugh 222
'Great World' 22, 25
Greater East Asia Co-prosperity Sphere 45, 63, 119, 140, 144, 151, 164
Gregory (estate manager & wife) 15-19
Gregson (wing commander) 23, 25, 26, 43, 44, 57, 63, 67, 76, 77
Gula Malacca 67

Hakko ichiu (world domination) 58
Happy World 22, 25
Hardwick, Sid 65
Harries, Dave 108, 191,199
Haruku 53, 84, 86, 91, 92, 93, 95, 96, 99, 103, 105, 106-159, 160, 161, 165, 166, 175, 177, 179, 185, 189, 193, 194, 195, 198, 199, 200, 201
Hawaii 13
headmen 46, 84
Hengie (Heldermam, Dutch POW) 63, 68, 75, 76, 184

Hirohito, Emperor 233
Hitler, Adolph 12
Horse Face (guard) 114
Hudson bombers 44
Humphrey 155
Hurricane fighter 32, 34, 35, 41, 43, 69, 114, 205, 229

Ienaga, Saburo 214
Indomitable 34
insanity 68
Ipoh, SS 31

Jaar Markt 75, 79, 80, 169, 184
Japanese Government 221
Jakarta, see Batavia
Java 31, 32, 35, 36, 37, 38, 42, 43, 45, 46, 51, 52, 53, 54, 55, 57, 58, 59, 63, 68, 71, 75, 76.
'Java Balls' 68, 117, 129
Jean Nicolet 218
Jenny (penpal) 66, 67, 68
Jim 44, 70, 74, 77, 78, 182, 184, 189, 191, 192, 193
Joan (Kerilla Estate) 16-19
Joe 108
Johore 27, 29, 33

Kallang 14, 22
Kasiyama 'Slime' 103, 104, 105, 107, 117, 118, 124, 129, 136, 163, 181, 185, 189, 198
Kavieng Massacre 212
Kelantan Province 14, 27
Kelantan River 16
Kemmis-Betty, Peter 227
Kempetai (military police) 66, 68, 82, 164
Kendari, Celebes (Sulawesi) 159, 160
Kerilla Estate 14
King William School 34, 52
Kinloch, Robert 21, 192
Kittyhawk fighter 32, 44
Kota Bharu 15, 17, 18, 19, 32

Kuala Krai 18
Kuala Lumpur 14, 20
Kurashima (camp officer) 115, 117, 142

latrines 88, 89, 95, 96, 97, 123, 151
Lee, Geoff 200
Legi line 72
Leigh, Dixie 65, 66, 69, 73, 77
Leleh, Mrs. 200
Liang (POW Camp Ambon) 152
lice 82, 119, 129
Lodestar (aircraft) 44, 46, 51
Lombok 89
Lyceum school 56, 81

MacArthur, Gen. D. 229
Macassar POW Camp 180, 183, 186, 193
Madura 82
malaria 56, 68, 69, 72, 75, 76, 97, 100, 107, 108, 115, 139, 146, 156, 157, 182
Malaya 15-21, 186, 188
malnutrition 68, 72, 117, 138, 146, 183
Mandarin Night Club 13
Marcel (Dutch POW) 100, 101, 102, 200
Matador, Operation 223
Midway, battle of 67
Mitchell, Elsie 229
Moluccas Islands 90, 149
Mori, Gunso 85, 91, 102, 103, 104, 105, 107, 112, 113, 115, 116, 117, 118, 121, 124, 127, 129, 133, 140, 142, 144, 163, 181, 185, 189, 198
Mukden Incident 198
Muna Island & Camp 160, 183, 194, 199
Munsell, Sgt. 69
Musashi, Battleship 220, 231

NAFFI (Navy, Army, Air Force Institute) 28, 29, 33

New Britain 72
New Guinea 89, 90, 91, 106, 118, 134, 152, 159, 195
New World 22

P1 and P2 (airstrips) 34
Palembang 34, 35, 205, 206
Palomar 13
Pearl Harbour 13, 84
Pelau 98, 118, 122, 148, 199
Penang 14
Penny (Sgt Penteney) 44, 57, 62, 70, 77, 101, 113, 114, 126, 155
Percival, A.E. 225
Perth 194, 203
Peter 44
Phillips, Admiral Sir Thomas 229
Philps Dr. 63, 68, 72, 76, 77, 146, 147, 166
Pittam, Curly 62
Pitts, Sqd Leader 85, 107, 142, 198
Portuguese 63
President Taft 11, 13
Prince of Wales 36
Purwakarta 37

Qualicum Beach 12
quinine 68, 76, 112, 156, 157, 165, 173

RAF 11, 22, 23, 24, 25, 26, 33, 34, 38, 39, 40, 41, 42, 43, 44, 49, 51, 52, 54, 57, 58, 60, 62, 128, 129, 138, 190, 193, 203, 206
Raffles Hotel 13, 14, 19, 25
Red Mac 112
Robbie (uncle) 12
Royal Malayan Air Force 20
Royal New Zealand Air Force (RNZAF) 21, 26, 52
Rumah Tiga 152

Sambawang 21
Samurai 35, 36, 117, 132, 152, 153, 159, 163, 187

San Francisco 13
Seletar Transit Camp 23, 44
Semarang 57, 59, 60, 64, 67, 68, 72, 75, 76, 80, 81, 122, 166, 193
Shanghai 13
Shimada Dr. 156, 209
Shinano, Battleship 220, 231
Siam (Thailand) 15, 16
Singapore 11-33, 119, 188, 190, 191, 192, 193, 194
Singapore Harbour Board Police 195
Slaughter, Todd 104, 126, 155
'Slime' (Camp Officer). *See* Kasiyama
Sourabaya 54, 60, 71, 75, 81, 96
South Africa 23
South East Asia 45, 47
South West Pacific 92
Springer, Dr. 104, 113, 146
Steadman W/C 51
Steve 182, 184, 186, 189, 191
Sukarno 63, 188
Sumatra 34, 58, 195, 204, 210
Sumbawa 89
Sunda Strait 36
Swallowfield Farm 12
Sydney 80, 86
syphilis 76, 102, 103

Taffy 38, 39, 44, 46, 51, 56, 62, 73, 96, 126, 155
Tammy 173
Tanah Rata 12
Tanglin Club 14, 22
Tasik Malaja (aerodrome) 42, 52, 54, 55, 56, 60, 67, 76
Tengah aerodrome 21, 30, 192
Thailand *see* Siam
Thomas, Shenton 224
Thompson automatic 31
Titch 53
Tjideng (women's camp) 190
Tjilatjap 38, 41, 42

tobacco 37, 174, 180
toilet paper 98
Tom (Kerrilla estate) 16, 18, 19
Tsuji, Colonel 229, 232

ulcers 6, 99, 104
'unsinkable aircraft carriers' 92
US blockade 91

Van de Post, Laurens 198
Vancouver 12, 15
Vandergaast, Van 224
Visitors' Day (Semarang Camp) 67
Vyner Brooke 11, 32, 35

Wards, Col. G.T. 226
Wavell, General 35, 165, 203
Wei Jami 151, 184
Wejak 89
Whiskers 112
Whiskers (Japanese officer). *See* Amani, Lt.Col.
Whitic, Wing Comm 81

Yamato, Battleship 220, 231
Yoshijiro, Umezo 230

Zero fighters 19, 30, 33, 69, 71, 75, 90, 229